D1261029

*The Fatal Mirror*

# THE FATAL MIRROR

*Themes and Techniques in the Poetry of*

*Fulke Greville*

RICHARD WASWO

UNIVERSITY PRESS OF VIRGINIA
CHARLOTTESVILLE

The University Press of Virginia
Copyright © 1972 by the Rector and Visitors
of the University of Virginia

First published 1972


ISBN: 0-8139-0392-0
Library of Congress Catalog Card Number: 75-188603
Printed in the United States of America

# Contents

# Preface

THE purpose of this study is to examine Fulke Greville's nondramatic —primarily his lyric—verse in relation to the philosophical, literary, and religious contexts from which it springs, and to show how its style is successively influenced by these contexts. The governing assumption throughout is that ideas have consequences, that, in this specific case, certain kinds of metaphysic generate certain kinds of poetic practice. This assumption proceeds from the more general scholarly conviction that "ideas have an effect on literature which can be traced, often with great probability, and sometimes with certainty."[1]

It is, I suppose, obvious enough—even platitudinous—that a man's vision or definition of reality will condition the language in which it is expressed; and that, conversely, the structure of the language will implicitly contain and reveal the structure of that reality. But platitude or not, this principle seems to me the most useful in arriving at a full understanding of literature, especially the literature of the English Renaissance, a period bristling with intellectual speculation, with confident assertions of new truths and impassioned defenses of old ones, with competing and fully articulated theories on every subject from the nature of God to the observation of natural stress in the iambic line.

Applied to Greville, the principle will delineate the choices made by the poet among the competing theories of his time, and will demonstrate how his language is disciplined accordingly. The investigation will thus reveal some qualities of his writing seldom or never explored: his subtly ironic use of conventional literary mannerisms, his refinement of traditional conceptions and forms of lyric poetry, and the relation of his particular religious beliefs to the style and structure of his great religious poems.

Such an investigation must necessarily stand on the shoulders of the critical and historical scholars who have made it possible. The obligations thus incurred will find, I hope, adequate acknowledgement both in the text and in the notes, where I have tried my best to distinguish plunder from contention. I have sought to view the poetry of one man

---

[1] C. S. Lewis, *English Literature in the Sixteenth Century* (New York, 1954), p. 56.

from the several perspectives provided by modern scholarship in the attempt to explain the nature of Greville's achievement as a poet and to offer such a reassessment of his poems as has recently been called for by James Reeves and Martin Seymour-Smith.[2] With few exceptions, modern interest in Greville has tended understandably to confine itself to description and analysis of his ideas. I have tried to use such analysis to illuminate some of the distinctive features of his style.

My chief concern throughout is with the poetry as poetry: to obtain as complete and rounded an estimate as possible of its merits, its defects, and its reasons for being the kind of poetry that it is. This aim, I trust, controls such excursions as are required into the various intellectual and religious "backgrounds." When discussing individual lyrics, I have usually tried to see them simultaneously with respect to idea and style, to keep the focus neither on theme nor technique to the exclusion of one or the other, but on the crucial relation of the two. The success with which Greville often creates and manipulates this relation constitutes the principal distinction and the lasting value of his verse, which emerges from an understanding both of what its materials are and of how they are used.

I first studied the poetry of Fulke Greville some years ago with the late Yvor Winters, who impressed many of his students at that time less by his notoriety as a critic than by his skill and power and obvious delight in the oral reading of poems. What he tried to teach us about meter, accent, and the whole aural texture of verse is set forth only incidentally in his published criticism. As a living voice he awakened us to the wide and subtle range of expressive possibilities in rhythmic, spoken words. For that experience, and for the impulse to investigate how it may occur, I am much indebted to him.

The first version of this study was patiently awaited and kindly criticized by Professors Daniel Seltzer and Herschel Baker. I hope I have profited from Mr. Baker's elegant instruction, and am additionally grateful for his help in giving me my first opportunity to teach.

Any student of Greville owes thanks to his modern editors, Geoffrey Bullough and G. A. Wilkes, for providing the essential texts. Occasional exception to their views implies no disrespect for their labors. The verse treatises on *Monarchy* and *Religion* are quoted from Wilkes's edition of *The Remains* (Oxford, 1965) by permission of the Oxford University Press, New York. The other treatises, on *Humane Learning, Fame and Honour*, and *Warres*, the plays *Alaham* and *Mustapha*, and the sonnet sequence *Caelica* are quoted from Bullough's two-volume edition of the *Poems and Dramas* (New York, 1945) by permission of the editor.

---

[2] *A New Canon of English Poetry* (New York, 1969), p. 314.

Greville's *Life of Sidney* is quoted from the edition of Nowell Smith (Oxford, 1907). Citation of all these editions is made parenthetically in the text by stanza number in the treatises, poem number in *Caelica*, and page number in the *Life of Sidney*. In all quotations from these and other original sources I have normalized the use of *u*'s and *v*'s, *i*'s and *j*'s, and have silently deleted italics, expanded contractions, and corrected obvious misprints. For permission to quote from their unpublished dissertations, I am grateful to Professors Marie H. Buncombe, Burnham Carter, Jr., and James L. Rosier.

Other individuals have been generous with the kind of personal aid and comfort that can find no mention elsewhere. I am grateful for courtesies extended and insights shared by Ronald Rebholz of Stanford University, Wilbert O. Crockett of San Jose State College, and James Reeves of Lewes, Sussex. Margaret Selley, of Routledge, Kegan Paul, was kind enough to send me a proof copy of Joan Rees's informative new critical biography, *Fulke Greville, Lord Brooke, 1554–1628*, to consult in the final stages of preparing my own manuscript. The preparation itself was faciliated by a grant from the Research Committee of the University of Virginia. Various chapters have benefited from the scrutiny of my present colleagues Edward I. Berry, Hoyt N. Duggan, William A. Elwood, Alan B. Howard, Robert Kellogg, and especially from the discerning stylistic sense of Leopold Damrosch, Jr. The entire manuscript was improved by the meticulous criticism of Lester A. Beaurline. The gracious efforts of all these gentlemen have spared the reader sundry errors, obscurities, and infelicities. Such is the nature of original sin, however, that one is likely to persevere in evil despite the best advice, and is justly regarded as responsible for doing so. Merits may have been imposed upon me, but faults are mine alone.

*Charlottesville, Virginia*                                                         R. W.
*July, 1971*

*The Fatal Mirror*

# I "A Sense of Declination"

I KNOW the world and believe in God"—this famous remark of Fulke Greville, first Lord Brooke, tersely indicates his principal concerns as statesman and thinker. To most of his commentators, the remark additionally implies the dualistic conflict of these concerns: the irreconcilable opposition between heaven and earth, the apparently unbridgeable gap between the realms of grace and nature.[1] Greville's starkest statement of this theological dichotomy is the following:

> Mixe not in functions God, and earth together;
> The wisdome of the world, and his, are two;
> One latitude can well agree to neither;
> In each, men have their beinges, as they doe:
>     The world doth build without, our God within;
>     He traffiques goodnesse, and she traffiques sinne.
>                                   (*Religion*, 98)

The position of man in this moral ontology is of course uniquely ambivalent: potentially, at least, he alone can participate in both worlds. Greville's anguished questioning of this state provides the summary statement for those seeking the mainspring of his thought:

> Oh wearisome Condition of Humanity!
> Borne under one Law, to another bound:
> Vainely begot, and yet forbidden vanity,
> Created sicke, commanded to be sound:
> What meaneth Nature by these diverse Lawes?
> Passion and Reason, selfe-division cause:
> Is it the marke, or Majesty of Power
> To make offences that it may forgive?[2]
>                     (*Mustapha*, "Chorus Sacerdotum," 1–8)

[1] Typical views of the conflict are found in: Geoffrey Bullough, ed., *Poems and Dramas* (New York, 1945), I, 1; C. S. Lewis, *English Literature in the Sixteenth Century*, p. 525; David Daiches, *A Critical History of English Literature* (London, 1960), I, 202; N. Orsini, *Fulke Greville tra il mondo e Dio* (Milan, 1941), p. 10.

[2] The first few lines of the passage were slightly misquoted by Aldous Huxley as an epigraph to *Point Counter Point*, and are, perhaps for that reason, Greville's best known words. The last two lines seem best understood, in keeping with the an-

This anguish clearly results from perceiving the virtual impossibility of realizing the potential of the higher law, man's ethical dilemma as summed up by St. Paul, "For I know that in me (that is, in my flesh,) dwelleth no good thing: for to will is present with me; but how to perform that which is good I find not" (Rom. 7:18).

The Pauline ethical emphasis appears here, however, in a context that filters it through what is probably the chief philosophical crux of the high Renaissance: man's changing view of nature, which has been generally accepted as one of the intellectual watersheds between the medieval and the modern world. The "Chorus Sacerdotum" concludes a Senecan closet drama dealing with Turkish despotism, a work designed "to trace out the high waies of ambitious Governours, and to shew . . . that the more audacity, advantage, and good successe such Soveraignties have, the more they hasten to their owne desolation and ruine" (*Life of Sidney*, p. 221). It immediately follows the "Chorus Quintus" of Tartars, which pungently ridicules all religion as vain superstition and draws the appropriate inference with a final sarcastic understatement:

> Man should make much of Life, as Natures table,
> Wherein she writes the Cypher of her glorie.
> Forsake not Nature, nor misunderstand her:
> Her mysteries are read without Faiths eye-sight:
> She speaketh in our flesh; and from our Senses,
> Delivers downe her wisdomes to our Reason.
> If any man would breake her lawes to kill,
> Nature doth, for defence, allow offences.
> She neither taught the Father to destroy:
> Nor promis'd any man, by dying, joy.

This Nature is not the glass wherein man can discern the workings of a benevolent and divine providence; she refers to nothing beyond her tangible self. She is not the normative and genial universe that we have been taught to associate with Shakespeare, Hooker, and the Elizabethan world picture. What is more, the priests of the play do not deny her, but merely use her to describe the "selfe-division" of fallen man. She is "le monde où l'homme est placé, la situation pénible dans laquelle il se trouve. Mais c'est aussi le Pouvoir qui décide les conditions de l'épreuve qu'il doit subir."[3] And the priests utter their profound complaint that these conditions virtually preclude salvation, which is to be sought, they hint, not "With pompe of holy Sacrifice and rites," but in the individual's

---

tithetical structure of the whole, if "marke" is taken to mean "target" or "aim." Cf. Jonson's "Though beauty be the mark of praise."

[3] Jean Jacquot, "Religion et raison d'état dans l'oeuvre de Fulke Greville," *Études Anglaises*, V (1952), 222.

inward experience of God ("Chorus Sacerdotum," ll. 19–24). Greville utters the same agonized complaint elsewhere, in his own person:

> The word is cleare, and needs no explanation,
> Onlie the councell is a mysterie;
>   Why God commanded more then man could doo,
>   Beinge all things that he will, and wisdome too?[4]

> Why came our Saviour, if fleshe could fulfill
> The Lawe enjoynd? Or if it must transgresse,
> Whence tooke that justice this unequall will,
> To binde them more, to whom he giveth lesse?
>
> (*Religion*, 76–77)

Primarily because his conception of nature is closer to ours: not what ought to be, but only what is, this acute consciousness of the Christian dilemma marks Greville as something of a modern. But his expression of it in *Mustapha* marks him as preeminently a man of his age. There, he takes popularized material from contemporary, but prudently remote, history; casts it into a fashionable classical form; uses it to examine problems of statecraft and tyranny that were central to the Renaissance; views these problems in terms of orthodox Elizabethan political theory and with a medieval seriousness of moral purpose; and brings to bear on the entire treatment a grandeur of conception largely provided by the avant-garde theological and philosophical currents of his day.[5] It is therefore small wonder that most of the scholarly interest in Greville, until very recently, has tended to concentrate on the explication of his ideas, to see him as a microcosmic example of the educated Englishman of his time. This tendency is naturally reinforced by the facts of his career: his adult life spanning the reigns of Elizabeth, James, and Charles I; his attendance at court and political service under all three monarchs; his numerous friendships with and patronage of some of the leading churchmen, thinkers, scholars, and writers of his age[6]—all these encourage a view of Greville as, intellectually, a kind of minor English Montaigne, a funnel through which the sixteenth century flowed into the seventeenth.

---

[4] In our own day, Reinhold Niebuhr poses exactly this question as "The Relevance of an Impossible Ethical Ideal," in *An Interpretation of Christian Ethics* (New York, 1935), ch. IV. Lewis calls Greville an "Existentialist" (p. 525). Geoffrey Bullough suggests that "Moods momentary in *Hamlet* and *Lear* were habitual to Greville" (*Poems and Dramas*, II, 61).

[5] See Bullough's Introduction, *Poems and Dramas*, II, 7–38, 58–61; and also the penetrating summary of the play by Joan Rees, *Fulke Greville, Lord Brooke* (Berkeley, Calif., 1971), pp. 170–71.

[6] Many of the scattered biographical data have been narrated and intelligently interpreted by Miss Rees, chs. 1–4. The sketch in *Biographia Britannica*, III (1750), is still helpful. Ronald Rebholz has a full biography currently in press at Oxford.

Our present interest in Greville's ideas, however, is prefatory to an examination of how he uses them in his best poetry, and how they, in turn, influence his poetic style. As a thinker, he was not distinguished; it is rather as a typical representative of one kind of intelligent response at a pivotal period in intellectual history that he is valued. In the world of ideas, "Greville war kein Führer."[7] His interest in ideas, though extensive, was clearly not that of the professional speculator, but rather that of the gentleman amateur, the man of letters, the practical moralist. He contemned "idle theoricke" (*Monarchy*, 225) and sought rather to apply his ideas to the judgment of his experiences of life. This application and the grounds on which it is habitually made will be our principal concern.

Greville's vision of life is fundamentally conditioned by a view of human nature that sees all that takes place within it as a consequence of original sin. *A Treatise of Religion* provides the fullest exposition:

> But there remaines such naturall corruption
> In all our powers, even from our parents seed,
> As to the good gives native interruption;
> Sense staines affection; that, will; and will, deed:
>    So as what's good in us, and others too
>    We praise; but what is evill, that we doe.[8]

                                                             (st. 13)

On this earth corruption is natural; the frustration of the good is "native." Yet our perception of this unhappy condition, of our divided selves, is itself evidence of the "feeble bit of light" left in us:[9]

> Questions againe which in our harts arise
> (Sinne lovinge knowledge, not humilitie)
> Though they be curiouse, Godlesse, and unwise,
> Yet prove our nature feeles a Deitie:
>    For if these strifes rose out of other grounds,
>    Man were to God, as deafnesse is to soundes.

                                                             (st. 9)

Even so, we cannot fully comprehend our unhappy state: self-love turns our guilt into fear of punishment and moves our wit to invent super-

---

[7] H. W. Utz, *Die Anschauungen über Wissenschaft und Religion im Werke Fulke Grevilles* (Bern, 1948), p. 118.

[8] The couplet paraphrases St. Paul (Rom. 7:19) and perhaps echoes Ovid, "video meliora proboque, deteriora sequor" (*Metamorphoses*, VII.20–21), who is quoted by Calvin, *Institutes of the Christian Religion*, trans. John Allen, ed. Benjamin B. Warfield (Philadelphia, 1936), I, 305 (II.ii.23).

[9] John Calvin, *Commentaries*, trans. and ed. Joseph Haroutounian and Louise P. Smith (Philadelphia, 1958), p. 131 (on John 1:5). On the partial "perspicuity in the human understanding," which "immediately terminates in vanity" see also *Institutes*, I, 293 (II.ii.12).

stitious rituals to avoid punishment (19–30), and we repine at the justice of God.[10] We find no peace until "a grace inspired . . . a spirit not of earth, Fashioninge the mortall to immortall birth" "leades us to our Savior" (3, 105), who takes upon himself the burden of our crimes, bestowing on us faith in him, which alone is true wisdom.[11] These truths, made evident in "good life," are implemented only by "that litle flocke, Gods owne elect," for whose sakes "God doth give restraininge grace To his seene Church, and to the heathen too," so that they might not be wholly destroyed by the unregenerate. God also favors the elect with help in overcoming temptation (110–13).

These doctrines, as such, are the doctrines of Calvinism—derived largely from St. Augustine and generally too well known to need comment—and Greville has, of course, been commonly regarded as a Calvinist. How and in what sense he is so, that is, the meaning of that label in a literary context, requires some clarification. Passages like those above could be, and have been, indefinitely multiplied, and juxtaposed with the appropriate dogmas from Calvin's *Institutes*, or from any of the voluminous *Commentaries*. Marie H. Buncombe, who has done this, presents Greville as a solid Calvinist by enumerating his convictions that original sin infects both mind and will; that restraining grace curbs the excesses of the reprobate; that election is predestined; that unmerited grace alone saves the elect and preserves them in faith.[12] Claiming these as cardinal points in Calvin's theology, she must nonetheless admit that only the first two receive direct analysis in Greville's poetry.[13] Of the others, the necessity for free grace was stressed by all Protestants (and used especially as a stick for beating Catholics), and in any case the poet is much more interested in the effects of grace than its doctrinal promulgation. With regard to preserving grace, only a small part of this doctrine gets a passing mention from Greville. The question of predestined election is even more problematic. Greville's latest editor denies that he takes Calvin's view of predestination, and claims that he rather defines the elect as "those who choose to accept God's calling."[14] This contention seems plausible, although the passage in question (*Religion*, 41–46) is such that would not, I think, preclude the assumption of pre-

[10] On dread of punishment as initial stimulus to conversion see Calvin, *Institutes*, I, 656 (III.iii.7).

[11] On Christ as mediator, and the moral impotence of man without him see Calvin, *Institutes*, I, 367–68 (II.vi.1), and I, 551–58 (II.xvi.1–5).

[12] "Fulke Greville's *A Treatie of Humane Learning*: A Critical Analysis," Ph.D. Diss., Stanford University, 1966, p. 119. The five points are roughly the famous five articles imposed by the strict Calvinists on the Synod of Dort.

[13] Buncombe, p. 91.

[14] G. A. Wilkes, "The Sequence of Writings of Fulke Greville, Lord Brooke," *Studies in Philology*, LVI (1959), 264.

destination. If one wished to assume it, one might cite Greville's use of "election" in two love poems (Sonnets 4, 75), where he takes it to mean wholly willful choice, having nothing to do with either "worth" or "reason." The problem here, again, is that Greville's poetry is not directly concerned with how, on what basis, grace is vouchsafed or denied, but rather with its effects—and with these, more specifically, as they are contrasted to the vain behavior of the unregenerate.

Looking at the doctrines from a more historical perspective, another scholar denies that Greville can even be called a Calvinist. Burnham Carter, Jr., reviews the Thirty-nine Articles and the two books of Elizabethan Homilies to show how they temper the letter of Calvin's law by omitting the grimmer statements of predestined election and reprobation, and hinting that man's own moral efforts are not wholly futile. He detects these omissions and these hints in Greville, and therefore sees him as a solid Church of England man. "Nevertheless," Mr. Carter admits, "echoes of the spirit of John Calvin do occur in Greville," most notably "in moments of extreme conviction of sin."[15] All this is very well, but it assumes an impossibly pure definition of "Calvinist" that narrows the word to uselessness: taken as Mr. Carter takes it, in terms of the historical modification of his doctrines, no one was a Calvinist but Calvin. By the same reasoning, Marx would have begot no Marxists, and Freud no Freudians.

On the other hand, the historical perspective can also generate the almost infinite extension of the word: while acknowledging the Church of England's "tendency to retreat from the extremes of predestinarian ideology," we can emphasize its "basically Calvinist" theology, and so call everyone in it—from Cartwright to Hooker—a "Calvinist," or for that matter, an "Anglican." This position, taken by two historians, is based on a survey only of clerical writings, and maintains that no distinctions of doctrine can be drawn between Calvinist (or Puritan) and Anglican prior to 1640.[16] From this point, the controversy has developed through intellectual history to concerns more directly relevant to social history than to literature.[17]

[15] "The Intellectual Background of Fulke Greville," Ph.D. Diss., Stanford University, 1955, pp. 32ff., 40–44, 64.

[16] Charles George and Katherine George, *The Protestant Mind of the English Reformation, 1570–1640* (Princeton, N.J., 1961), pp. 70, 7.

[17] The Georges' position contradicts the earlier analyses of William Haller, *The Rise of Puritanism* (New York, 1938), and of Perry Miller, *The New England Mind: The Seventeenth Century* (Cambridge, Mass., 1939). It has since been explicitly refuted in two different ways: John F. H. New, *Anglican and Puritan: The Basis of Their Opposition, 1558–1640* (London, 1964), finds deep doctrinal divisions between the two in four broad areas—the nature of man, the Church, the sacraments, and ethics; Christopher Hill, *Society and Puritanism in Pre-Revolutionary*

Perhaps enough has been said, though, to suggest that defining the "Calvinist" in England on the basis of doctrines per se is a very slippery business. What makes it so is precisely that historical fact which is the starting-point for all the rival interpretations: the celebrated *via media*, the compromise between reformed (to whatever arguable extent) doctrine and traditional ecclesiastical structure, which permitted the vast diversity within Elizabeth's church. It should also be emphasized that this diversity was inherent in the original Protestant impulse. The ability of Protestantism generally, as a religion—even apart from its connections with national politics and economics, which make the whole phenomenon so complex—to proliferate in sect and schism is commonplace. It is clear that to feel the unutterable majesty of God and the exhilarating liberation of faith in him as Luther and Calvin felt it could produce a wide range of attitudes toward experience in this world. And it is on the basis of these attitudes, all of them contained in some variety of theological Calvinism, that a distinction between Calvinist and Anglican has been found that is inclusive enough to be useful, and specific enough to be discernible.

We may approach this distinction by noticing one possible range these attitudes may take in Greville's work. He is summarizing his view of knowledge with his usual talent for compendious expression:

> The chiefe Use then in man of that he knowes,
> Is his paines taking for the good of all,
> Not fleshly weeping for our owne made woes,
> Not laughing from a Melancholy gall,
> Not hating from a soule that overflowes
> With bitternesse, breath'd out from inward thrall:
>     But sweetly rather to ease, loose, or binde,
>     As need requires, this fraile fall'n humane kinde.
>
> Yet Some seeke knowledge, meerely but to know,
> And idle Curiositie that is;
> Some but to sell, not freely to bestow,
> These gaine and spend both time, and wealth amisse;
> Embasing Arts, by basely deeming so:
> Some to be knowne, and vanity is this:
>     Some to build others, which is Charity;
>     But these to build themselves, who wise men be.
>                             (*Humane Learning*, 143–44)

On the latter stanza, the editor comments, "It is astonishing to find so direct a statement of the Puritan view which sets the salvation of one's

---

*England* (London, 1964), merely dismisses the Georges' conclusions (pp. 13–14), and proceeds to document exhaustively the relationship they cannot establish between ideology and social history.

own soul above all other works, even above altruism."[18] More astonishing, perhaps, is that this very altruism—the true concern for the other that was Luther's constant moral imperative—is expressed in the preceding stanza. What Greville is insisting on there is the direct moral function of knowledge: its proper application to helping our fellow sinners as opposed to lamenting, ridiculing, or despising them. The next stanza discriminates the motive for this application, ultimately that of moral self-regeneration as opposed to material gain, self-aggrandizement, or knowledge for its own sake. The whole passage at first glance appears to modify strict Calvinism by its assumption that man can "build" himself. But not really: we shortly discover that the means by which he does so, true learning, is simply "the truth and good to love, and doe them .../ When gifts of Grace, and Faith" allow him to be inwardly converted (149). This knowledge is something like the lowly wisdom that Milton was later to recommend: both writers arrive at a conception of wisdom designed to chasten the pride of life that the various energies of the period evoked, to limit man's curious searchings and focus his attention on moral values, the "things that most concern" (*Paradise Lost*, VIII. 196).

The attitude in question here is that fallen men are much more in need of binding than easing. It proceeds from a predisposition to see all experience in moral terms—terms that are derived from the Augustinian ontology so strenuously revived by Calvin, which posits the absolute sovereignty of God at the expense of man's reason as a moral agent.[19] It is this attitude that allows Calvin to devote an entire chapter to the assertion that everything proceeding from man's "Corrupt Nature" is "Worthy of Condemnation."[20] The attack on the traditional "axiom of knowledge"—that Thomistic synthesis of rational truth and moral goodness, with its consequent view of grace as perfecting what man's natural capacities can begin—is clear.[21] The attack was certainly clear to Hooker,

---

[18] Bullough, *Poems and Dramas*, I, 310.

[19] This brief discussion of a very large subject is founded on Herschel Baker's *The Wars of Truth* (Cambridge, Mass., 1952). Professor Baker there examines Calvinism under several different headings as a chapter in the history of thought. He sees the emancipation of God from reason and of nature from Grace as ironically contributing to what it was supposed to forestall: the growing secularization of politics and natural philosophy.

[20] *Institutes*, I, 312–33 (II.iii).

[21] The phrase is Professor Baker's, p. 4. His view of the conflict is supported by Robert Hoopes, (*Right Reason in the English Renaissance* [Cambridge, Mass., 1962], p. 97), who sees fideism (which he calls an "attitude of mind" that deems reason morally useless) as a principal antithesis to *recta ratio*. Virgil K. Whitaker also sees Calvinism in general and Greville in particular as undermining right reason: *Francis Bacon's Intellectual Milieu* (Los Angeles, 1962), pp. 22–24.

who, when it came time to formulate a rationale for the *de facto* institution of the Church of England, perceived that the immediate controversy over church government had its ultimate basis in a disagreement on the first principles of metaphysics and ontology. Hooker therefore began his defense of the hierarchical, analogical fabric of Church and State with his famous restatement (in Book I of the *Laws of Ecclesiastical Polity*) of the ancient concept of natural law by which a rationally perfect God governs a universe that is thus rationally apprehensible to man.

It is in this large area of philosophic attitude that intellectual historians and literary scholars have found a distinction between Calvinist and Anglican that is both adequate and highly significant for literature because it depends not on doctrine as such, but rather on the quality and habits of the minds that react to and develop the doctrine. I do not mean to deny the importance, nor the interest, of the doctrines themselves, but simply to emphasize this more fundamental difference. Greville's specific doctrines will be discussed as they appear in specific poems, and his treatment of them will be contrasted to that of other writers who share them. Given the broad doctrinal agreement between the Thirty-nine Articles and the Westminster Confession, the universal need of the age for logical articulation and the universal training in rhetoric that facilitated it, and the universally accepted Aristotelian faculty psychology that supplied the terms of analytic discourse, the distinction becomes a matter of differing temperamental valuations of the natural world and of man's natural capacities. In a literary context, this fundamental distinction between separate philosophic viewpoints gathered under the same doctrinal umbrella has become sufficiently established for Greville's latest commentator merely to assume that "To call a man of the sixteenth or seventeenth century a Calvinist is to indicate an attitude of mind rather than adherence to a formal set of doctrines."[22] For Calvinist or Anglican, then, man's moral predicament—his pivotal position in creation between the beasts and the angels—remained the same; but the perspective from which it was viewed and the ways in which it might be resolved could differ greatly. As Greville's cry *de profundis* in "Chorus Sacerdotum" echoes the ethical insight of Calvin's favorite authority, St. Paul, it establishes a perspective that is largely foreign to Hooker. The "laws" to which Greville sees us bound are merely the irreconcilable demands of our moral nature, which our reason can perceive but is impotent to resolve. They are not those Thomistic assurances of the divine regulation of the world which our reason can both perceive and teach

[22] Rees, p. 182.

us to obey. Greville's assumption here of the extreme Calvinistic opposition of nature and grace, with its corollary of reason's moral incapacity, produce in the poem a kind of agony that is not possible from Hooker's point of view.[23] For the agony results from our perception of the utter futility of our moral efforts: our reason can only show us that no matter what we do, we do wrong; and it cannot show us how to do right.

The thoroughness with which Greville examines life from this debilitating perspective sets the tone that distinguishes his development of Calvinistic premises. If "the wisdome of this world, and [God's], are two" (*Religion*, 98), and if we cannot attain the second, even in part, by means of our natural light of reason, then all that reason can illuminate is the privation, the literal nothingness, of the first; and all the moral guidance it can provide is an unremitting and tormented consciousness of sin.[24] From this point of view, even our "saving God" becomes a "fatall mirrour of transgression" (Sonnet 99) in which we can perceive only the distorted image of our own perversion. Greville holds this mirror up to nature and records what he sees there with a consistency that Emerson would doubtless have deplored. It is this very consistency that makes merely doctrinal summaries of Greville's verse, such as the one given above of *A Treatise of Religion*, somewhat misleading. The direct introductory and concluding statements of the doctrines are but the framework from which Greville "moves out to censure alternative courses and to condemn the world that fails the test of his standards."[25] The censure, the condemnation, is a primary goal.

It might be objected that to identify this habitual negative perspective as proceeding from Calvinism we do the memory of the great reformer some injustice. Calvin, after all, has something to say of the joys and rewards of faith, and there is great potential optimism in the concept of Christian liberty for the community of saints. On the other hand, Calvin's role as polemicist directed his greatest eloquence (as well as the greater part of his writings) to the denunciation of man's overweening pride and the false idols it creates. In any case, we do not pretend to define Calvinism as a theology by describing one predominant effect of the vision of life that he made popular. We intend merely to specify the literary consequences of that vision, and to distinguish them from those of the more moderate Anglican position. As we shall see, Greville, along with other writers, extends some of Calvin's premises beyond Calvin's own development of them. Were it less awkward, we might more exact-

[23] John F. H. New discusses the difference between the dialectical and perfecting views of grace as characteristics of Puritanism and Anglicanism, pp. 36–40.

[24] Ivor Morris seems to suggest that the necessity for this kind of affliction is "The Tragic Vision of Fulke Greville," *Shakespeare Survey*, XIV (1961), 66–75.

[25] G. A. Wilkes, ed., *The Remains: Being Poems of Monarchy and Religion* (Oxford, 1965), p. 17.

ly refer to Greville henceforth as an "ultra-Calvinist";[26] at least we may think of him as such.

With respect to the popularity of the negative perspective, C. S. Lewis has reminded us how fashionable Calvinism was at the court of Elizabeth, how it appealed to the young, the progressive, the doctrinaire, and how nothing seemed "more *comme il faut*, than the censorious."[27] For those who took it seriously, as Greville did, this contemporary relish for the castigation of vice was connected with larger issues of traditional Christian pessimism—the so-called Jacobean melancholy, or the theory of the world's decay—issues which were themselves "contained within Augustinian terms and adapted to Augustinian purposes."[28] It was surely inevitable that Calvin's emphasis upon these terms and purposes should result in a general tendency to accentuate the negative: not merely because of the exigencies of controversy, but because by definition our reason can perceive within us nothing but pollution, and without us nothing but abomination.

Although to Greville theoretical disputation was an arid thing, he was a logical man as well as a practicing politician, and was concerned both to explore the grounds of his convictions and to apply them to the problems he knew best. His most philosophical and best known effort of this sort is *A Treatie of Humane Learning*. The strategy of the poem is an interesting illustration of how Greville supplied his Calvinistic cannon with a whole arsenal of current intellectual ammunition.

He begins by asserting the infinitude of knowledge in an implied contrast to "The Mind of Man," which is finite, "this worlds true dimension" (1). Although these first two stanzas appear laudatory, the contrast provides the logical foundation for the real definition of knowledge which follows:

> This Knowledge is the same forbidden tree,
> Which man lusts after to be made his Maker;
> For Knowledge is of Powers eternity,
> And perfect Glory, the true image-taker;
>    So as what doth the infinite containe,
>    Must be as infinite as it againe.
>
> No marvell then, if proud desires reflexion,
> By gazing on this Sunne, doe make us blinde,
> Nor if our Lust, Our Centaure-like Affection,

---

[26] I adapt the term from Miss Rees: "It is very plain that his outlook is ultra-Protestant" (p. 113).

[27] Pp. 42–44.

[28] Baker, p. 77.

> Instead of Nature, fadome clouds, and winde,
> So adding to originall defection,
> As no man knowes his owne unknowing minde.
>
> (st. 3–4)

Man's very desire to know everything is of course sinful in the context of the Pauline emphasis on the great myth of original sin that lies at the center of Greville's thought. Man's pride in thus seeking "to be made his Maker" results in continual self-deception and ignorance. The story of Ixion who, seeking to embrace Juno, begot the race of centaurs on clouds or mist, is a recurring ironic metaphor of Greville's for the mental and emotional self-deception caused by the desire for self-aggrandizement (cf. Sonnets 66, 42). With such a motive we cannot hope to fathom nature.

Having stated his thesis, Greville summarizes in the next fifteen stanzas the natural imperfections which are the means of this self-deception. He begins with sense, and ascends through all the traditional knowing faculties of the soul. With respect to the external senses, the source of all knowledge, man is inferior to beasts; unlike them, he is born wholly impotent and never develops senses as sharp as theirs. Moreover, the senses are not only deceptive, but they produce in everyone different reactions, according to temperament, health, or age. Man's internal epistemological apparatus is also in dreadful shape: the imagination does not at all reflect what the senses (however erroneously) present to it, because it is "so shadowed with selfe-application," and colored by our individually variable affections (10–11).

> Hence our desires, feares, hopes, love, hate, and sorrow,
> In fancy make us heare, feele, see impressions,
> Such as out of our sense they doe not borrow;
> And are the efficient cause, the true progression
>     Of sleeping visions, idle phantasmes waking,
>     Life, dreames; and knowledge, apparitions making.
>
> (st. 13)

Memory, whose office is to retain these impressions and mold them into arts, is obviously worthless: it can only perpetuate the "disguis'd intelligence" it receives (14). Finally, the understanding,

> which though it containe
> Some ruinous notions, which our Nature showes,
> Of generall truths, yet have they such a staine
> From our corruption, as all light they lose;
>     Save to convince of ignorance, and sinne,
>     Which where they raigne let no perfection in.
>
> (st. 15)

The consequence of this analysis is that "mans bankrupt Nature is not free,/By any Arts to raise it selfe againe" (16). Even if "these faculties of apprehension" were perfect, as they were at creation, the senses of the bodies they must use as instruments would insure error (18). The paradox of mental and physical aging is adduced as an effect of original sin to conclude this section:

> Yea of our falne estate the fatall staine
> Is such, as in our Youth while compositions,
>     And spirits are strong, conception then is weake,
>     And faculties in yeeres of understanding breake.
>
> (st. 19)

Greville has here presented in highly condensed fashion the principal doubts of reason and man's perceptual capacities that were entertained by the philosophical skepticism much in vogue at the turn of the century.[29] The blueprint for this skeptical procedure can be found in Sextus Empiricus' discussion of the "Ten Modes" and the huge palace constructed along its lines in Montaigne's "An Apologie of Raymond Sebond."[30] The unreliability and weakness of the senses—usually argued by invidious comparisons to beasts—and the emotional distortion of perception, with all the resulting contradictory opinions and customs of mankind, were the standard weapons of the skeptics in their assault on the anthropocentric universe. Bacon of course classified these debilities most succinctly as the Idols of the Tribe and the Cave. He also noticed the similarity of the negative beginning of his program for the sciences to "a sort of suspension of the judgment" but explicitly distinguished his purpose from that of the skeptic philosophers: "I do not take away authority from the senses, but supply them with helps; I do not slight the understanding, but govern it."[31] Greville's purpose, however, is much closer to Montaigne's, for he recapitulates in minuscule compass at the beginning of *Humane Learning* the arguments that Montaigne expansively flows into and out of in the "Apologie": the initial ambiguous tribute to knowledge as an ideal; the impotent human infant and the sensuous superiority of beasts; the total inaccuracy of "our intellec-

---

[29] Miss Buncombe cites the appearance of these doubts in such writers as Donne, Chapman, Davies of Hereford, Raleigh, and Greville's more particular friends, Sir John Davies and Samuel Daniel (pp. 12ff).

[30] *Outlines of Pyrrhonism*, trans. R. G. Bury, Loeb Classical Library (London, 1933), I, 25–93 (I.36–163); and *Essayes*, trans. John Florio, Modern Library (New York, n.d.), pp. 385–547 (II.xii). The other Renaissance encyclopedia of skepticism, which Greville also uses, is Cornelius Agrippa's *De Incertitudine et Vanitate Scientiarum*. Bullough discusses this and other sources: *Poems and Dramas*, I, 55–56.

[31] *Works*, ed. James Spedding, Robert Leslie Ellis, and Douglas Denon Heath (London, 1857–74), IV, 54–60, 111–12 (*The New Organon*, I.xli-lviii, cxxvi).

tuall and sensible faculties," with the consequent universal disagreement (23–24) and lack of self-knowledge.[32] As they thus undermine
reason, both writers also exalt faith—Montaigne's of course being a
repose upon the authority of the Church that Greville regarded as the
whore of Babylon. Pyrrhonism could naturally cut both ways. Richard
H. Popkin has described its use by French Counter-Reformation Catholics to attack the "authorities" of Calvinism—Scripture and the inner
light.[33] The fideism that skepticism supported only established faith itself as a ground for belief: faith in exactly what was another matter.

But if Greville and Montaigne share the same broad philosophical procedure, their motives, as well as the tone of their literary approaches, are
very different. To doubt reason because, upon exhaustive examination
of its operations and conclusions, reason seems dubious is one thing; to
doubt it because of an a priori assumption about its nature is quite another.[34] Greville keeps the disaster of the fall constantly before our eyes
in a way that Montaigne never does. Montaigne's whole enigmatic
"defense" of Sebond (which could be aptly described today as a "put-
on") is merely an excuse for his delighted, garrulous application of the
skeptical method as described by Sextus Empiricus: "To every argument investigated by me which establishes a point dogmatically, it seems
to me there is opposed another argument, establishing a point dogmatically, which is equal to the first in respect of credibility and incredibil-
ity."[35] In another essay Montaigne, speaking of physicians, virtually
paraphrases this remark: "Loe heere how they in all their discourses
juggle, dally, and trifle at our charge, and are never able to bringe mee
a proposition, but I can presently frame another to the contrary of like
force and significance."[36] At one point in the "Apologie" he gleefully
cites the conflicting opinions of twenty-seven ancient philosophers on
the divinity that rules the universe, and exclaims, "Trust to your Phi-
losophie, boast to have hit the naile on the head; or to have found out
the beane of this Cake, to see this coile and hurly-burly of so many
Philosophical wits."[37] He also claims that this confusion instructs him
into humility, but of this we see little evidence.

The net effect of his colossal attack on man as the measure of all

---

[32] *Essayes*, pp. 385–86, 402, 505–10 (II.xii, *passim*). Greville was apparently well-
acquainted with Montaigne's English translator: see Frances A. Yates, *John Florio*
(Cambridge, 1934), pp. 48, 92–93.

[33] *The History of Skepticism from Erasmus to Descartes* (New York, 1964),
ch. IV.

[34] The same distinction is drawn by Hoopes (p. 116), discussing the historical
interrelation of fideism and skepticism.

[35] *Outlines of Pyrrhonism*, I, 121 (I.203).

[36] *Essayes*, p. 696 (II.xxxvii).

[37] *Ibid.*, pp. 459–61 (II.xii).

things is to reach virtually the viewpoint of modern anthropological relativism, which would effectively demolish Sebond's rational theology along with Montaigne's own lip-service to the notion that nature herself manifests her great Christian Architect. Montaigne is clearly enchanted by the method, by means of which he charms us, and has a pleasant disregard of its logical implications. Greville on the other hand clearly subordinates the method to his theology, using the "skeptical arguments as a logical means for asserting religious dogma,"[38] and even allows the logic of the arguments, as will be discussed below, to modify that dogma. This contrast between the two writers can be summarized by Bacon, who criticizes with his usual lucidity what he sees as a consequence of skepticism: "yet still when the human mind has once despaired of finding truth, its interest in all things grows fainter; and the result is that men turn aside to pleasant disputations and discourses and roam as it were from object to object, rather than keep on a course of severe inquisition."[39]

Despite this essential difference in temperament and intention, Greville and Montaigne appear to share a certain quality of mind that could partly account for "the way in which impulses originally fideistic and impulses originally skeptical often blend in the minds of sixteenth-century thinkers to produce the same result."[40] The result referred to is the denial of reason's ability either to arrive at certainty or to exert moral control. And the common quality of mind that can produce this antithesis to right reason is simply literalism. On the fideistic side, the text-torturing of the Puritans produced on the stage such comic butts as Malvolio and Tribulation Wholesome, and caused no less a historical analyst than Bacon to trace the origin of his "first distemper of learning, when men study words and not matter," to the "more exquisite travail in the languages original" of the ancients who were revived by the early Protestant reformers in their battle against the schoolmen.[41] Bacon's identification of Protestantism with what we should nowadays see as the independent and earlier phenomenon of humanism reminds us of their common antipathy to medievalism, to its religious doctrines, its Latin style, and its vernacular literature. When Roger Ascham finds nothing in chivalric romance but manslaughter and bawdry he is echoing a moral objection to the genre that had been made throughout the Middle Ages by men

---

[38] Buncombe, p. 131. Apropos of this contrast, Howard Schultz finds that "If arts failed of their purpose to repair the damage that Adam had done to the human intellect, Greville more sincerely than Montaigne found sin at fault, darkening the understanding": *Milton and Forbidden Knowledge* (New York, 1955), p. 31.

[39] *Works*, IV, 69 (*The New Organon*, I.lxvii).

[40] Hoopes, p. 97.

[41] *Works*, III, 283–84 (*Advancement of Learning*, I).

(like Dante and Petrarch) who were scarcely literal-minded.[42] But he, along with the whole generation of mid-sixteenth-century humanists, had acquired new weapons for the old battle in a literal-minded confinement of Aristotle's newly recovered doctrine of imitation to a "narrow concept" of wholly credible reproduction of empirical reality.[43] Humanistic literalism of this kind bridged the religious chasm: Ascham's staunchly Protestant sentiments are echoed by Montaigne, who is proud not to have sullied himself in his youth with such "wit-besotting trash of bookes" as those of King Arthur, Lancelot, and Amadis.[44] Greville, to judge by the "finer moralities" he singles out for praise in the *Arcadia* and by his apology for its having been an entertainment, would most likely have agreed (*Life of Sidney*, pp. 11–18).

But there is a more thoroughgoing literalism which perhaps underlies the textual or the pedagogical, and which provides the assumptions that can credit the arguments and the procedure of skepticism. When Greville denies the ability of arts to contain "infallible" scientific truth, he calmly proposes

> For proofe, What grounds so generall, and known,
> But are with many exceptions overthrowne?
>
> (*Humane Learning*, 23)

To disavow the whole notion of generality because exceptions can be found is to demand a certitude so absolute that it is, indeed, possible only "to the Deity" (22), and to demand it, moreover, in literal terms. In philosophy such terms of course constituted the nominalist challenge to the realists. If men wished to poke holes in the fragile synthesis sustained by the syncretic, figurative, analogical universe of the medieval rationalists, one way to do so was to focus attention on the particular, discrete data of sense and to deny that language could permit discourse of anything else. The mental habit thus engendered, and the object to which it was directed, provided a vague common ground for the later blending of fideism and skepticism. The blend is apparent, for example, in the thought of Cornelius Agrippa. The habit—refusing to order observations by mind—has been suggested as a way to reconcile Agrippa's lifelong pursuit of both magic and science with his fideist repudiation of knowl-

---

[42] Roger Ascham, *The Whole Works*, ed. J. A. Giles (London, 1864–65), II, *Toxophilus*, p. 7; see also III, 159 (*The Scholemaster*, I).

[43] Alban K. Forcione, *Cervantes, Aristotle, and the "Persiles"* (Princeton, N.J., 1970), pp. 31–32. See also his critique of "Renaissance Interpretations of Mimesis," pp. 45–48.

[44] *Essayes*, p. 138 (I.xxv). Such literalism seems partly responsible for Montaigne's most ungracious moments, as when he criticizes the penchant of antiquity for deifying human characteristics as having proceeded "from a meere and egregious sottishnesse . . . of mans wit," p. 461 (II.xii).

edge: "Empiricism without theoretical guidance practically guaranteed the belief he showed in magical phenomena."[45] All data are equivalent; all testimony not disproved by concrete experience must be accepted.

Only a literal mind could be troubled by the fact that beasts are better equipped with teeth, claws, skin, strength, speed, and agility than men are. It is instructive to hear Hooker dismiss this subject:

Beasts are in sensible capacity as ripe even as men themselves, perhaps more ripe. For as stones, though in dignity of nature inferior unto plants, yet exceed them in firmness of strength or durability of being; and plants, though beneath the excellency of creatures endued with sense, yet exceed them in the faculty of vegetation and of fertility: so beasts, though otherwise behind men, may notwithstanding in actions of sense and fancy go beyond them; because the endeavours of nature, when it hath a higher perfection to seek, are in lower the more remiss, not esteeming thereof so much as those things do, which have no better proposed unto them.[46]

Hooker can allow himself the luxury of seeing beyond the discrete phenomena to the idea of the great chain of being that embraces them all, which is based on the Aristotelian principle that all things tend to perfection in their several kinds. Sir Thomas Browne dismisses the subject in a similar fashion by seeing it as a part of God's "equity" in dealing with all his creatures: "Thus have wee no just quarrell with Nature, for leaving us naked, or to envie the hornes, hoofs, skins, and furs of other creatures, being provided with reason, that can supply them all."[47] Hooker can also discriminate degrees of certitude, which are of course fatal to the all-or-nothing of skepticism:

The greatest assurance generally with all men is that which we have by plain aspect and intuitive beholding. Where we cannot attain unto this, there what appeareth to be true by strong and invincible demonstration, such as wherein it is not by any way possible to be deceived, thereunto the mind doth necessarily assent, neither is it in the choice thereof to do otherwise. And in case these both do fail, then which way greatest probability leadeth, thither the mind doth evermore incline.[48]

"O false and treacherous Probability," cries Greville, which only loses "obedience in the pride of wit" until "the vayles be rent, the flesh new-borne" (Sonnet 103).

[45] George H. Daniels, Jr., "Knowledge and Faith in the Thought of Cornelius Agrippa," *Bibliothèque d'Humanisme et Renaissance*, XXVI (1964), 332–33. Admitting that Agrippa was influenced by Pyrrhonism, Daniels denies that he was a proper skeptic, and compares him rather to Occam and Hume.

[46] *Of the Laws of Ecclesiastical Polity*, in *The Works*, ed. John Keble (Oxford, 1845), I, 217 (I.vi.2).

[47] *Religio Medici*, ed. L. C. Martin (Oxford, 1964), p. 19 (Sec. 18).

[48] *Laws*, I, 268 (II.vii.5).

One final contrast may be mentioned between the literal or descriptive and the symbolic or normative views of nature. Montaigne speaks of man's "superfluous and artificiall" desires: "It is wonderfull to see with how little nature will be satisfied, and how little she hath left for us to be desired. The preparations in our kitchins, doe nothing at all concerne her lawes. The Stoikes say, that a man might very well sustaine himselfe with one Olive a day."[49] This is precisely the sort of argument that Shakespeare often puts in the mouths of his villains. When Goneril and Regan urge it against Lear, his famous reply assumes the whole philosophical tradition that saw splendor, not sustenance, as truly natural to the dignity of man:

> O, reason not the need! Our basest beggars
> Are in the poorest thing superfluous.
> Allow not nature more than nature needs,
> Man's life is cheap as beast's.
>
> (II.iv.263–66)

The fatal mirror can produce no such reflection. After Greville discredits the several arts and sciences, he restates the ground for his conclusion:

> Againe, if all mans fleshly Organs rest
> Under that curse, as out of doubt they doe;
> If Skie, Sea, Earth, lye under it opprest,
> As tainted with that tast of errors too;
>     In this Mortalitie, this strange privation,
>     What knowledge stands but sense of declination?
>
> (*Humane Learning*, 48)

The "Rhapsody of questions controverted" (49) by "Wit, a distemper of the braine" (20), cannot discover positive truth; it can reveal only the sin from which it springs and the haste with which the world is moving toward its final conflagration. "Wit" is almost always used by Greville as a pejorative term for the craft, cunning, pedantry, or web-spinning subtlety of the unregenerate reason. Throughout Greville's castigation in *Humane Learning* of the futility of philosophy, medicine, grammar, music, mathematics, rhetoric, law, and government, he applies the perspective (systematically unfolded in *A Treatise of Religion*) that he does not state explicitly until the end of the poem: true wisdom as inward, moral regeneration. Two examples will suffice: physicians are mere "Word-sellers," who "have no power to cure/The Passions, which corrupted lives endure" (30). Similarly, grammarians spend lifetimes wrangling over rules

[49] *Essayes*, p. 417 (II.xii).

> For some small sentence which they patronize;
>    As if our end liv'd not in reformation,
>    But Verbes, or Nounes true sense, or declination.

(st. 31)

The grim pun on the key term, "declination," is typical. Everything we do that has not the direct, immediate, and literally conceived purpose of serving or glorifying God is not worth doing.

Several commentators have noticed that in his rigid and literal application of this perspective Greville, in effect, out-Calvins Calvin.[50] Paul H. Kocher presents the fullest statement:

Greville reposed certitude only in faith and explained the loss of certitude in every other activity as due to the curse of the Fall. This was skepticism Christianized, but Christianized in a way that neither Catholicism nor Protestantism approved, since both these theologies assigned no such drastic consequences to the doctrine of original sin. . . . No other Elizabethan poem [than *Humane Learning*] was based on a skepticism so profound, consistent, and thoroughly reasoned.

Professor Kocher also mentions *Nosce Teipsum* and Montaigne as

more extreme in describing the disaster of the Fall than was Calvin himself. And it is not impossible that they and others like them were misapprehending the new Reformation doctrine of human depravity, not recognizing that the great reformers themselves restricted it to matters of faith and morals, and therefore applying it in the field of practical sense and reason, to science in short, where it was never intended to apply.[51]

Perhaps not intended—but it is difficult to see this restriction, in the light of Pauline theology, as anything but arbitrary. Calvin proposes that within our partly destroyed faculty of reason "there is one understanding for terrestrial things, and another for celestial ones" (the latter being totally blind and stupid), and stakes off the areas that each concerns. But he does not maintain this distinction at all clearly in a cognitive sense. It is surrounded, for example, by Saint Augustine's statements on the corruption of even our natural talents, which would seem to debilitate the "terrestrial" reason also. But Calvin then extols as "gifts of God" the intellectual achievements of the ancients in law, politics, mathematics, and science for their "acuteness and perspicacity in the investigation of sublunary things," only to deny such exercises "in the sight of God . . . a solid foundation of truth." Here he is still, apparently, speaking of the

[50] Bullough, *Poems and Dramas*, I, 62. Greville's extension of the effects of the fall from ethical to scientific reason and his consequent epistemology of the sinful is a major point of Miss Buncombe's (pp. 74, 120, *et passim*).

[51] *Science and Religion in Elizabethan England* (San Marino, Calif., 1953), pp. 56, 58.

"terrestrial" understanding, for not until later does he begin to address the problem of reason's blindness in matters of faith.[52] The ambiguity of the entire crucial passage naturally provided his enemies with ammunition, and his followers with endless controversy. I do not think it unfair to suggest that Calvin's powerfully humanist education momentarily got the better of the logical implications of his theology.

Greville certainly uses the logic of skepticism to extend the consequences of original sin; yet he also, it seems to me, in his consistent application of the tacit equation of wisdom with moral virtue, merely allows the logic of original sin to extend itself. For one who felt the Pauline ethical dilemma as keenly as Greville did, it was an inevitable inference that if reason could not grasp moral truth, it could not grasp any truth. If we, with Paul, stop calling knowledge (the exercise of natural reason) virtue and start calling virtue (a supernatural gift) knowledge, our definition precludes us from knowing anything in the ordinary way. "I will destroy the wisdom of the wise, and will bring to nothing the understanding of the prudent. . . . Hath not God made foolish the wisdom of this world?" (I Cor. 1:19–20). Greville does not flinch from the logical and literal application of the Apostle's words. Like Hooker with the opposite viewpoint, he wished to see truth as one and indivisible, and did not care to divorce cognitive from ethical truth as Calvin had imperfectly attempted. Francis Bacon was only too glad to supply the deficiency.

Bacon's confident and ambitious plan for the reform of learning may now direct our attention to Greville the practical man and practicing Protestant who, though he must strive not to be of the world, must nonetheless live in it. Having demonstrated in the first sixty stanzas of *Humane Learning* "the Vainenesse, and Defect / Of Schooles, Arts, and all else that man doth know" (60), Greville rejects the counsel of ignorance that such a demonstration might imply and cautiously begins to offer his program for plucking the "grapes sprung up among the thornes" of learning (62). He makes the purpose of this program unmistakably clear at the outset:

> For as the World by time still more declines,
> Both from the truth, and wisedome of Creation:
> So at the truth she more and more repines,
> As making hast to her last declination.
> Therefore if not to cure, yet to refine
> Her stupidnesse, as well as ostentation,
>     Let us set straight that Industrie againe,
>     Which else as foolish proves, as it is vaine.

(st. 63)

[52] *Institutes*, I, 292–97 (II.ii.12–16, 18).

From this "Industrie" the elect, "Gods Children . . . these pure soules (who only know his voice)" and "Have no Art, but Obedience, for their test," are significantly exempt (64). Greville's program is only a stopgap, a curb for the vanity and foolishness of the unredeemed; it cannot pierce the mysteries of truth and has nothing to do with questions of ultimate value. Hence, just as the inwardly converted are above the demands of the law, so do they transcend the epistemology of the wicked.

The key words in Greville's program are "use," "practice," and "action." Since "God made all for use . . . / The World should therefore her instructions draw / Backe unto life . . . / To make them short, cleare, fruitfull unto man" (71). Knowledge for its own sake is of course anathema: what Greville calls for is the development of technology. We should study nature, not books, and use our knowledge of natural causes, gained by experiment, to produce effects (73–75). Terms in each course of study should be precisely defined and stable,

> To which true end, in every Art there should
> One, or two Authors be selected out,
> To cast the learners in a constant mould.[53]
>
> (st. 78)

Likewise, each national state should use its outward church to impose conformity in religious matters, and its laws, "meere Children of disease" (91), to punish those who deviate from it, thereby insuring domestic tranquility and obedience to the sovereign (79–95). Throughout this discussion, Greville emphasizes that the earthly institutions of church and state despise the truth and hate the good; their harsh—and wholly orthodox—regimen is justified despite its wrong motives by its socially beneficial effects,

> Since when, from Order, Nature would decline,
> There is no other native cure but terror.
>
> (st. 92)

Greville was assuredly no Puritan in political affairs; as servant to Queen Elizabeth and councillor to King James he could not afford to be. His interpretation of Christian liberty was exclusively inward. The visible church is utterly irrelevant to salvation; it is a product of fallen nature, and its principal function is, with civil law as its enforcing power, to maintain society in what appears to the twentieth-century observer as

[53] We should remember that this seemingly fanatical demand for precision was not wholly unwarranted by the wide-ranging and haphazard curiosity of Elizabethan learning. Louise C. T. Forest nicely documents the chaos of one major field in "A Caveat for Critics against Invoking Elizabethan Psychology," *PMLA*, LXI (1946), 651–72.

a state of *rigor mortis*. This repressive response to the rapidly increasing social changes of the late sixteenth century was typical (then, as now) for members of the establishment. Although Sidney, unlike Greville, seems to accept the right of subjects to rebel against a tyrant under carefully defined circumstances, he is amused and appalled by the spectacle of frankly competing interests uncontrolled by a hierarchical principle:

For the Artisans, they would have corne and wine set at a lower price, and bound to be kept so stil: the plowmen, vine-laborers, and farmers would none of that. The countrimen demaunded that every man might be free in the chief townes: that could not the Burgesses like of. The peasants would have the Gentlemen destroied, the Citizens (especially such as Cookes, Barbers, and those other that lived most on Gentlemen) would but have them reformed.[54]

Order—of the old style—or chaos appeared to most men as the only alternatives. Hooker defended the order as ideal; Greville as expedient.

Greville restricts the terminal arts (most of what we should now call philosophy and science) to probability (96–101), suggesting that government exert some control over political theory, and he urges the radical simplification and the severely practical application of the instrumental arts (102–23). He then leaves this "vanity, with her Sophistications" (127) to return to a discussion of how the elect can renounce it all as false wisdom, and submit willingly to their temporal prince (128–38). He concludes the poem by reiterating some of the abuses of learning (one of which seems to be the "dissolving" contradictions of skepticism) and by explicating the idea of true wisdom as moral regeneration (139–51). This perspective seems in fact to have instructed Greville into humility: his final words remind us not to be hastily prideful in scorning this world, since our nature has

> lost her being, ere she understood
> Depth of this fall, paine of Regeneration:
> By which she yet must raise herselfe againe,
> Ere she can judge all other knowledge vaine.
>
> (st. 151)

For many of the specific items in his program Greville is indebted to traditional and contemporary authorities, among them Seneca, Agrippa, Machiavelli, and Bacon. His debt to the latter seems the most pervasive, and has been subject to various assessments. Greville's views in *Humane Learning* have been seen as largely identical with Bacon's, as a "reply"

[54] *The Complete Works*, ed. Albert Feuillerat (Cambridge, 1922–26), I, 315 (*Arcadia*, II.xxvi). See W. D. Briggs, "Political Ideas in Sidney's *Arcadia*," *Studies in Philology*, XXVIII (1931), 137–61.

to him, and as "a neat summation, distinct from Baconianism, of neo-humanistic practicality."[55] In their contexts, these opinions are generally complementary. Greville and Bacon shared a dismal estimate of human capacities; the poet approved the usefulness of induction and experiment promoted by his friend, and thus, in effect, "took his place beside Ascham, Daniel, and Bacon as an apostle of action and a reformer of learning."[56] In terms of intention, however, Greville is certainly distinct from, or even antagonistic to, Bacon's belief in the value of empirical science and the "double truth" by which he formulated it.[57] The intention most concerns us here, the moral vision to which all else is subordinate and in the light of which Greville must counsel scientific reform and political obedience as virtually a hopeless hope: we may strive to make life bearable, provided only that we do not delude ourselves into thinking we can make it perfect.

Like other, and greater, Renaissance poets, Greville was concerned to evaluate, in his verse treatises, the major motive forces and human values of his time. Over all of them his ultra-Calvinism casts that "sense of declination" which makes them essentially illusions at the same time as it preserves them as practical necessities. Such was his view of rational knowledge itself, and such are his views of fame, military conquest, and politics.

The last infirmity of noble mind gets a verse treatise all to itself: *An Inquisition upon Fame and Honour*. Dismissing material gain and pleasure at the outset, Greville considers honor as man's chief "bayte," drawing him to noble action as Aristotle advised and as Hercules practiced (1–6).[58] But the poet immediately suggests, in a series of ironic questions, the egoism on which such action depends:

> For else, what Governour would spend his dayes,
> In envious travell, for the publike good?
> Who would in Bookes, search after dead mens wayes?
> Or in the Warre, what Souldier lose his blood?
>> Liv'd not this Fame in clouds, kept as a crowne;
>> Both for the Sword, the Scepter, and the Gowne.
>
> (st. 7)

[55] Whitaker, pp. 22–23; John Buxton, *Sir Philip Sidney and the English Renaissance* (London, 1954), p. 289; and Schultz, p. 31.

[56] Schultz, p. 30.

[57] Utz remarks that there was no such thing as "double truth" for Greville (p. 47). Similarly, Miss Rees sees Bacon's vision of man's dominion over nature as having "no place in Fulke Greville's assessment of man" (p. 186).

[58] Hallett Smith describes the allegorized Hercules as a type of the Renaissance epic hero: *Elizabethan Poetry: A Study in Convention, Meaning, and Expression* (Cambridge, Mass., 1952), pp. 300–303.

The summarizing metonymies in the couplet, as well as the succinct indictment, are typical. In this labyrinth of error, men are excited to accomplishment of any kind only for the sake of reputation. Even if we were capable of the disinterested pursuit of goodness or truth, the world would not honor it:

> No man yeelds glory unto him that makes him,
> For if he doe, he sees the world forsakes him.
>
> (st. 10)

In his darkened state, man "makes himselfe his end" (11), creating "strange oddes, betweene the earth and skie," so that

> Humours are mans religion, Power his lawes,
> His Wit confusion, and his Will the cause.[59]
>
> (st. 12)

To equate, therefore, fame with virtue is an hypocrisy of hell (18); but hypocrisy, "in this estate of Mans defection" (15), has its uses. Precisely because man is forever exiled from the good, states do well to encourage his thirst for self-glorification; if he will not be reformed, he can at least be constrained.

> In humane commerce, then let Fame remaine,
> An outward mirrour of the inward minde,
> That what man yeelds, he may receive againe,
> And his ill doing, by ill hearing finde:
>     For then, though Power erre, though Lawes be lame,
>     And Conscience dead, yet ill avoyds not shame.
>
> (st. 28)

Greville then leaves "these stormy orbs of passion" (29) to discuss the true ideal that fame violates:

> For Mans chiefe vertue, is Humilitie;
> True knowledge of his wants, his height of merit;
> This pride of minde, this Magnanimity,
> His greatest vice, his first seducing spirit;
>     With venimous infection of his fall,
>     To Serpent-like appearance ever thrall.
>
> (st. 33)

The remainder of the poem (some fifty stanzas) condemns fame by using a mundane analysis of its nature and origin (in the fickle opinion

---

[59] Throughout this treatise Greville's language exhibits one of its best characteristics: the compressed epigrammatic force that prompted C. S. Lewis to comment on its resemblance to the Augustan manner (p. 523).

of the mob), its motives (pride of heart, place, or praise), and effects ("hard gotten, worse to keepe," 71) to substantiate the theological judgment upon it. The reiteration of the latter is the conclusion:

> Who worship Fame, commit Idolatry,
> Make Men their God, Fortune and Time their worth,
> Forme, but reforme not; meer hypocrisie,
> By shadowes, onely shadowes bringing forth.
> (st. 86)

Greville's censure of war in *A Treatie of Warres* follows a similar procedure, except that it is largely unqualified by beneficial effects. The church can promote reverence and piety although it possesses them not; under the spur of fame, men may act rightly, even if for the wrong reasons—but the energies that war calls forth are seen as evidence of alliance with the devil. The poet begins this examination by showing how war reverses the advantages of peace, and by reviewing its ostensible causes in contrast to its real ones:

> Thus see we, how these ugly furious spirits,
> Of Warre, are cloth'd, colour'd, and disguis'd,
> With stiles of Vertue, Honour, Zeale, and Merits,
> Whose owne complexion, well Anatomis'd,
>   A mixture is of Pride, Rage, Avarice,
>   Ambition, Lust, and every tragicke vice.
> (st. 20)

Although these diseases on the part of rulers bring the destruction of war upon the people,

> Yet are not Peoples errors ever free
> From guilt of wounds they suffer by the Warre:
> Never did any Publike misery
> Rise of it selfe; Gods plagues still grounded are
> On common staines of our Humanity:
>   And to the flame, which ruineth Mankind,
>   Man gives the matter, or at least gives wind.
> (st. 23)

All of us are infected by "the humour radicall/Of Violence," so that

> Men would be Tyrants, Tyrants would be Gods,
> Thus they become our scourges, we their rods.
> (st. 25)

"By our fall" we have forsaken God and embraced the rebellious spirit of the devils, so that we war against each other, "Which Devils doe not; wherein worse we are" (26).

For proofe; this very spirit of the Devill,
Makes men more prompt, ingenious, earnest, free,
In all the workes of ruine, with the evill,
Than they in saving with the goodnesse be;
  Criticks upon all writers, there are many;
  Planters of truth, or knowledges not any.[60]

                    .    .    .    .    .

Yea even in Warre, the perfect type of hell;
See we not much more politicke celerity,
Diligence, courage, constancy excell,
Than in good Arts of peace or piety?
  So worke we with the Devill, he with us;
  And makes his harvest by our ruine thus.

                                               (st. 27, 29)

Having thus firmly located the cause of war in men's willful transgressions, Greville returns to and elaborates on the traditional historical
idea of war as a scourge of God. Remembering that the devil himself is
"Under the power of Heaven," we must "the hand of God confess, / In
all these sufferings of our guiltinesse" (31). War is caused by that for
which it is a punishment: God uses our unpleasant vices as instruments
to plague us. From the viewpoint of the Almighty, wars are just and
necessary. Greville pursues this point, as shown in the Old Testament
and in the cyclical rise and fall of nations, as proof of man's mortality,
that is, of God's intention that man shall not inherit the "time-made
World." Along with the "oppositions here below, Of Elements . . . / Of
constellations . . . / Of qualities in flesh," war is yet another of these
"Principles of discord" (48). As with these, its causes and effects

Lye close reserv'd within th'Almighties lap:
  Where fashion'd, order'd, and dispos'd they be,
  To accomplish his infallible decree.

                                               (st. 49)

Greville concludes the poem by suggesting the problematic consequences of the paradox of war as man's sin and God's decree. He distinguishes two kinds of war. The first,

Warre proceeding from the Omnipotence,
No doubt is holy, wise, and without error,
The sword of justice, and of sinne the terror.

                                               (st. 50)

---

[60] Greville continues this literary analogy for the destructive impulse as a result
of original sin in the next stanza, claiming that satire is more popular than lyric
or epic.

The second, "Warres of Men," will not be entered into by good Christians without extensive confirmations of their divine purpose by divine portents (52). This classification of wars "of God" and "of men" appears to be a restatement of the dual perspective the poem has taken on war, not a distinction between holy wars and others. I cannot take it—as Bullough seems to (I, 68, 70)—for unhesitating approval of a Crusade as the most just of all wars, since in the following stanza, wars "built on Piety" are regarded as one kind of "Warres of men."[61] And even though they are pious, they must be undertaken lawfully and mercifully (53–54). Greville then suggests, in a series of unanswerable questions, other highly problematic "warrants" for waging war. His conclusion is that they "Whose end in this World, is the World to come . . . / Can in the War find nothing that they prise" (59). A lament for Christian disunity and temporal ambition ("For to their own true Church they strangers are," 65) leads to the final couplet:

> Since States will then leave warre, when men begin
> For Gods sake to abhorre this world of sinne.
>
> (st. 68)

The implication in all this is that although war—especially religious war—may be just in the grand scheme of divine providence, our participation therein is never so, is always colored by sinful impulses, and is therefore best avoided.

At all events, Greville's strategy in *A Treatie of Warres* is basically the same as that in the treatises of *Religion* and of *Humane Learning* and in *A Disquisition upon Fame and Honour*. In all of them he establishes a theological perspective of stringent Calvinism which deprives his subjects of their customary value; he justifies the perspective by some logical means—by exposition of doctrine, by reference to a philosophical system, by historical example, or, most frequently, by inference from empirical observation—and thus revalues his subjects, to a greater or lesser extent, as necessary evils.

This procedure differs only in its proportions in his longest treatise, *Monarchy*; the controlling perspective is the same. Greville introduces this subject by describing at length "those goulden dayes" (2) when power ruled in justice, love, and truth, when good rulers had the heroes of myth to do their bidding and were deified after death, when even the

---

[61] This point is also made by Hugh N. Maclean, "Fulke Greville on War," *Huntington Library Quarterly*, XXI (1958), 106. Mr. Maclean's interpretation of the poem's dualistic view of war, which "encloses . . . rationalist views within an outlook characteristically voluntarist" (p. 109), generally supports my brief discussion.

spite of goddesses could not destroy "true worth" (13). But whether from
pride or envy, the golden age expired, and

> Tyme straight claym'd her succession in the brasse,
> And to her ends new instruments inspired,
> With narrow selfenes, stayning all that was.
>
> (st. 19)

The gods withdrew from the earth, leaving it to the anarchy of man's
discontent with authority, and afflicting it for the first time "With tem-
pests, earthquakes, fire, and thunders terrors" (21).

> In which confused state of declination
> Left by these Gods, mankinde was forc't to trust
> Those light thoughts, which were moulds of his privation,
> And scorning equalls, raise a Soveraigne must:
>     For frailty with it self growen discontent,
>     Ward-like must lyve in others government.[62]
>
>         .    .    .    .    .
>
> Let each then knowe by equall estimation,
> That in this fraile freehold of flesh and blood,
> Nature it self declines unto privation,
> As mixt of reall ill and seeming good;
>     And where mans best estate is such a strife,
>     Can order there be permanent in life?
>
> (st. 24, 27)

The consequences of the passage from the golden to the brazen age
are obviously those of the fall, and are described by Greville's usual
theological vocabulary in which the concept of the privation of good—
both in man and in external nature—is central. The identification of the
mythical golden age with the Christian paradise of Eden was a medieval
commonplace,[63] which here supplies Greville with an alternative means
of asserting that government is firmly rooted in original sin. But if such
an order cannot be permanent, it can at least prevent chaos by setting
bounds to the "endless Myne" (43) of man's desires through laws and
distinctions of degree. How these things are to be done and why monarchy is fittest of all forms of government to do them are set forth in
detail in the more than six hundred remaining stanzas of the poem. In

---

[62] Wilkes (p. 234) notes that the next stanza alludes to the Biblical account of the
origin of kingship (I Sam. 8:4–22). God prophesies that the Israelites' wished-for
king will abuse them, and that it will be their own fault.

[63] Edward Tayler traces and discusses this identification, mainly with reference
to its implications for pastoral poetry, in Nature and Art in Renaissance Literature
(London, 1964), pp. 96–101.

this presentation, political theory receives the most perfunctory treatment; Greville's main interest is in prescribing the proper uses of power, very much in the tradition of the vast advice-to-princes literature of the Renaissance. Although his purpose is thus less exclusively evaluative than in the other treatises, the evaluation, stated at the beginning and assumed throughout the poem (of war as the scourge of error by omnipotence, 522; of law as "but corrupt reason," 242; of the outward church as socially coercive hypocrisy, 238), is the same.

This evaluation proceeds from the irrevocable dualism which consistently controls Greville's vision of life, and which will provide a recurring theme even in his love poetry. He knew the difference between the wisdom of this world and God's, between necessity and truth, between earthly expediency and moral principle. The distinction must be clearly understood so that we will not be misled into finding "contradictory positions" in Greville's thought. His recent editor, G. A. Wilkes, sees *Religion* as repudiating the rest of the treatises and hence postulates a "development" of Greville's thought which proceeds from condoning to condemning the efforts of natural man. Partly on this basis, he argues for a chronological "sequence" of the treatises.[64] His evidence, however, depends on no such "development," but merely on the clear shift in subject matter between the earlier treatises and the later. But to say that Greville ceased dealing with the earthly battle of passion and reason to focus on man's radical corruption, or that "the preoccupations of the statesman yield to the preoccupations of the moralist," is by no means to say that he contradicts himself, or that he reaches a "new metaphysic."[65] He may well deny in *A Treatise of Religion* as morally efficacious what he has recommended in *A Treatise of Monarchy* as politically viable; this is not a conflict, but rather the same thing viewed from two different perspectives, the divine and the profane. As we have seen, Greville explicitly uses both perspectives in *Humane Learning, Fame and Honour*, and *Warres*. To ignore this dualism, which Greville is careful to maintain, in the pursuit of a conjectural notion of "development" is to overlook a principal source of irony and pathos in his writing: the premise that our seeming goods are real evils, and that of ourselves we are incompetent to remedy this condition.

Far from confusing when considered as a whole, his work best reveals itself when so taken, as the circumstances of its provenance virtually

[64] "The Sequence of the Writings," p. 489.

[65] Wilkes, pp. 16–17. There is almost no external evidence for dating either the treatises or the lyrics with any confidence or precision. Miss Rees, for these and other reasons, rejects Wilkes's view both of Greville's thought and of the chronology (pp. x, 207–12).

command.[66] *Certaine Learned and Elegant Workes* (including all that Bullough printed in his two-volume edition) appeared in 1633, five years after the poet's death, with the following information on the title-page: "Written in his Youth, and familiar Exercise with Sir Philip Sidney." *The Remains* appeared in 1670 with a publisher's note that tells us, "When he grew old he revised the Poems and Treatises he had writ long before, and . . . intended . . . to have had them Printed altogether." According to both his modern editors, the state of the manuscripts bears ample witness to this claim for revision. It seems highly unlikely that anyone with the leisure (for about ten years after the death of Elizabeth and again in the last few years of his life, he held no government office), the financial independence, the didactic purposes, and the literal mind of Greville would conscientiously prepare for publication works whose metaphysics would cancel each other out. It is rather more likely that he would, instead, leave some indication of how they were to be regarded, which is in fact the case. A note in Greville's own hand dictates the following placement of four of the treatises: (1) *Religion*, (2) *Humane Learning*, (3) *Fame and Honour*, (4) *Warres*, which order his editor rightly defends on grounds of relative importance.[67] The first does not invalidate the others, but rather "gives the foundation of all his beliefs," most clearly setting forth the opposition of heaven and earth upon which they depend.[68]

A final example may be given from a part of the poet's thought we have not yet discussed: it is true that Greville explicitly rejects in *A Treatise of Religion* (36) the Stoic *mens adepta* that he as explicitly recommends in "A Letter to an Honorable Lady."[69] The question is how and for what purpose does he counsel or deny Stoicism in each context? In the treatise Greville is discussing the nature and source of moral goodness, of which "Divine the Author, and the matter be," since

> Religion standes not in corrupted thinges,
> But vertues, that descend with heavenly winges.
>
> (st. 35)

---

[66] Wilkes asserts the confusion: "The Sequence of the Writings," p. 489. Miss Rees makes the same objection to his view: "It seems rather that [all the poems] have in general been so worked over that each presents a fully integrated statement of its author's mature attitudes and beliefs" (p. xi).

[67] Wilkes, *The Remains*, p. 16.

[68] Bullough, *Poems and Dramas*, I, 52. W. W. Greg has also shown that the printer of the first edition in 1633 intended to honor Greville's direction by placing *Religion* first, but that it was cancelled—no doubt for political reasons—during the printing: "Notes on Old Books," *The Library*, VII (1922), 217–19.

[69] Wilkes alleges this to be a conflict (*The Remains*, p. 17). The "Letter" is printed in *The Works in Verse and Prose Complete*, ed. A. B. Grosart (London, 1870), IV, 233–96.

From this viewpoint it is obvious that "heathen vertue," a mere "state of minde" (36), cannot possibly root out the evil in man; it can only balance it—"passion with her counterpassion peas'd" (38). In the "Letter," however, Greville is giving advice to a particular lady (whom Grosart conjectured to be Lady Penelope Rich) in a particular situation. The lady had evidently been mistreated by her husband and was contemplating some sort of reprisal against him. Greville, in his most graceful and coherent prose, displays keen sympathy for her position, coupled with a keener awareness of its difficulty in the eyes of the world he knew well: "Now if you will examine the preeminences of a husband's estate, you shall soone discover what huge armies of usurpation, custome, municipall lawes, are in this strife of mastering him against you; truth in some degree, fortune, and opinion universally."[70] Hence he cannot be mastered; he is too far gone to be mended, nor can she please him without corrupting herself. Having logically demolished the outward alternatives, Greville argues that the lady should bear her cross with obedience and a quiet mind, that she should cultivate in this world of flesh, this "purgatory of the soule," an inward peace.[71] He shows her "by reasone, that obedience is just and necessary; by example, that it is possible," and urges her not "to forsake herselfe, for his ill that hath already forsaken her." Thus she will attain by "this practice of obedience . . . a calmed and calming *Mens adepta*."[72]

Even if Greville had stopped at this point we could find no metaphysical conflict in this recommendation, simply because Greville is not speaking metaphysically. He is rather trying to show the lady what is her most practical and least damaging course of action in this less than best of all possible worlds. In fact, though, he does not stop here, but continues (before the letter breaks off unfinished) to suggest the achievement of true virtue. He proposes that the lady, having made peace with this world by Stoic calm, concentrate on winning the next by worshipping the only true God: "For in the one we worke with our owne strengths, which are but weaknesses: in this with His, that is omnipotent."[73] There can be no clearer statement that Greville was never confused about the ultimate value of the practically expedient. Virtue resides wholly in the giving up of self to God; no heathen philosophy can accomplish this, although a philosophy that trains us first to renounce the things of this

[70] *Works*, IV, 245.
[71] *Ibid.*, p. 256. We may recall that the elect willingly obey their king (*Humane Learning*, 136–38). Greville appeals to the same idea here: outward obedience is nature's tribute to power, and helps us to focus our energies on our inward reform (p. 259).
[72] *Ibid.*, pp. 283, 287.
[73] *Ibid.*, p. 296.

world may indeed be useful. Greville makes a similar statement in the sestet of Sonnet 86: man can merely "endure" his self-created ills, or he can "forsake" them by turning to heaven.

I have attempted to sketch in broad outline the general application of Greville's Calvinistic dualism, and to suggest, even more broadly, its relation to the thought of his time. Before we proceed to examine how he explores its constituent ideas and attitudes in his lyric poetry, and how they in turn affect some of the stylistic features of that poetry, it may not be amiss to comment on Greville's vision of life as such. Because that vision is so remote from our own, and because it finds expression in precisely those tones of uncompromising dogma and facile analogy that we have been taught to disdain, we are too easily lulled, when confronting it, into a sense of our superior sophistication. Something of this kind appears in much modern criticism of Renaissance verse, for example, Patrick Cruttwell's *The Shakespearean Moment*, the partial thesis of which is that Puritanism—not without help—destroyed the suspensive, syncretic mental attitudes that made the best Renaissance poetry possible. This is debatable, but is possibly in some sense true. The point is that to assert it, Mr. Cruttwell does not have to call the religious beliefs of the Puritans "nonsense."[74] If anything, this damages his argument, since the particular belief he speaks of was shared by all Protestants, certainly by Donne, who is Mr. Crutwell's poetic *ne plus ultra*. We may be convinced that predestined reprobation is nonsense, and that Juno's wrath against Aeneas, medieval courtly love, and Wordsworth's child-mysticism are nonsense too. But unless we are willing to dismiss Virgil, Chaucer, and Wordsworth because they believed what we do not, we cannot thus dismiss the Puritans. Assessing the effects of their beliefs is one thing; scorning them out-of-hand is quite another.

It is likely nonetheless that our attitude toward Greville's uncompromising brand of Calvinism is at best ambivalent: on one hand, we are repelled by its rigidity, literalism, and hostility to art or learning as valid modes of knowing truth; moreover, we may be repelled retroactively, as it were, by its subsequent and mutual development with Baconian utility into the mind-stifling middle class of yesterday and today. On the other hand, we are attracted to its salutary perspective of value, which does not sacrifice man to machine by allowing uniquely human desires and needs to be judged by mechanical standards. But whatever our feelings about Greville's fatal mirror, we can recognize that it contained for him distinctive reflections of human nature which he described in ways that make them worthy of our attention. No poem that lives—that substantiates a belief with the power of emotion, the evidence of experience, and

[74] *The Shakespearean Moment* (London, 1954), p. 142.

the discipline of logic—can possibly be a monument to dead ideas. For the very purpose of a poem (or, in Renaissance terms, the function of rhetoric ) is to provide its subject with a form that multiplies the possibilities of our response to it, enabling us at whatever remove of time or fashion to comprehend the perceptions that it offers.

It remains briefly to suggest the consequences of the dualistic vision for literary theory, as Greville saw them. Like all the other instrumental arts, poetry should be exclusively directed toward its particular use. Greville praises "those tymes"[75] when "Doinge and writinge" were the same, when men "who, what by sword they wan, / By pen as lively registred to man" (*Monarchy*, 486–88). He advises princes to "honor spiritts of Parnassus free, As knowinge best what fitts humanitie" (483), according to the following principle:

> All arts preferred by oddes of practicke use,
> The meere contemplative scorn'd as abuse.
>
> (st. 484)

This use—what best fits humanity—is of course moral direction, delivered in a certain way.

> For the true Art of Eloquence indeed
> Is not this craft of words, but formes of speech,
> Such as from living wisdomes doe proceed;
> Whose ends are not to flatter, or beseech,
>     Insinuate, or perswade, but to declare
>     What things in Nature good, or evill are.
>
> (*Humane Learning*, 110)

Greville here discredits the traditional aims of rhetoric because they do not necessarily serve truth, and can "with empty sounds" mislead us "to false ends" (107). Rhetoric can also mislead us by playing the wanton with metaphor, which, however, is a necessary resource of language (108).

> Whereas those words in every tongue are best,
> Which doe most properly expresse the thought;
> For as of pictures, which should manifest
> The life, we say not that is fineliest wrought,
>     Which fairest simply showes, but faire and like:
>     So words must sparkes be of those fires they strike.[76]
>
> (st. 109)

[75] Presumably the ancient; in any case, not those of the "wranglinge mouncks" (485).

[76] This view of language recalls the Idols of the Marketplace, and the whole nominalist-pragmatist attitude. Greville remains sufficiently of his age, or sufficiently intelligent, not to advocate the total abolition of metaphor as Hobbes later did.

Words should represent things as directly and accurately as possible, and should "declare" to us whether these things are good or evil.

To some extent, this theory of didactic plain statement seems part of the common reaction against Elizabethan Euphuism in verse and prose, which exercised the "flowers and figures" of rhetoric for their own sake, almost wholly neglecting matter in the pursuit of "a seeming finenesse."[77] More fundamentally, however, Greville's advocacy and practice of the theory proceeded from moral and ontological grounds that were not shared by his friend Sidney.[78] Greville compares music with poetry as "Arts of Recreation," whose end being "meerely" to delight, can move us, but cannot "enrich the Wit,/Or . . . mend our states by it" (111). The assumption is that these arts are decorative—for delicate tastes, not "solid Judgements"—the frosting on the cake of nature (112). Even so, both arts have their uses: music may stimulate the appropriate feelings when used in church services or in battles, and poetry,

> if to describe, or praise
> Goodnesse, or God she her Ideas frame,
> And like a Maker, her creations raise
> On lines of truth, it beautifies the same;
> And while it seemeth onely but to please,
> Teacheth us order under pleasures name;
>     Which in a glasse, shows Nature how to fashion
>     Her selfe againe, by ballancing of passion.
>
>                                            (st. 114)

In sum, poetry

> (like Nature) doth Ideas raise,
> Teaches, and makes; but hath no power to binde.
>
>                                            (st. 115)

The assumption of the moral purpose of poetry was universal; where Greville and Sidney disagree is on the question of its moral efficacy, or value, and therefore on its manner of presentation. One of Sidney's great contributions to the English criticism of his age in the *Defence of Poesie* was the Italianate equation of teaching with delighting, which enabled

[77] Sidney, *Works*, III, 42 (*Defence of Poesie*).

[78] This important distinction is demonstrated by Hugh N. Maclean in "Greville's 'Poetic,' " *Studies in Philology*, LXI (1964), 170–91. The same distinction is unconvincingly denied by Norman Farmer, Jr., "Fulke Greville and the Poetic of the Plain Style," *Texas Studies in Literature and Language*, XI (1969), 657–71. Miss Rees, independently of these articles, arrives at the view that Greville does not share Sidney's faith in the imagination, that he is "uneasy" with the *Arcadia*, and that his "whole approach to the business of poetry was fundamentally different from that of his friend" (p. 199).

him to give poetry the supreme place in moral education. It was superior to philosophy precisely because it delighted, because it could move the passions and so stimulate our sinful wills to virtuous action: "Who readeth Aeneas carrying old Anchises on his backe, that wisheth not it were his fortune to performe so excellent an Act?"[79] Sidney's faith that art can lead us not only to know but to do the good informs the entire argument of the *Defence*.[80] It was sustained by the rational idealism that Greville consistently denies. Sidney has the poet coming to us with a *tale* that holds children from play and old men from the chimney corner; Greville has him *describing* goodness, and while he *seems* to please, what he is really doing is teaching. The difference in diction is vital: it is the whole difference between "discursive" and "representational" literature.[81] The delight of an enthralling narration is for Sidney the key to the moral power of literature; for Greville nothing has real moral power but the grace of God. Hence he regards all the arts as "useful chiefly to . . . shore up the *status quo* of the human condition, certainly not to draw men upward toward spiritual perfection."[82] Poetry cannot "mend our states"; it "hath no power to binde." What delight it offers is clearly separable from the benefits it confers: it "beautifies" the literal statement of the truth. The difference in mode of presentation implies a difference in subject which again reflects the differing ontological assumptions: Sidney's theoretical poet gives us the golden world, the ideal hero as an object of imitation; Greville's shows us how to balance the passions of our unruly nature.

It is Greville's distrust of delight that accounts, I think, for his uneasiness in presence of the *Arcadia*, and for his persistent treatment of that book in terms of his own theory, not of Sidney's. After giving a detailed catalogue of the political *exempla* to be found there, Greville concludes that Sidney's

purpose was to limn out such exact pictures, of every posture in the minde, than any man being forced, in the straines of this life, to pass through any straights, or latitudes of good, or ill fortune, might . . . see how to set a good

[79] Sidney, *Works*, III, 20.

[80] His stress on *praxis* as the end of art is mentioned in J. W. H. Atkins' discussion of why late sixteenth-century Englishmen felt the need to defend poetry and how they did so: *English Literary Criticism: The Renascence* (London, 1951), pp. 102–3, 349.

[81] The distinction is discussed by R. S. Crane, "Literature, Philosophy and the History of Ideas," *Modern Philology*, LII (1954), 80. It is ignored by Miss Rees in her account of Greville's didacticism (p. 192).

[82] Maclean thus summarizes the function of art as Greville saw it ("Greville's 'Poetic'," p. 176), and suggests its affinities with the "Platonic mode" of some Italian theorists (p. 191).

countenance upon all the discountenances of adversitie, and a stay upon the
exorbitant smilings of chance.

*(Life of Sidney*, p. 16)

This eloquent description does not falsify; it merely selects. What it
selects are not positive examples of lofty behavior, but rather directions
for the "ballancing of passion." Greville had no hope that any of us
could be excited to truly virtuous deeds by any mortal means; in his
view we are all in trouble—more so in good times than in bad—and what
we need are exact and straightforward instructions on how to get out of
it. Greville apologizes that "the first project of these workes" was "to
please others," and declares that Sidney,

when his body declined, and his piercing inward powers were lifted up to
a purer Horizon . . . then discovered, not onely the imperfection but vanitie
of these shadowes, how daintily soever limned: as seeing that even beauty it
self, in all earthly complexions, was more apt to allure men to evill, than to
fashion any goodness in them.[83]

*(Life of Sidney*, p. 16)

It has frequently been observed that the dramatic tension in Sidney's
work results from the conflicting claims of the ideal and the actual;
beauty for him could be both a means to moral edification and a temptation to sin. For Greville, it was almost exclusively the latter, and he
was at pains to praise his friend for convictions congenial to his own.
Hence he tells us that Sidney's purpose in the *Arcadia* "was not vanish-
ing pleasure alone, but morall Images, and Examples, (as directing
threds) to guide every man through the confused Labyrinth of his own
desires, and life" (*Life of Sidney*, p. 223). This, at any rate, is certainly
Greville's purpose in writing the life of Sidney, whose death is just such
a guide:

In which passage, though the pride of flesh, and glory of Mankind be commonly so allayed, as the beholders seldome see any thing else in it, but objects

---

[83] As evidence for this, Greville cites Sidney's "memorable testament" as leaving
instructions to burn the "unpolished Embrio" (*Life of Sidney*, p. 17). But no reference whatever is made to the *Arcadia*, or to any of his own writings, in Sidney's
will (*Works*, III, 310–16). There was, however, a seventeenth-century tradition
that Sidney, dying, directed that the *Arcadia* be burned. The story is told, with the
addition of *Astrophil and Stella* to the condemned list, by Thomas Moffet, *Nobilis;
or, A View of the Life and Death of a Sidney*, ed. and trans. V. B. Heltzel and
H. H. Hudson (San Marino, Calif., 1940), p. 11. Moffet's editors trace the tradition
to a reported remark of Sidney's wife (p. 117). Again we should remember that
Greville is selecting for emphasis a tendency that we can certainly find in Sidney.
Neil L. Rudenstine reminds us that in Arcadia, as well as in the courtly world of
Astrophil, "love and leisure invariably lead to trouble": *Sidney's Poetic Develop-
ment* (Cambridge, Mass., 1967), p. 273.

of horror, and pittie; yet had the fall of this man such natural degrees, that the wound whereof he died, made rather an addition, than diminution to his spirits. So that he shewed the world, in a short progress to a long home, passing fair, and wel-drawn lines; by the guide of which, all pilgrims of this life may conduct themselves humbly into the haven of everlasting rest.

*(Life of Sidney,* pp. 127–28)

Greville's very insistence on all these points betrays his discomfort with an art he regarded as ornamental, and his fear lest it not serve our higher purposes but "possesse our hearts" (*Humane Learning,* 115).

The discomfort and the fear are amply evident in Greville's comments on his own writing as well as in his treatment of Elizabethan history. On three occasions, in fact, he uses the word "poetical" as a synonym for "false" or "lying" or "unreal" (*Life of Sidney,* pp. 46, 50, 156).[84] He disavows any intention to excel as belletrist: the treatises, he tells us, grew out of the choruses of the tragedies, "yet being the largest subjects I could then think upon ... I preferring this generall scope of profit, before the self-reputation of being an exact Artisan in that Poeticall Mystery, conceived that a perspective into vice and the unprosperities of it, would prove more acceptable to every good Readers ends" (*Life of Sidney,* pp. 150–51). In the course of explaining why he did not intend his plays for the stage, he sees his literary object in "ordaining, and ordering matter, and forme together for the use of life," and specifies, in his well-known and accurate description of himself, what kind of use he means:

> For my own part, I found my creeping Genius more fixed upon the Images of Life, than the Images of Wit, and therefore chose not to write to them on whose foot the black Oxe had not already trod, as the Proverbe is, but to those only, that are weather-beaten in the Sea of this World, such as having lost the sight of their Gardens, and groves, study to saile on a right course among Rocks, and quick-sands.
>
> *(Life of Sidney,* p. 224)

He writes, in short, with that overwhelming "sense of declination" which sees man as lost beyond his own remedy in a maze of evil, and the writer as but the cartographer of these nether regions.

It should be emphasized that Greville's clear but casually formulated literary theory seems not only to follow from his Calvinistic dualism, but also to be a conscious choice. When it came to practice, as we shall

---

[84] Lawrence A. Sasek, in his concise survey of the opinions of Puritan divines, shows that "poet" and "poetical" are regularly used "as though they had unfavorable connotations": *The Literary Temper of the English Puritans* (Baton Rouge, La., 1961), p. 64. He locates such vague hostility to literature as art less in their religious creed than in "the narrrow pragmatism which some puritans shared with some non-puritan humanists and with many devotees of the new science" (p. 126).

see, he could on occasion turn out a sugared sonnet that rivals Sidney in fluency or Spenser in rhetorical elaboration. We may not admire his taste for literal didacticism, but we can recognize that his practice of it proceeded from his deepest convictions—which give it its characteristic expression and its power—and cannot impute it to simple lack of skill.

Professor Bullough thinks that "in Greville was lost a great moral and political essayist" (II, 62), which seems dubious to me. Surely few who have read Greville's prose regret that he did not write more of it. For all the vaunted obscurities and dull passages in the treatises, their stanzaic form at least provides pegs to hang the thought on. In contrast, the prose (except for pithy or eloquent moments, which are far more frequent in the verse) sprawls and rambles mercilessly.[85] Simply because the verse has a stanzaic backbone of rhythm and rime, which compels a kind of orderly progression, it can tolerate syntactical distortion and grammatical ellipsis in a way that prose cannot. We can appreciate Greville's thought in its stanzas; had he set it down in his prose, it is doubtful that we could even unravel it. If in our view "he made verse do the work of prose,"[86] we must remember that it is the kind of work that prose has only since Greville's time become universally capable of doing. Douglas Bush remarks that "Elizabethan prose, while it encouraged both poetic elevation and homely raciness, had not become a tempered and reliable instrument"; Yvor Winters less diplomatically calls the prose of the period, with few exceptions, a "crude instrument" in contrast to its poetry, in which "metrical form . . . provided guidance to syntactic structure and variation."[87] Of Greville's contemporaries, only a Hooker or a Bacon could wield the vernacular as an efficient expository tool; the achievements in prose that are best known are in other genres: in popular polemic, in exhortation, in personal meditation. The expository verse essay, on the other hand, was sanctioned by centuries of ancient and medieval practice, was currently being discussed and revived by Greville and his friends Daniel and Davies, and would in a hundred years become one of the dominant genres in English poetry. It was, along with the lyric, Greville's most natural idiom. A recent critic cites his verse as an example of the "nicety of statement" that is T. S. Eliot's first requirement for good poetry: the "perfection of a common language," economy, precision, perspicacity—the virtues of good prose,[88] virtues that Greville's own prose

---

[85] See, for example, the paragraph beginning "Nay more it pleased," *Life of Sidney*, p. 195. There is much there, but it requires much digging to sort out.

[86] Bullough, *Poems and Dramas*, II, 61.

[87] Bush, *English Literature in the Earlier Seventeenth Century*, 2d ed. (New York, 1962), p. 192; Winters, *Forms of Discovery: Critical and Historical Essays on the Forms of the Short Poem in English* (Chicago, 1967), p. xvi.

[88] Donald Davie, *Purity of Diction in English Verse* (London, 1952), pp. 67–68.

does not usually share. Since his ideas, as such, are largely unoriginal, had he explored them in prose he would be of interest today solely to historians. His mode of expression provides his primary distinction, and it is as a poet that Greville can command a wider audience.

In the light of his own literary theory, to argue for the merits of his poetry is to be put in the not unusual position of saying that he wrought better than he knew.[89] In part he did; but in larger part the strengths of his lyrics result from sources that do not fall under his strictures on poetry simply because he took them for granted: the early example of Sidney, which gave him both themes and techniques that he developed in his own way; the thorough training in rhetoric that he shared with every Renaissance schoolboy; and above all the passionate religious convictions that supplied his profoundest inspiration. Greville's success as a poet may be modestly suggested by his final remarks on his own work:

But he that will behold these Acts upon their true Stage, let him look on that Stage wherein himself is an Actor, even the state he lives in, and for every part he may perchance find a Player, and for every Line (it may be) an instance of life, beyond the Authors intention, or application, the vices of former Ages being so like to these of this Age, as it will be easie to find out some affinity, or resemblance between them, which whosoever readeth with this apprehension . . . let him use it freely, [and] judge . . . moderately of me, which is all the returne that out of this barren Stock can be desired, or expected.

*(Life of Sidney,* pp. 224–25)

[89] Which is merely to say that our critical standards are different from and broader than his own.

# II   The Ironic Petrarchan

THE variety and scope of *Caelica* both in subjects and forms were often a source of exasperation to earlier critics, one of whom suggested that the sequence should "be treated as a series of independent lyrics."[1] The collection indeed seems to be a kind of individual miscellany, a convenient repository for the shorter poems that Greville was writing, so far as we know, throughout his life. Clearly occasional addresses to his real or imagined mistresses (whom he calls Myra, Caelica, and Cynthia), which vary in tone from adoration to contempt, are interspersed with poems of general reflection on politics or society. Introspective poems seriously examining the emotional gamut of love are gradually replaced by clever and cynical performances before the courtly coterie. Two fabliaux are told; elegant (and perhaps intimate) praise is offered the Queen; and meditative religious and philosophical poems dominate the end of the sequence. Fewer than half of the 109 poems are 'true' sonnets; one-third employ the popular Elizabethan six-line iambic pentameter stanza, riming *a b a b c c*.[2] Of the rest, some use any of five other stanzaic forms, some tetrameter couplets, one poulter's measure; one is an experiment in rimed sapphics and another in poorly maintained trochaics.

The miscellaneous character of the collection suggests a chronological order for the poems,[3] although we cannot know to what extent they were later revised or rearranged. There are, however, two important signs of conscious arrangement—both notes in the manuscript.[4] The first, in Gre-

---

[1] Sidney Lee, *The Cambridge History of English Literature*, ed. A. W. Ward and A. R. Waller (New York and Cambridge, 1910), III, 267. He could find no narrative thread of biography, and hence neither passion nor sincerity in *Caelica*. George Saintsbury deplored it for not employing "quatorzains" exclusively: *A History of English Prosody* (1908), II, 91.

[2] Sometimes called the "sixain" by the Elizabethans, and today often called the "Venus and Adonis" stanza, which is historically misleading. I shall discuss Greville's use of this form in chapter III, and refer to it henceforth simply as "the six-line stanza."

[3] After Bullough presents his own and other arguments for this (*Poems and Dramas*, I, 35–38), he goes on to suggest, on the basis of references to "Myraphil" and "Caelica" in the Oxford *Exequiae* on Sidney, that the first seventy-six poems were written by 1586 (I, 41).

[4] Bullough, *Poems and Dramas*, I, 275.

ville's hand, refers to Sonnet 82: "this to (come?) after with the rest." The second indicates that Sonnet 83, a long poem in poulter's measure lamenting the poet's frustrations in love, should follow Sonnet 76. It seems clear that Sonnet 82, a moralistic address to the reader, is intended to introduce "the rest" of the poems in the sequence—beginning with 84, the farewell to Cupid—which deal largely with religious subjects, and to which 83 is irrelevant.[5] The obvious general shift in subject from the "heavens" as objects of earthly desire to the "heavens" as objects of moral passion is thus emphasized. The ironic play of the dualistic perspective on his title is characteristic of Greville, and suggests the dry mockery of profane love, which proceeds from its incompatibility with the divine, as a broad principle of thematic order in *Caelica*.

It has been plausibly suggested that the title is additional evidence of Greville's youthful poetic competition with his friend Sidney.[6] In a poem first printed in *A Poetical Rhapsody*, Sidney describes himself as "Striving with my Mates in Song," and the mates are identified in the margin as Dyer and Greville.[7] If Sidney addressed his love poems to a "star," Greville would go him one better by addressing his to a whole galaxy. The relationship of the two poets thus suggested "is not imitation, but deliberate rivalry, adaptation of another mood and personality."[8] It is the atmosphere of the poetic contest (as in the *Arcadia*) that pastoralism made popular, and in which, as we shall see, similar materials are used for very dissimilar purposes.

The rivalry, however, while it can reveal the great temperamental difference between the two poets, does not suggest the central problem that they shared: how to evaluate the fashion of Petrarchan love. Sidney is of course explicitly absorbed in the literary aspects of the problem in a way that Greville is not;[9] but the movement of Astrophil as he slides back and forth between ideal devotion and carnal desire and carefully examines the effects of each upon himself is duplicated by Greville in *Caelica*. Both writers "raise the problem of arriving at a definition of love

[5] This interpretation is also offered by Douglas L. Peterson, *The English Lyric from Wyatt to Donne* (Princeton, N.J., 1967), pp. 270–71. The date of these last poems is entirely hypothetical: Bullough (I, 52) thinks that they were all written by 1600; Wilkes ("The Sequence of Writings," pp. 499, 503) tentatively places them after 1610–14.

[6] By Frances A. Yates, in a letter to the *Times Literary Supplement*, August 7, 1937, p. 576.

[7] *The Poems of Sir Philip Sidney*, ed. William A. Ringler, Jr. (Oxford, 1962), *Other Poems* 7. All subsequent references to Sidney's poetry, taken from this edition, will be cited parenthetically in the text, using Ringler's titles and numbers.

[8] Bullough, *Poems and Dramas*, I, 45.

[9] David Kalstone speaks of his "excessive consciousness of style" as a symptom of the decay of the whole European Petrarchan tradition: *Sidney's Poetry: Contexts and Interpretations* (Cambridge, Mass., 1965), p. 180.

which adequately distinguishes between a selfless esteem for the beloved and a selfish desire to possess the beloved as an object of appetite."[10] In *Astrophil and Stella*, Sidney, admitting the claims of both, does not resolve the problem; Greville does, by denying the possibility of realizing ideal love in this world.

If Astrophil's unresolved conflicts furnished Greville with a set of themes, Sidney's experiments in the *Arcadia* with elaborately patterned verse of the ornate style no doubt suggested to him the kinds of techniques by which they could be embodied. In addition to some specific technical interests—in classical meter and in the use of feminine rimes —Greville seems to have acquired from his friend a definite sense of how to use formalized, balanced, and amplified rhetorical eloquence as a vehicle of meaning.[11] The meaning for each writer is of course different. In accordance with his theories in the *Defence*, Sidney seems most interested in exploiting stylized patterns of language for their ability to achieve the *energia* of style, the forcible, moving presentation of action or passion which was for him the source of the power and value of fiction, and which he found sadly lacking in the amorous versifiers of his day, those that "if I were a mistresse, would never perswade mee they were in love."[12] Greville, distrusting exactly this kind of power, tends to use the rhetorical patterns of the ornate style either to illustrate his general concepts, or to modify in audacious and subtle ways the very attitudes toward experience that the style itself implies.

We may begin by following Greville's introduction of the theme of Petrarchan love, with its consequent emotional conflicts, in the first series of poems in *Caelica*. Sonnet 1 is a finely balanced, conventional presentation of the Petrarchan mistress as an object of ideal devotion in the ideal world of Neoplatonic harmony:

> Love, the delight of all well-thinking minds;
> Delight, the fruit of vertue dearely lov'd;
> Vertue, the highest good, that reason finds;
> Reason, the fire wherein mens thoughts bee prov'd;
>     Are from the world by Natures power bereft,
>     And in one creature, for her glory, left.
>
> Beautie, her cover is, the eyes true pleasure;
> In honours fame she lives, the eares sweet musicke;
> Excesse of wonder growes from her true measure;

[10] Peterson, p. 266.

[11] That this was a primary accomplishment of Sidney is demonstrated by two excellent studies: Robert L. Montgomery, Jr., *Symmetry and Sense: The Poetry of Sir Philip Sidney* (Austin, Tex., 1961), pp. 26–27; and Neil L. Rudenstine, ch. VI.

[12] Sidney, *Works*, III, 41.

Her worth is passions wound, and passions physicke;
   From her true heart, cleare springs of wisdome flow,
   Which imag'd in her words and deeds, men know.

Time faine would stay, that she might never leave her,
Place doth rejoyce, that she must needs containe her,
Death craves of Heaven, that she may not bereave her,
The Heavens know their owne, and doe maintaine her;
   Delight, Love, Reason, Vertue let it be,
   To set all women light, but only she.

It would be difficult, I think, to find another poem that presents as economically the rationale, effects, and literary methods of Renaissance courtly love. In each stanza the elaborate rhetorical and syntactic parallelism of the quatrains builds and focuses the praise exclusively upon the lady in the couplets. The parallelism of the whole, recapitulated by the word-figure in line 17, and emphasized by the rhythmic variation in the line, is the audible rendering of the metaphysic on which the emotion depends: the rational admiration of virtue enshrined in beauty is the true pleasure of love. The successive links between these faculties and feelings are expressed by the deft use of climax, or the figure of reduplication, in the first stanza: the series of clauses, waiting in suspense for the verb that will unite them in the lady, ascends to this unity in gradual steps by means of the successive postponement in the first three lines of the word to be repeated. The paradoxes inherent in the hyperbolic praise—"Excesse" resulting from proportion, cure from "wound"—are themselves subsumed by the dense texture of assonance in the second stanza. The asyndeton in the third stanza is reinforced by the double alliteration in the fourth foot of the first three lines, and varied, as the poem proceeds to its concluding summary, by the successive postponement of the caesurae in lines three and four. The light texture of assonance on the rime-sounds *v* and long *a* is linked with the dominant sound of the preceding stanza in "craves" and "Heavens," subtly reinforcing the emphasis, provided by the varied caesurae, on the title of the sequence: the lady is heavenly. All the grammatical, rhetorical, and prosodic techniques of the poem constitute the "balanced and ample style" that creates the symmetry requisite to a concept of love which "grasps its object as harmoniously proportioned."[13]

   In this ideal harmony, there is of course one potentially disquieting

---

[13] The phrases are from Montgomery's discussion of Petrarchan idealism, p. 59. The brevity and concision of Greville's poem exemplify Rosemond Tuve's interpretation of what "ample" means (*Elizabethan and Metaphysical Imagery* [Chicago, 1947], pp. 89–90): it does not mean mere expansion or abundance or repetition, but rather intensification, heightening; the "amplification" of modern audial electronics is, she suggests, the proper analogue.

implication: its sheer exclusiveness. Since the convention of Petrarchan love required that the lady be exalted as the sole possessor of all possible virtues, it entailed grave consequences for the lover whose "one creature," whose "only she," did not look with favor upon his devotion. The resultant frustration and suffering provided the rest of the staple themes of the genre, which could be developed in two major ways: as psychological self-analysis or as complaint of the lady's cruelty. Greville touches on both of these in Sonnet 2, in terms of a metaphor that suggests a relationship far removed from the harmonious ideal he has just presented. He addresses the lady as

> Faire Dog, which so my heart dost teare asunder,
> That my lives-blood, my bowels overfloweth.

Cupid has long pursued him, but she has given him "that fatall wound" which causes him to request either death or pity. The metaphor supplies him with a concluding argument that she is capable of the latter, "since Nature hath revealed, / That with thy tongue thy bytings may be healed." The lover languishing unto death from the disdain of the beloved is one standard pose he may assume; but Greville has assumed it by taking the stock notion of "wounds" and placing it within the implied metaphor of the hunt, which suggests the savagery of physical appetite. This kind of passion does not unite man's faculties, but divides them; it destroys innocence and binds "reason to her servant humor." It is not a reflection of order, but rather creates disorder. Accordingly, the style of the poem is in startling contrast to the carefully symmetrical rhetoric of Sonnet 1: Sonnet 2 contains no figures of syntax, no rhetorical parallelism whatever; it develops a single metaphor with graphic and unpleasant imagery. It is important to observe that the metaphor of dying, which was the conventional source of hyperbole and paradox to describe the magnitude of the lover's suffering, is here developed by Greville in order to focus rather on the source of that suffering, explicitly physical deprivation, and to suggest its internally divisive psychological consequences.

The first two poems of *Caelica* thus suggest the conflict between the higher and lower loves which was central to Astrophil, who, acknowledging that beauty, reason, and virtue all coexist harmoniously in Stella's perfection, still hears the cry of Desire: "give me some food" (*AS* 71). Greville proceeds to explore the conflict in the next several poems, suggesting some alternative attitudes that the lover can adopt to resolve it. The first of these is to ignore it by seeing the lady, as in the first poem, exclusively through the rose-colored glasses of ideal devotion. The restatement of this vision in Sonnet 3 is accomplished by a return to the patterned style that enforces it:

> More than most faire, full of that heavenly fire,
> Kindled above to shew the Makers glory,
> Beauties first-born, in whom all powers conspire,
> To write the Graces life, and Muses storie.
>     If in my heart all Saints else be defaced,
>     Honour the Shrine, where you alone are placed.
>
> Thou window of the skie, and pride of spirits,
> True Character of honour in perfection,
> Thou heavenly creature, Judge of earthly merits,
> And glorious prison of mans pure affection,
>     If in my heart all Nymphs else be defaced,
>     Honour the shrine, where you alone are placed.

The series of hyperbolic appositives to describe the lady in each quatrain builds to the refrain that, like a psalm, reiterates her exclusive praise in each couplet. She exemplifies "the Makers glory," and is honored, like him, with a kind of liturgy. It is typical of Greville's habit of compression that he implies the lady's superiority to all other representatives of divine perfection in both Christian and pagan terms. It is also typical of his precise control of all aspects of language that the grammar of the poem makes it a plea for favor at the same time that it is a hymn of praise: it is addressed to the lady, and asks her to honor the poet's heart, the shrine of devotion to her alone.

What this attitude of religious worship ultimately imposes on the lover is made explicit in the next poem, which continues the play upon the ideas and images inherent in the title of the sequence.

> You little starres that live in skyes,
> And glory in Apollo's glorie,
> In whose aspects conjoined lyes
> The Heavens will, and Natures storie,
> Joy to be likened to those eyes,
> Which eyes make all eyes glad, or sorie,
>     For when you force thoughts from above,
>     These over-rule your force by love.
>
> (Sonnet 4)

The lady's eyes are compared with stars in three concisely suggestive ways: the first is scientific and implies that the lady reflects divinity as the stars reflect sunlight; the second is ontological and implies that she represents the divine order of the universe; the third is astrological and implies her power—the love she inspires can "over-rule" the influence of constellations. The poet then prays to this love, "which in these eyes/ Hast married Reason with Affection, "to lend him wings, that he

> may rise
> Up not by worth but thy election;
> For I have vow'd in strangest fashion,
> To love, and never seeke compassion.

The religious vocabulary of adoration naturally, and most effectively, culminates in the religious idea of unmerited election: the lover of the Petrarchan ideal can only worship; he cannot sue for reciprocation of his love on the basis of his deserving, but must put away all desires of his own and hope for grace. The precision with which Greville controls the complex and various philosophical and religious concepts and the metrical fluency with which he weaves them together into a graceful song have made Sonnet 4 one of his most frequently anthologized lyrics. In context, however, the poem accomplishes even more, by using the conventional vocabulary to draw out the logical implication of the conventional attitude. And in so doing, it employs conventional stylistic devices: the parallel personified address in each stanza; the identical initial rime linking both stanzas; two word-figures of repetition ("glory" and "force" used in pairs as noun and verb) emphasizing the concepts that praise the lady. Thematically, Sonnet 4 is both a logical consequence of the preceding poem and a logical premise of the following one, which will combine the stylistic elements of both its predecessors but will use them for a different purpose.

For in Sonnet 5 Greville begins to suggest the inadequacy of the complete self-abnegation demanded by the conventional pose. He offers himself as an example that the attitude of worshipful hope results merely in betrayal. The rhetorical strategy is anachinosis—inviting the judgment of the reader:

> Who trusts for trust, or hopes of love for love,
> Or who belov'd in Cupids lawes doth glory;
> Who joyes in vowes, or vowes not to remove,
> Who by this light God, hath not beene made sory;
>     Let him see me eclipsed from my Sunne,
>     With shadowes of an Earth quite over-runne.
>
> Who thinks that sorrowes felt, desires hidden,
> Or humble faith with constant honour armed,
> Can keep love from the fruit that is forbidden,
> (Change I doe meane by no faith to be charmed,)
>     Looking on me, let him know, loves delights
>     Are treasures hid in caves, but kept with sprites.

The polysyndeton in each quatrain states the conventional pose, which is discredited in each couplet by an image. With reference to the preceding poems, the images are ironic: the lover's sun is now in eclipse; the delights of love are hidden and jealously guarded. The first image suggests the idea of the lady's change which is made explicit in the next stanza; the second reinforces the idea of coy capriciousness implicit in the mention of the "light God" in the first stanza. Also ironic is the stress upon the conventional pose provided by the word-play on "trust," "love," and "vowes." The symmetrical structure and the rhetorical figures are used to express the reverse of what they customarily imply: instead of harmony, discord; instead of rapture, sorrow. The poem contains two implications that Greville will develop explicitly and often in later poems: that women are faithless, and that therefore worship of them is but self-deception. For the present, however, he continues to explore the psychological consequences of the conventional conflict.

One such result of the lover's position as willing slave achieves smooth and subtly modulated expression in the rimed sapphics of Sonnet 6.[14]

> Eyes, why did you bring unto me those graces,
> Grac'd to yield wonder out of her true measure,
> Measure of all joyes, stay to phansie-traces,
>> Module of pleasure?

The question is not rhetorical; the answer begins to be implied in the next two stanzas, which describe the effects of those "graces" on the lover. They enthrall his thoughts, make his senses traitors and his reason a "disease,"

> So that all my powers to be hers, obey me,
>> Love be thou graced.

The harshly pejorative epithets that have described the process make this concluding statement almost sarcastic: it is as if he were asking, "Is this mental and emotional servitude, this loss of volition, the privilege, delight, and commendation of love?" The potential sarcasm is neatly sidestepped by the final stanza, which makes the answer explicit: "Grac'd by me Love? no, by her that owes me." What gives love its value is not his condition, but simply her "Angells spirit": she exemplifies the ideal. Although this is the conventional resolution, the structure and the language of the poem suggest ironies that betray dissatisfaction with it. Again, the obtrusive word-figures stress not proportion, but excess (the play on "measure" is clearly ironic); the most frequently reiterated word play on the idea of "graces" and "graced" is deliberately set up in oppo-

---

[14] Bullough (*Poems and Dramas*, I, 233) notes the superiority of the poem to all experiments, including Sidney's, in this meter before Campion. In his discussion of the first six poems of *Caelica*, Peterson (pp. 253–57) does not examine their style, but I am indebted to him for the general outline of my view of their thematic progress. Although I take exception to some of his views on style generally, and on Greville's religious verse particularly, I owe him much throughout.

sition to the inward bondage being described. In addition, the falling dactyllic and trochaic meter, reinforced by the consistent feminine rimes, establishes a mournful rhythm that is the precise audible equivalent of the lover's emotional state as he struggles to accept the ideal while he acknowledges its unhappy effects on him. The delicate and exact examination of such paradoxes is made possible only by the modes of perception inherent in the ornate style as exercised by a fine talent in the service of an acute intelligence.

If Greville can use the rhetorical orotundity of the eloquent style to establish a counterpoint of tension to the view of love that it assumes, he can also use it to suggest attitudes very much opposed to the role it demands. This role has produced misery; in Sonnet 8 Greville consoles himself for this suffering by imagining the revenge that time will wreak on its cause.

> Selfe-pitties teares, wherein my hope lyes drown'd,
> Sighs from thoughts fire, where my desires languish,
> Despaire by humble love of beauty crown'd,
> Furrowes not worne by time, but wheeles of anguish;
>   Dry up, smile, joy, make smooth, and see
>   Furrowes, despaires, sighes, teares, in beauty be.
>
> Beauty, out of whose clouds my heart teares rained,
> Beauty, whose niggard fire sighs' smoke did nourish,
> Beauty, in whose eclipse despaires remained,
> Beauty, whose scorching beames make wrinkles florish;
>   Time hath made free of teares, sighs, and despaire,
>   Writing in furrowes deep; she once was faire.

The rigorously symmetrical structure of the poem is achieved by two variations on the figure of collectour: not only are the previously explained terms repeated, but the verbs that complete their suspended syntax are also listed in series in the couplet of stanza one; and the terms are again repeated, in reverse order, in the couplet of stanza two. In both stanzas, the couplets conclude the careful asyndeton of the quatrains, which is established by the rhythmic aid of anaphora in the second stanza. The elaborate syntactic and rhythmic parallelism of the poem is of course integral to its meaning: beauty is subject to the identical miseries she causes. It will also be noticed that Greville is still exploiting, here ironically, the imagery latent in his title. The figurative language used to describe the effects of beauty is drawn from the attributes of the sky, especially of the sun, the reflection of whose glory by the lady made her formerly a symbol of divine perfection. Now, its eclipse represents her disdain, and its "scorching beames" her power to inflict anguish.

The highly formalized language and rhetoric of the whole poem lends great contrasting force to the simple and direct statement that concludes it: "she once was faire." What is thus suggested is the kind of vindictiveness, only much milder, that Donne was once thought to have a monopoly on, as exemplified in such a poem as "The Apparition."[15] But Donne usually attacked the servile pose of the Petrarchan lover by refusing to use the rhetorical structures of his style. By using these structures ironically, Greville can slyly undercut the pose with a rational, if temporary, solution to the self-pity that it requires.

This self-pity is of course an "essential motif of Petrarchan idealism: the necessary frustration of the lover who turns to a model of perfection. His pain and suffering must match in intensity the quality of his lady's beauty and virtue. . . . The lover, always hungry for divine excellence, must always content himself with frustrated despair, and these two conditions circumscribe his universe."[16] Greville has expressed impatience with the obsessive lamentation that the self-pity can produce; but he also understood that it could produce genuine analysis of the experience from which it arises. He offers such analysis in Sonnet 9, in terms that by implication criticize the mood of Sonnet 8. Addressing "Love, thou mortall sphere of powers divine," he complains of it as a tyrant who maintains sovereignty by fear. The political metaphor provides the subsequent argument:

> If I by nature, Wonder and Delight,
> Had not sworne all my powers to worship thee,
> Justly mine owne revenge receive I might,
> And see thee, Tyrant, suffer tyrannie.

But he has sworn to worship love, and hence cannot in justice obtain revenge for what love imposes on him any more than subjects can lawfully rebel against their ruler. He must accept sorrow, which consumes his life and overthrows his reason, if sorrow is decreed:

> So as while love will torments of her borrow,
> Love shall become the very love of sorrow.

The self-pity of the conventional pose is here given a rational and a psychologically accurate explanation: the poet is subject to love, so if love disdains him, he must love to be disdained. When passion fails of an object to which it is irrevocably committed, it must willingly embrace the failure, which is the only sign of the commitment, as the only way

---

[15] Donne's position, however, as "original" anti-Petrarchan has been assailed most provocatively by Donald L. Guss (*John Donne, Petrarchist* [Detroit, 1966]), who argues, unconvincingly I think, that "The Apparition" is an example of the "poise and propriety" of one strain in the Petrarchan tradition itself (p. 60).

[16] Montgomery, pp. 61–62.

it can be reaffirmed. This insight into the tenacity of human emotion is supplied by the convention, and is asserted by Greville in terms of a developed metaphor that suggests its logic, and of briefer metaphors— "tragedies," "orbe," "ruins"—which suggest its quality and force. The consequence of this analysis is that the lover has no recourse but supplication, and Greville concludes the poem with a prayer to love, to

> Move her to pitty, stay her from disdaine,
> Let never man love worthiness in vaine.

The style of the poem is wholly directed to the analysis of the emotion; its word-figures stress the key terms of the analysis, both in small patterns within the stanzas and in larger ones (especially the repetition of "powers," "sorrow," "love") throughout the poem.

To analyze the psychological validity of the conventional attitude, however, does not necessarily justify it, does not reconcile the theoretical glory of love with the actual wretchedness it can impose. Greville attacks this paradox directly in Sonnet 10, which gathers up some of the implications in the preceding poems, and provides a logical motive for the radical shift in attitude of the following ones. He addresses love, who, having been enticed from his mind by admiration of the lady's beauty and virtue, failed to win her and has now returned to what can only be called a disaster area:

> Within which minde since you from thence ascended,
> Truth clouds it selfe, Wit serves but to resemble,
> Envie is King, at others good offended,
> Memorie doth worlds of wretchednesse assemble,
> Passion to ruin passion is intended,
> My reason is but power to dissemble;
>     Then tell me Love, what glory you divine
>     Your selfe can find within this soule of mine?

The rhetorical question, its irony underscored by the grammatical ambiguity of "divine" (which can be taken as adjective or verb), is exactly the one he only hinted at in Sonnet 6.

This is indeed the problem, and Greville proceeds to resolve it by developing one part of the conventional philosophy which denies the other. He tells love to go back to the "heavenly quire" of the lady's beauties, "And there in contemplation feed desire," because

> those sweet glories, which you doe aspire,
> Must, as Ideas only be embraced
>     Since excellence in other forme enjoyed
>     Is by descending to her Saints destroyed.

The lady, as ideal, cannot be embraced in any earthly sense; she can only be contemplated, for the ideal simply does not exist in the flesh.

Small wonder, therefore, that the lover is doomed to miserable frustration when he tries to possess her. Greville has arrived at the explanation for the contradictory implications of Sonnets 4 and 5—the worshipful hope and its betrayal, along with the underlying conflict between flesh and spirit implied by the first two poems. The explanation is discovered in Greville's habitual and here explicitly Platonic dualism, by which he denies the Neoplatonic pretensions to create a continuum, a unity of flesh and spirit in this world. The precise philosophical terms of the poem continue and intensify the irony of adoration: if the descent of excellence from the heaven of Ideas or Forms destroys her, then her saints are spurious and their worship far from divine.

Robert Montgomery has suggested that Sidney's unique distinction lies in his fusing these two motifs of courtly love: Petrarchan suffering and Platonic idealism.[17] Greville, in contrast, uses the latter to explain the paradoxes of the former, and ultimately to discredit the Petrarchan pose altogether: suffering under an impossibility is absurd. The same perception of the lover's chaotic frustration that prompted Cardinal Bembo to climb the famous ladder of love will prompt Greville to saw it in two. The Platonic dualism that sees ideal love as a proper object only of contemplation also, of course, frees earthly love as an object of physical desire; putting the ideal above possession, we may strive to possess what we can without incurring such frustration. All these implications are developed in subsequent poems of *Caelica*; the idea that generates them is arrived at in Sonnet 10 as the solution to the emotional conflicts inherent in courtly love, which have received careful analytic exploration in these first ten poems.

Although the character of *Caelica* is a good deal more miscellaneous than that of most other Elizabethan sonnet sequences, and though it contains no single thread of narration, it is very much a "sequence" in the same thematic sense as are the sonnets of Sidney or of Shakespeare. The introductory poems we have examined are not the random flexings of an apprentice's muscles; they are serious explorations of experience conducted by a mature craftsman with a full command of the available tools. They represent, in little, what Northrop Frye has described in the large:

The Renaissance poet was not expected to drift through life gaining "experience" and writing it up in poetry. He was expected to turn his mind into an emotional laboratory and gain his experience there under high pressure and close observation. Literature provided him with a convention, and the convention supplied the literary categories and forms into which his amorphous emotions were to be poured. Thus his imaginative development and

[17] P. 53

his reading and study of literature advanced together and cross-fertilized one another.[18]

In Greville's case the process of cross-fertilization was no doubt accelerated by his poetic rivalry with Sidney. Both writers used the conventions of their time to probe and evaluate problems of thought and feeling common to all times; both learned to manipulate the conventional style in order to modify the conventional attitude. Both wrote sonnet sequences that are records of developing awareness, in which individual poems suggest moods or implications that cast new light on what has gone before, and foreshadow what is to come.

The direction that Greville's modification of the convention will take can be thrown into exemplary relief by comparing his use of some traditional Cupid lore to Sidney's. Long ago, Morris Croll was the first to list the specific poems in *Astrophil and Stella* and in *Caelica* that make use of similar Anacreontic legends about Cupid.[19] One of these is the tale of his migration from the tropics to the colder climates of the north. Sidney motivates his flight by an allusion to the contemporary conquest of Cyprus by the Turks, and has him taking refuge from the cold in the face of Stella, whose beauty promises warmth (*AS* 8). This promise, however, is deceptive, for her chastity soon drives him into the poet's heart, where "He burnt unwares his wings, and cannot fly away." Sidney's poem is a graceful blending, in Alexandrines, of several conceits to express the conventional paradox of the lady "most faire, most cold"; and the chilly Cupid provides a witty, oblique statement of his devotion to her.

Greville motivates the same flight by a mythological allusion whose imagery immediately identifies Cupid with cuckoldry and the directly physical aspects of sex. The remainder of the sonnet is a penetrating analysis of what we should now call the psychology of repression, as Greville describes Juno's expectations of Cupid's frustration and their disappointment:

> Juno, that on her head Loves liverie carried,
> Scorning to weare the markes of Io's pleasure,
> Knew while the Boy in Aequinoctiall tarried,
> His heats would rob the heaven of heavenly treasure,
> Beyond the tropicks she the Boy doth banish,
> Where smokes must warme, before his fire do blaze,
> And Childrens thoughts not instantly grow Mannish,
> Feare keeping lust there very long at gaze;

---

[18] *Fables of Identity* (New York, 1963), p. 91.

[19] *The Works of Fulke Greville* (Philadelphia, 1903), pp. 8–9. The permutation and combination of the numerous sources in individual poems can now be found more conveniently in the notes of both Bullough and Ringler.

> But see how that poore Goddesse was deceived,
> For Womens hearts farre colder there than ice,
> When once the fire of lust they have received,
> With two extremes so multiply the vice,
> As neither partie satisfying other,
> Repentance still becomes desires mother.
>
> (Sonnet 11)

Shame in northern ladies begins merely by postponing sexual indulgence, and ends by contributing to it. The story that Sidney used as a statement of personal devotion Greville has here transformed into an etiology for the rapacious joylessness of lust, which invites comparison to Shakespeare's direct treatment of the same theme in "Th' expense of spirit in a waste of shame" (Sonnet 129). Though Shakespeare's poem presents a far more powerful impression of the rapacity, it does not reach the final insight of Greville's—that guilt itself enhances the savor of the transgression.

In their treatments of the more general motif of the runaway Cupid, we can observe a less extreme but no less ironic difference between Greville and Sidney.[20] The blind and naked Cupid given harbor in the poet's heart was a common conceit which both poets use to complain of ingratitude shown to love's service (*AS* 65; *Caelica* 12). Sidney calls him "unkind," describes how he gave him shelter and eyesight, and suggests the resultant suffering in the final conventional metaphor: "Thou bear'st the arrow, I the arrow head." Greville calls him "naughtie," describes how he gave him eyesight and clothed him in reason, and immediately implies that this charity is foolishness: "Fye Wanton, fie; who would shew children kindnesse?" Cupid has clouded his eyes "with a seeing blindnesse" and made "reason wish that reason were forgotten." Then, in the sestet, Greville has him flying to Myra's eyes,

> Where while I charge him with ungratefull measure,
> So with faire wonders he mine eyes betrayeth,
> That my wounds, and his wrongs, become my pleasure;
> Till for more spite to Myra's heart he flyeth,
> Where living to the world, to me he dieth.

Sidney suggested only the suffering; Greville suggests in addition the willed acceptance of it that he has previously analyzed. Such acceptance, however, is less inevitable than sad and mildly ridiculous in this context, where gratitude from children cannot be expected, and where Myra loves all men but him. By emphasizing the childishness of Cupid, Gre-

---

[20] This fugitive is discussed, as to origin and as to his use in English poetry, by Lisle Cecil John, *The Elizabethan Sonnet Sequences: Studies in Conventional Conceits* (New York, 1938), pp. 69–77.

ville here develops his mischievous ingratitude into conscious spite, which he uses as an implied indictment of Myra's promiscuity. The twist in the couplet, which ironically devalues the emotion that the conceit ordinarily prescribes, is of course wholly absent from Sidney's poem.

Another popular myth of the fugitive Cupid—his exile for displeasing his mother—shows Greville at work in a similar way on material that Sidney uses for the conventional purpose. Here is Sidney's octave:

> His mother deare Cupid offended late,
>> Because that Mars, growne slacker in her love,
>> With pricking shot he did not thoroughly move,
> To keepe the pace of their first loving state.
> The boy refusde for feare of Marse's hate,
>> Who threatned stripes, if he his wrath did prove:
>> But she in chafe him from her lap did shove,
> Brake bow, brake shafts, while Cupid weeping sate.
>
>> (*AS* 17)

And here is Greville's:

> Cupid, his Boyes play many times forbidden
> By Venus, who thinks Mars best manhood boyish,
> While he shot all, still for not shooting chidden,
> Weepes himselfe blind to see that sexe so coyish.
>
> And in this blindnesse wandreth many places,
> Till his foe Absence, hath him prisonner gotten,
> Who breaks his arrowes, bow and wings defaces,
> Keepes him till he his Boys play hath forgotten.
>
>> (Sonnet 13)

Sidney is very careful to keep our sympathies with Cupid by motivating his offense in the domestic quarrel: he is threatened; a child, caught between contradictory commands, he has no choice, and weeps at the injustice of his punishment. There is no implied injustice, nor even any punishment, in Greville, who is more concerned to present the effects of Cupid's exile than its domestic drama. Like Sidney's, Greville's Cupid is damned if he does and damned if he doesn't—but only because of his mother's feminine inconsistency, which is the cause of both his weeping and his blindness. The idea of inconsistency suggests the antagonist of love, Absence, who in Greville's poem temporarily deprives Cupid of his power, which itself is twice referred to by the contemptuous epithet, "Boys play."

In his sestet, Sidney is able to exploit the sympathy he has built up for Cupid: we share his delight when his grandmother, Nature, replaces his broken weapons with Stella's eyes and brows. This homely pleasure

effectively sets us up for the twist in the couplet, where Cupid, armed
with Stella's beauties, "Like wags new got to play, / Fals to shrewd
turnes, and I was in his way." The personal application abruptly redi-
rects the emotion without materially changing it—the pleasure at Cupid's
recovery becomes the poet's delight at being injured with Stella's weapons
—and rounds off the whole gracefully formed compliment to the lady.
Greville's sestet, however, describes the consequences, implied by the
character of Venus in the octave, of Cupid's captivity by Absence. Love
remains blind, is restored full power but no constancy, and is released,
"no God of yeeres, but houres." The cynical devaluation is completed in
the couplet, which implies Cupid's own original capriciousness:

> Ladies, this blind Boy that ran from his Mother,
> Will ever play the wag with one or other.

In accordance with his celebratory purpose Sidney portrays the runaway
as victim; Greville, intending to criticize, as incipient libertine.

   The contrast between Greville and Sidney shows us two fine poets
working in the same convention and manipulating the same myths to
achieve their different purposes. A long-enduring prejudice—dating from
the nineteenth century when many critics went to the Renaissance
seeking the pretty effusiveness they admired in Shelley or Keats and
found it in Sidney and Spenser—has obscured Greville in the shadow of
his great friend, dismissing him for not writing the way Sidney was supposed to have been writing. Because this view, although fortunately
dying, is not quite dead, it is worth remarking that the three pairs of
poems we have discussed do not constitute a prima facie case for the
superiority of either poet. If Sidney's language is more conversational and
flowing, Greville's is more condensed and precise; if Sidney's emotional
range is more delicate, Greville's has greater complexity; if Sidney presents the conventional attitudes in fresh and original ways, Greville is
equally original in using the conventional material ironically. In accordance with his purpose, Greville uses tighter logical structures and
has more intellectual depth. This is not to say that Sidney is "decorative"
or "trivial." It is merely to insist that the poets are doing different things,
which must be understood before they can be judged.

   The other poems in *Astrophil and Stella* that make use of Cupid (11,
12, 13, 19, 20, 43) all see him in the more or less playful Anacreontic way,
and use him for the conventional ends: to praise by hyperbole, or to suggest the debilitating power and frustration of loving the physically en-
ticing but chaste Stella. Even when Sidney calls him "that murthring
boy," "theefe," and "Tyran" (*AS* 20), the intention is not to devalue the
experience he represents, but rather to assert its dramatic force. When
Astrophil falls into a carnal or cynical mood, he tends to express it direct-

ly, never placing Cupid, as Greville often does, in explicit opposition to
reason or virtue. Sidney does not, in short, use the myths ironically; nor
does he play on the pejorative, trifling connotation of the word "boy."
There is also in Greville another kind of Cupid—the malevolent Ovidian
knave—who never appears in Sidney.[21] The consciously spiteful child
and the light god of cuckoldry are already on the way to becoming in
later *Caelica* sonnets the deliberate deceiver (27), the jealous fool (20),
or the frankly cynical libertine (28, 31) who is loftily amused by man's
passionate sufferings over infidelity (76).

Just as Greville has previously used the rhetorical structures of the
ornate style to suggest ironic modifications of the conventional attitude,
he has in the three poems on Cupid we have examined (Sonnets 11, 12,
13) used the conventional myths virtually to deny the validity of the
experience they traditionally described. In context, the three poems function as justifications of the principle enunciated in Sonnet 10: they all
present examples of how ideal love, an "excellence in other forme enjoyed, / Is by descending to her Saints destroyed." In this world, that
love is destroyed by lust, ingratitude, or inconstancy. To complain of the
fickleness of women was of course a commonplace of the tradition; but
to use the complaint to discredit the whole traditional pose was not,
at least not until Donne made the mockery itself fashionable.

From this point in the sequence Greville goes on to examine the consequences of the conflict between ideal and actual love as he has dualistical-
ly defined it: the two loves are simply incompatible. We cannot pursue
all the ramifications of this examination here, but only outline its major
themes. These are (1) that the ideal per se is not discredited by its failure
to be realized; (2) that the failure proceeds both from attempts to express
the ideal devotion carnally, and from the unworthiness of its objects; (3)
that the devotion itself is therefore a kind of self-deception that entails
a variety of psychological consequences; (4) that, finally, earthly love is
best regarded as an urbane game that offers its own limited kind of satisfaction, which is not to be confused with other kinds.[22] Throughout his

---

[21] Miss John discriminates two species of Cupid: the mischievous, playful Anacreontic, and the vindictive, tyrannical Ovidian, from the latter of which the
medieval liege lord of lovers is derived (pp. 39–42). Greville uses all of these in
his own variations, one of which includes the reversal of the medieval derivation:
Cupid as the vassal of the lover (Sonnet 71).

[22] Peterson does not go into Greville's psychological development of these
themes, but he describes succinctly the dualistic position that generates them: "No
daughter of Eve could possibly embody the ideals of virtue and beauty that the
neo-Platonists insist upon, nor could any son of Adam worship such ideals in a
woman without finding his own fallen nature an unsurmountable obstacle"
(p. 258).

progressive reevaluation of the Petrarchan tradition, Greville generally
continues to use both its myths and its stylistic structures in ironic ways.

Immediately after his initial use of the Cupid stories to show that
women are lustful, ungrateful, and inconstant, Greville hastens to re-
assure himself that his mistress is nonetheless ideal. The abrupt series of
rhetorical questions in Sonnet 14 asserts a fine indignation toward the
previous cynicism by restating the logic and fitness of ideal devotion:

> Shall feare make reason from her right depart?
> Shall lacke of hope the love of worth forbeare?
>
> Love is a tribute to perfection due,
> Reason in selfe-loves-liverie bondage showeth,
> And hath no freedome, Myra, but in you.

But despite its justice, this attitude merely begins the vicious circle once
again: when he pays the tribute in Sonnet 15, his worship brings him
only frustration. The poet gives Cupid his eyes, and cuts "selfe-loves
wings to lend him fethers," only to find that

> His heate in her chast coldnesse so confoundeth,
> As he that burnes must freeze, who trusts must feare.[23]

The paradox which compels these paradoxical sufferings is succinctly
apprehended: "Honour and Beauty reconcil'd togethers" in the lady
constitute "the birth, the fatall tombe and story" of love. What one stimulates, the other forbids.

Although Greville explores and manipulates these paradoxes central
to the articulated feeling of Petrarchan love, his was not the kind of mind
or temperament that could finally content itself with such ambivalence.
Sonnet 16 passes the final dualistic judgment upon the worship/frus-
tration syndrome in terms of a simile asserting the dichotomy between
heaven and earth that lies at the center of all Greville's convictions on
whatever subject. Just as the earth is deceived by its own shadow, which
creates night, into thinking the heavens dark, so desire is deceived by its
own unhappiness into thinking love less than ideal:

> Fye foolish Earth, thinke you the heaven wants glory,
> Because your shadowes doe your selfe be-night?
> All's darke unto the blind, let them be sory,
> The heavens in themselves are ever bright.
>
> Fye fond desire, thinke you that Love wants glory,
> Because your shadowes doe your selfe benight?

---

[23] This poem, using the waggish Cupid to express the paradoxes of love's suffering, is Greville's single closest approach in theme and tone to the usual practice of
Sidney.

The hopes and feares of lust, may make men sorie,
But love still in her selfe finds her delight.

Then Earth stand fast, the skye that you benight
Will turne againe, and so restore your glory;
Desire be steady, hope is your delight,
An orbe wherein no creature can be sorie;
    Love being plac'd above these middle regions,
    Where every passion warres it selfe with legions.

Hope is the only reward of devotion to the ideal; we are simply mistaken
to think that we can possess it in a carnal fashion. Our suffering is therefore the result of self-deception, and in no way reflects upon the quality
of the ideal. The elaborate parallelism of syntax, rhythm, diction, and
rime is the formal realization of the cosmic analogy that does not inte-
grate, but rather isolates the ideal from the sublunary sphere. And there
it will remain: what Greville has done in these last three poems is to
recapitulate the analysis of the first ten, reasserting and developing the
solution first proposed in Sonnet 10. The solution is now final: Greville
attempts no further to assume the Petrarchan attitude, but instead anatomizes the various fallacies that result from its pretension to find the ideal
in the real.

With the ideal irrevocably beyond our grasp, our adoration of it becomes either futile or absurd, depending on its object. In the case of
"Cynthia, whose glories are at Full for ever," it is the former (Sonnet
17).[24] After stating his desire for her and her displeasure with it, Greville employs two different myths to suggest both the futility of adoration and its possible cause in considerations of reputation:

Are you afraid, because my heart adores you,
The world will thinke I hold Endymion's place?
Hippolytus, sweet Cynthia, kneel'd before you,
Yet did you not come downe to kisse his face.
    Angells enjoy the heavens inward Quires:
    Starre-gazers only multiply desires.[25]

Despite the careful ambiguity of the stanza—by which the allusion to
Hippolytus may also be taken as an oblique plea for favor, a counterargument to the suggestion in the reference to Endymion—its final em-

---

[24] This opening line, as well as the cautious, ambiguous tone of the whole sonnet, have suggested the conjecture that it was addressed to the queen. If this seems
plausible, we might even press it further: is "Endymion" Leicester? is "Hippolytus"
Raleigh?

[25] It is tempting to see in this line a sly criticism of Astrophil's (the star-gazer's)
whole progress, the finally unresolved tension of all his multiplied desires.

phasis is clear: only the angels can hear the harmony of the spheres; we who gaze from below can only wish to. Again, the imagery of *Caelica* is exploited for an ironic purpose. We are now firmly bound to the sublunary world, where selflessness in love is neither desirable nor possible. Caelica is now changeable and contemptuous; she adroitly and deliberately perverts the ideal into an excuse for her own promiscuity, and is neatly replied to in kind:

> I grudge, she saith, that many should adore her,
> Where love doth suffer, and thinke all things meet,
> She saith, All selfe-nesse must fall downe before her:
> I say, Where is the sauce should make that sweet?
>
> (Sonnet 18)

The absurdity of adoring such a female, expressed by the justly crass insistence on a *quid pro quo*, implies the larger absurdity in the whole notion of selfless service as it existed in the literary convention: it virtually prohibited reciprocation or mutuality of feeling.

The common-sense notion of the necessity for reciprocation in love as we can know it receives explicit expression in one of Greville's most graceful songs. It begins by urging an easy, take-it-or-leave-it attitude toward Cupid's capricious decrees:

> Away with these selfe-loving Lads,
> Whom Cupids arrow never glads:
> Away poore soules, that sigh and weep,
> In love of those that lye asleepe:
>     For Cupid is a meadow-God,
>     And forceth none to kisse the rod.
>
> (Sonnet 52)

Love is neither to be rejected nor languished over; not to enjoy it or to be made miserable by it are equally silly. But it must be enjoyed on its own terms, which, like destiny, can declare "causeless good or ill." The next two stanzas give an example of the proper attitude: when Cynthia gives him her ring, he carves her name in a tree and sings her praises; when she asks for it back, he merely blots "her name out of the Tree." The final stanza states the principle with fine ironic word play on the notion of "worth":

> The worth that worthinesse should move,
> Is Love, that is the bow of love,
> And Love as well thee foster can,
> As can the mighty Noble-man.
>     Sweet Saint 'tis true, you worthy be,
>     Yet without Love nought worth to me.

In this justly well-known song, the pleasant ridicule of the Petrarchan pose is accomplished by an ironic use of its vocabulary and by a deceptively tight logical structure.

In another frequently anthologized lyric, Greville offers a more personal and poignant expression of the inconstancy of Myra, which still by implication discredits the worshipful pose. The rhetorical strategy of the first stanza is repeated in the next three:

> I with whose colors Myra drest her head,
> I, that ware posies of her owne hand making
> I, that mine owne name in the chimnies read
> By Myra finely wrought ere I was waking:
>     Must I looke on, in hope time comming may
>     With change bring backe my turne againe to play?
>
> (Sonnet 22)

In each stanza the shared pleasures and gestures of past love are listed by anaphora and asyndeton in the quatrain, while the couplet rhetorically questions what the poet's attitude should be toward their loss. This structure, with its precise and particular evocation of the now lost affection, produces a charming melancholy; but the ironic language of the questions is an implicit denial of the selfless pose at the same time as it is a condemnation of the lady's lightness. Am I fool enough, Greville asks, merely to wait my turn to play? To hope idly for impossible miracles? To languish, sighing, until "dead love" resurrects itself? To hang around, suppressing jealousy, watching her show her favors to others?

> Was it for this that I might Myra see
> Washing the water with her beauties, white?

Both the melancholy and the irony are magnificently fused in this hyperbolic image adapted from Sidney (*Old Arcadia* 29, l. 107). Uncharacteristically, but with perfect taste, Greville ends the poem on this note of emotional poise, recalling Myra's refusal to commit herself in writing as a kind of anticipatory caution:

> Mad Girles must safely love, as they may leave,
> No man can print a kisse, lines may deceive.

The poem is a remarkable example of the delicacy and range possible within the ornate style manipulated by a master hand. The elaborate symmetry of its rhetoric, syntax, and rhythm, the pastoral gestures and the myths of the convention, are all employed not merely to express the emotional quality of the experience, but also to suggest, by means of irony, a judgment upon it grounded in its cause.

Greville, however, is seldom quite so delicate. More frequently, he suggests the unworthiness of the supposedly ideal object in more acrimonious ways. In directly denouncing women, both in general and in particular, he can evoke a frank and bitter sensuality that would do Donne credit. With a clever figure of implied insult he introduces the theme of one poem: "Sathan, no Woman, yet a wandring spirit" (Sonnet 21). He then gives, in the octave, two examples of the proper response to natural contradictoriness: Satan wants no part of sailors, who can move a ship "two wayes with one wind"; the satyr wants no part of men, who can use their breath both to warm and to cool. In the third quatrain, Cupid represents the guile of women, who command "all the Arts of Change." The implied comparisons are gathered up in the figure of collectour for the punning twist in the couplet:

> Saylers and Satyres, Cupids Knights, and I,
> Feare Women that Sweare, Nay; and know they lye.

The specifically sexual infidelity of women is the subject of both the fabliaux that Greville tells. Merlin laughs at a funeral procession in which a father mourns the death of a child whose real father is the monk who leads the procession. The final couplet implies the delight that women take in such deceptions with a crude but appropriate pun:

> True fathers singing, supposed fathers crying,
> I thinke make women laugh, that lye a-dying.
>
> (Sonnet 23)

Scoggin overheard his wife tell her lover that only her backside belonged to her husband; consequently

> Her breast and bellie he in cavasse dresst,
> And on her backe-side fine silke did bestow,
> Joying to see it braver than the rest.
>
> (Sonnet 50)

The extended moral of the story is obvious:

> If Husbands now should onely decke their owne,
> Silke would make many by their backs be knowne.

Greville's most complex and interesting development of this theme is accomplished by an elaborated metaphor which implies two additional dimensions in the idea of feminine infidelity: his own carnal desires and their frustration by gossip. Caelica's heart is compared in the first quatrain to the Garden of Eden, where the poet had part "Of every fruit and flower":

> But curious Knowledge, blowne with busie flame,
> The sweetest fruits had downe in shadowes hidden,
> And for it found mine eyes had seene the same,
> I from my paradise was straight forbidden.

> Where that Curre, Rumor, runnes in every place,
> Barking with Care, begotten out of feare;
> And glassy Honour, tender of Disgrace,
> Stands Ceraphin to see I come not there;
>    While that fine soyle, which all these joyes did yeeld,
>    By broken fence is prov'd a common field.
>
> (Sonnet 38)

The sensual tone established by the agricultural diction throughout underscores the acrid irony in his complaint of "glassy Honour," which prevents only him from further enjoyment of what is now free to others. The accusation of hypocrisy is intensified if we accept the implication that it is he who originally broke the fence. The audacious blasphemy of the metaphor and the whole quality of the sentiment might well have inspired Donne to similar performances.

In this world where women are fickle, reputation but hypocrisy, and love frankly sensual and capricious, the Petrarchan pose results in self-deception. Greville makes the point in a variety of ways and emotional tones. The Biblical metaphor of the Tower of Babylon provides a simultaneous condemnation of her unfaithfulness and his idolatry. The story of how "The pride of Flesh" sought "to over-reach the skye" and was punished by God is told in the octave and applied to the poet and Caelica in the sestet:

> So I that heavenly peace would comprehend,
> In mortall seat of Caelica's faire heart,
> To babylon my selfe there, did intend,
> With naturall kindnesse, and with passions art:
>    But when I thought my selfe of her selfe free,
>    All's chang'd: she understands all men but me.
>
> (Sonnet 39)

The metaphor of course asserts that his punishment is just; moreover, the nature of the punishment suggests yet another fallacy of the pose: it prohibits communication. All the arts of passion and devotion allow none to "tell his fellow what he thought." The irony is that in seeking a heavenly object where it cannot be found, he fails even of the mortal object. In Sonnet 41 this irony is analyzed with explicit, somber sarcasm.

> Alas poore soule, thinke you to master Love,
> With constant faith; doe you hope true devotion
> Can stay that God-head, which lives but to move,
> And turne mens hearts, like Vanes, with outward motion.

The questions are answered in the negative: the hope is false, and is accused by Honor of wasting time and corrupting reason. To this accusation, the poet cannot plead that he has "erred out of Love":

No hereticke, thou Cupid dost betray
And with religion wouldst bring Princes under;

By merit banish Chance from Beauties sky,
Set other lawes in Womens hearts, than will;
Cut Changes wings, that she no more may flye,
Hoping to make that constant, which is ill;
    Therefore the doome is, wherein thou must rest,
    Myra that scornes thee, shall love many best.

The Erastian metaphor here asserts the self-deception of imagining love to be anything but ungovernable chance or will. Cupid is a prince, not a priest; power, not principle. The brief but logically complex economic ("Honours Audit"[26]) and political-religious metaphors build to Greville's most direct and powerful statement of the natural frailties that make ideal love a real impossibility, and therefore a false god, in whose service sacrifices deserve and receive punishment.

Yet another self-deception that the misconceived pursuit of ideal love imposes on us concerns the value of the emotions that result from the inevitable frustration. Greville has of course expressed these before, ringing the usual changes on their paradoxes. His long poem in poulter's measure is in fact wholly devoted to their expression (Sonnet 83). Desire wil not die; it creates only self-perpetuating despair: his thoughts are but a "prey / To worth" because "My Saint hath turn'd away her face, and made that heaven my hell." He embraces, and is defined by, these woes—the point is made by punning on his name:

Let no man aske my name, nor what else I should be;
For Greiv-Ill, paine, forlorne estate doe best decipher me.

Sonnet 54 analyzes the inefficacy of exactly this kind of grief:

Light Rage and Griefe, limmes of unperfect love,
By over-acting ever lose their ends;
For Griefe while it would good affection move,
With self-affliction doth deface her friends;
    Putting on poore weake Pitties pale reflexion,
    Whereas Good-will is stirr'd with good complexion.

The poem treats in a serious vein the same subject that Suckling handles humorously in "Prithee, why so pale." Raving and self-pity are self-defeating; they succeed only in making one miserable and cannot possibly persuade the lady to affection. Striving is silly, since love is but the product of "idle Chance." Desire must discipline itself to conquer "by

---

[26] Probably sugggested by "Reasons audit" (*AS* 18). The resultant bankruptcy, however, is embraced in Sidney's sonnet by just the appeal to "love" that Greville here considers and rejects.

close invasion" and must learn "hope; not rage, feare, griefe, / Powers as unapt to take, as give reliefe." From the pragmatic perspective of the fallen natural world, the feelings that the convention prescribes are seen as wholly ineffective, and the love that motivates them as "unperfect."

The prescribed feelings can also deceive us in other ways. Greville describes Philocell seized with tongue-tied confusion on finding Caelica alone, sitting in a window. She seems to acknowledge his look of love, and then becomes properly coy, which has the usual effect:

> But like flames throwne on the fire,
> Shames restraints, enflam'd Desire:
> Desire looks, and in her eyes,
> The image of it selfe espies,
> Whence he takes selfe-pitties motions
> To be Cynthia's owne devotions.

Even so, fear overcomes him and he cannot speak; on which Greville comments:

> But silent love is simple wooing,
> Even Destiny would have us doing.
> Boldnesse never yet was chidden,
> Till by Love it be forbidden,
> Myra leaves him, and knows best,
> What shall become of all the rest.
>
> (Sonnet 74)

The poet, by the way, calls the lady by all three names in this poem; he is similarly, though not so thoroughly, inconsistent elsewhere. This kind of thing caused the biography-hunters to throw up their hands in despair. The identities are of course irrelevant; Greville is writing about the nature of emotion, not about personalities, and uses whatever name suits the convenience of his meter, imagery, or theme. In Sonnet 74 the conventional situation ends in ironic ambiguity: he will never know whether she might have reciprocated his feeling or not. The implication is that she probably would not: what he sees in her eyes is only his own craving for compassion. And even this fails to move him to action. Here the deception is double: adoration makes us see what may not exist at all, and then prostrates us before it so that we can never find out.

If desire can produce this enervating timidity, it can also produce an opposite kind of persistence that has, ironically, the same deceptive effect. Greville likens himself trying to hold the love of Caelica to Pelius hanging on to Thetis while she changed herself into various monsters and elements (Sonnet 42). Pelius' perseverance was of course rewarded; Greville's only deceives him: Caelica's heart is first turned to stone by Venus' girdle of inconstancy, then into a cloud,

> And I poore Ixion to my Juno vowed,
> With thoughts to clip her, clipt my owne desire:
> For she was vanisht, I held nothing fast,
> But woes to come, and joyes already past.

The cloud then becomes a stream,

>                              in whose smooth face,
> While I the Image of my selfe did glasse,
> Thought Shadowes I, for beautie did embrace.

Still faith holds fast, "like foyles where stones be set, / To make toyes deare, and fooles more fond to get." Greville has here used three additional myths to create an allegory that destroys the promise of the first. The allegory is a powerful figurative expression of the ability of love's imagination to ignore what it does not wish to perceive, to go "Against the streames of reall truthes." Having asserted the deception in mythical terms, Greville states this general conclusion directly and vows to "hold no more." The poem is very tightly constructed, with careful and varied repetition of the phrase "hold fast" in the couplets to underscore the full extent of his perseverance in the false perception, and to evoke the extreme emotional difficulty of facing the truth. The parallelism of both the rhetorical structure and the rimes (four of which are repeated, one twice) reinforces the idea that the hope contains at the outset its own doom. And the reason for this is implied by the final allusion to Narcissus: the hope springs from a desire that is fundamentally a self-obsession.

Greville explores this latter insight in one of his most unusual and fascinating poems, Sonnet 56.[27] It is a dream-vision (which takes place within a waking action), and has an appropriate mesmeric, incantatory quality, created by the rhythm of emphatic, regular, and mostly headless tetrameters. The incantation modulates toward the end, however, into gnomic irony that explicitly sees the dream-vision as a metaphor for the debilitating self-absorption of a love whose delusive power is suggested by certain myths. The poem is quoted entire in order to include a section crucial to its theme (the twenty-four lines following l. 24). The passage appears only in the Warwick MS, which most of Greville's editors have chosen to print only in their notes,[28] and which is wholly omitted from other currently available editions of *Caelica*.

---

[27] Yvor Winters describes the poem as "an attack on the courtly concept of love and of love poetry," which "employs the mythological ornament of the concept, but only to discredit it" (*Forms of Discovery*, p. 47).

[28] Bullough, *Poems and Dramas*, I, 257; Grosart, IV, 373; Thom Gunn, ed., *Selected Poems of Fulke Greville* (London, 1968), p. 84.

All my senses, like Beacons flame,
Gave Alarum to desire
To take armes in Cynthia's name,
And set all my thoughts on fire:
Furies wit perswaded me,
Happy love was hazards heire,
Cupid did best shoot and see
In the night where smooth is faire;
Up I start beleeving well
To see if Cynthia were awake;
Wonders I saw, who can tell?
And thus unto my selfe I spake;
Sweet God Cupid where am I,
That by pale Diana's light:
Such rich beauties doe espie,
As harme our senses with delight?
Am I borne up to the skyes?
See where Jove and Venus shine,
Shewing in her heavenly eyes
That desire is divine:
Look where lyes the Milken way,
Way unto that dainty throne,
Where while all the Gods would play,
Vulcan thinkes to dwell alone.
Shaddowing it with curious art,
Nettes of sullen golden haire,
Mars am I, and may not part,
Till that I be taken there.
There withall I heard a sound,
Made of all the parts of love,
Which did sence delight and wound;
Planetts with such musicke move.
Those joyes drewe desires neare.
The heavens blusht, the white shew'd redd,
Such redd as in skyes appeare
When Sol parts from Thetis bedd.
Then unto myself I said
Surely I Apollo am,
Yonder is the glorious maide
Which men doe Aurora name,
Who for pryde shee hath in mee
Blushing forth desire and feare,
While she would have no man see,
Makes the world know I am there.
I resolve to play my sonne,
And misguide my chariott fire:
All the skye to overcome,

And enflame with my desire:
I gave reynes to this conceipt,
Hope went on the wheele of lust:
Phansies scales are false of weight,
Thoughts take thought that goe of trust,
I stept forth to touch the skye,
I a God by Cupid dreames,
Cynthia who did naked lye,
Runnes away like silver streames;
Leaving hollow banks behind,
Who can neither forward move,
Nor if rivers be unkind,
Turne away or leave to love.
There stand I, like Articke pole,
Where Sol passeth o're the line,
Mourning my benighted soule,
Which so loseth light divine.
There stand I like Men that preach
From the Execution place,
At their death content to teach
All the world with their disgrace:
He that lets his Cynthia lye,
Naked on a bed of play,
To say prayers ere she dye,
Teacheth time to runne away:
Let no Love-desiring heart,
In the Starres goe seeke his fate,
Love is onely Natures art,
Wonder hinders Love and Hate.
   None can well behold with eyes,
   But what underneath him lies.

There is a brilliant and careful progression in the celestial imagery and the myths, which implies the specific judgment Greville subsequently passes on his own condition. The whole fantasy is facilitated by the idealizing vision of cosmic harmony, but Greville makes the carnal motive clear by the language he employs and the myths he chooses, all of which project delusions of sexual grandeur, in conquest, expression, or possession. The poet deifies himself first as Mars committing adultery with Venus. Her eyes may be heavenly, but that is not where the poet is looking: the "Milky Way" between the lady's breasts, leading to the alabaster mound of paradise, became a standard item of the blazon after Sidney used it in a poem immensely popular with the Elizabethans (*Old Arcadia* 62, 58–61). What begins as pure eroticism shades, as the very heavens blush with passion, into more generalized, though still sexually derived, hallucinations of power. The poet hears (impossible for a mere mortal) the music of the spheres; becoming Apollo, he congratulates himself that Aurora blushes for him, announcing his presence to the world. But the whole cosmos must be witness to his erotic ambition, so, as Phaeton, he resolves to set the sky afire. It is a marvelous comedy of expanding megalomania. It is briefly suspended while Greville accurately judges it as his own illusion. The judgment prepares the way for the intrusion of reality, which has of course already been incorporated into his vision: the naked body of Venus is that of Cynthia transfigured by his imagination. The climax occurs as he steps forth to touch, not the lady, but "the skye"—and she runs away. The denouement brings us down gradually from the illusory heights: first in a conventional simile that focuses the celestial imagery on this earth and describes the lover's loss; then in a grimmer simile that forsakes the cosmic connotations for criminal ones, suggesting his guilt for that loss while introducing its moral lesson.

The generalized conclusion is familiar: "Starre-gazers only multiply desires" (Sonnet 17); they do not realize them. But in this poem the sexual *doubles entendres* reinforce the colossal irony of the fantasy: it prevents us from achieving exactly what it dreams of. The final couplet, in addition to its neatly cynical reversal of the climactic action (the poet's attempt to touch the sky), suggests the perceptual error that causes "wonder" to hinder love. This kind of idealization does not perceive reality because it is not really interested in reality: it is interested only in self. The use of myth as self-deification is, I think, Greville's most penetrating criticism of the Petrarchan pose: the love that it requires is a love not of a person, but of one's own emotional intoxication. What is intended to be selfless devotion to an ideal becomes, because selflessness is not possible in this world, but a dream of self-aggrandizement. The poet's desire to possess Cynthia has, ironically, very little to do with Cynthia: in his mind she becomes Venus—not, in this context, the symbol of divine harmony, but of sublimated sexual self-glorification.

The conclusion of this poem is a reasonably accurate statement of Greville's general view of love. In *Caelica*, the view is of course never wholly static, but shifted and modified throughout the sequence until the entire subject is explicit renounced in Sonnet 84. We have seen how it proceeds from the dualistic premise that Greville consciously formulates at the beginning, and how it develops, within this premise, psychological insights that are parallel to those of Baconian pragmatism, as it anatomizes the numberless ways in which our noblest desires can deceive us. The bitter cynicism it can produce has been discussed, but should be qualified by equal insistence on the more urbane attitude of acceptance that is often expressed. To an audience of gentlewomen who have objected to his view, Greville says,

> Faire Nymphs, if I wooe Cynthia not to leave me,
> You know 'tis I my selfe, not she deceaves me.
> Masters that aske their Schollers leave to beat them,
> Husbands that bid their Wives tell all they know,
> Men that give Children sweet meates not to eate them,
> Ladies, you see what destinie they goe:
> > And who intreats, you know intreats in vaine,
> > That Love be constant, or come backe againe.
>
> > > (Sonnet 53)

This "sophisticated response to the dilemmas of love," reconcilement to a serious problem by means of wit, has been described as Astrophil's principal weapon, and as a habitual technique with Sidney.[29] Greville also employs it regularly, in his own way. Such sophistication, whether vindictive or urbane, has, moreover, long been regarded as a common ground between Greville and Donne. Almost seventy years ago Croll saw this ground as their mutual renunciation of ornament, liking for "realistic" images, and "extraordinary richness and subtlety of thought."[30] Very recently Douglas Peterson has seen all three poets working in the same tradition of the secular lyric: "In content and attitude *Caelica* reflects the processes of intellectualization that are evident in *Astrophil and Stella* and which reach significant fulfillment in Donne's *Songs and Sonets*." Peterson pictures Sidney as wrestling within the Petrarchan "norms of feeling," while Greville and Donne usually mock them for their unrealistic and "fatuous ways of viewing amorous experience." In Greville's case, the evidence is his "mockery of constancy, his denial of the feminine ideal, his perverse praise of absence as an erotic stimulant, and his candid explorations of erotic experience."[31]

Qualified by the necessary stylistic distinctions, and also by a recognition of Donne's own brand of erotic idealism, this view seems generally accurate. But it underestimates, I think, the extent to which Greville wrestles within the Petrarchan norms, thus ignoring how much he learned from Sidney and somewhat misrepresenting the full range of his achievement. Greville can, on occasion, suggest even the inadequacy of the mocking sophistication. He does so, in fact, in the very poem that praises absence. Its beneficial effects are succinctly analyzed: it preserves a passion that might otherwise spend itself; it lessens the anguish of proximity; it allows us to savor pleasures in recollection and to make literature of them; it sharpens the edge of appetite:

[29] Rudenstine, pp. 180–81.

[30] P. 28. Felix Schelling echoed Croll's views in *English Literature during the Lifetime of Shakespeare* (New York, 1910) by finding in both Greville and Donne "a fullness and intricacy of thought and a disdain for prevalent conventional poetical mannerisms" (p. 125).

[31] Pp. 265–66.

> Absence doth nurse the fire,
> Which starves and feeds desire
> With sweet delayes.[32]

(Sonnet 45)

Compared to the obsession of presence, absence frees our thoughts. But this freedom is a two-edged sword; with it, thoughts can destroy themselves. Addressing them, Greville concludes:

> The absence which you glory,
> Is that which makes you sory,
> And burne in vaine:
> For Thought is not the weapon,
> Wherewith thoughts-ease men cheapen,
> Absence is paine.

Greville can perceive both the fallacies of the fashionable attitude, and those of its mockery. Despite the careful rationalizations, absence is still painful. The final assertion of the unavoidable claim of feeling in the teeth of a chain of reasoning that would deny it is of course a strategy that Sidney made famous (*AS* 21, 71). If the rationales of honor or philosophical idealism fail to argue Astrophil out of his honest admission of feeling, the counter-rationale of sophisticated, carnal analysis fails equally to argue Greville out of his.

I have tried to show that Greville's achievement in the love poetry of *Caelica* is broader and richer than has usually been recognized. His mockery of the Petrarchan attitudes arises in the context of a close and continuing examination of their implications. With the best Elizabethans, he exploits the modes of perception latent in the courtly tradition and the eloquent style; he also uses that style ironically to analyze the inadequacies of the tradition, arriving at themes and attitudes which were to become the stock-in-trade of the Cavaliers. In his secular lyric poetry as in his thought, Greville straddles the Tudor and Stuart ages, converting old tools to new uses within the framework of a consistent vision, and announcing that vision in a voice that is uniquely his. We shall consider the development and the distinctive features of this voice in the next chapter.

---

[32] This phrase, used to conclude two stanzas, recalls—if only by coincidence—Milton's splendid description of Eve yielding to Adam "with coy submission, modest pride, / And sweet reluctant amorous delay" (*Paradise Lost*, IV.310–11).

# III  The Traditional Stylist

ALTHOUGH Greville's Calvinistic dualism produced a literary theory that would sanction a rather crude form of medieval homily, his secular lyrics show us that his practice contains all the stylistic sophistication made possible by the classical learning and the linguistic preoccupations of the Renaissance. If he could not share Sidney's faith in the morally enlightening power of fiction, he could nonetheless profit from Sidney's conscious attempts to elevate vernacular poetry by applying to it the disciplines of logic and rhetoric so strenuously revived by the humanists.[1] Much of this application was, of course, traditional. The English Middle Ages largely identified rhetoric with poetry and largely confined rhetoric to elocutio, or the embellishment of a discourse.[2] This tradition saw poetry as versified doctrine, or beautified truth, in a way thoroughly congenial to Greville's moral conviction that we need instruction far more than we need entertainment. Some historians of criticism and literature have deplored this view as debasing the classical theories and maintaining a false and simplistic dichotomy between form and content. On the other hand, it has been suggested that the Renaissance development of the medieval theory transcends these limitations. Before looking at Greville's use of rhetoric, we shall deal briefly with these conflicting claims concerning the nature of rhetoric itself.

Thomas Wilson's *The Arte of Rhetorique* (1553) was the most popular and complete vernacular text on the subject. Wholly derived from the great authorities, Aristotle, Cicero, and Quintilian, as understood by their humanist commentators, it is a good summary of late medieval Ciceronianism.[3] Speaking of the book as representative of Renaissance rhetoric generally, one critic has commented on its "artificial" rhetorical distinction: "Wilson does not consider style as the final clarification of

---

[1] Ringler (pp. xvii–xix) discusses Sidney's training in these subjects at Shrewsbury (where he first met Greville) and Oxford, and its value for his writing.

[2] See Donald L. Clark, *Rhetoric and Poetry in the Renaissance* (New York, 1922), ch. V. Clark's book is generally neutral and informative, although he does in part see rhetoric as doing more harm than good to literature, as C. S. Baldwin, *Renaissance Literary Theory and Practice* (New York, 1939) wholly does.

[3] According to Wilbur S. Howell, *Logic and Rhetoric in England, 1500–1700* (Princeton, N.J., 1956), pp. 100–101.

thought. Conceiving of eloquence as something added to content, he perpetuates the dichotomy between style and content."[4] In her massive and classic account of how Renaissance rhetoric influenced poetic imagery, Rosemond Tuve admitted the crass appearance of Wilson's didacticism—winning the attention of the ignorant by fables—but attributed it merely to the concrete terms in which it is expressed, which naturally put us off "by innumerable differences in social outlook."[5] Throughout her book she argues for the happy marriage of poetry and rhetoric by explicitly denying that it produced any split between subject and style: Renaissance writers rather ask, " 'What is the poem for?' and 'How has that been accomplished?' That is, they consider a poem with respect to end and with respect to means, a consideration which does not bifurcate it."[6] In this view, a poem, like an oration, has a particular purpose—to praise or dispraise, to prove or disprove, to define, to judge—in which all its elements, ideas, images, sounds, are equal partners. Form and content are therefore integrated into a larger context where both are controlled by and contribute to the elucidation of a total meaning.

In terms of its usefulness for analyzing and understanding the poetry of the age, Miss Tuve's insistence on this kind of teleology is unexceptionable. Despite criticism of some of her particular extensions of it, her general view has been justly and widely influential; it or something very like it has provided some basic premises for many subsequent studies, including this one. Walter J. Ong has recently restated the growing scholarly conviction of the importance of rhetoric for all literature as training in both mind- and word-play, in developing "any word or idea systematically. Tudor exuberance of language and expression was not accidental, it was achieved." Similarly, but from a different angle, Brian Vickers stresses the functional importance of rhetorical figures "for expressing emotional and psychological states."[7] Subsequent scholarship has thus followed Miss Tuve's lead in examining the assumptions on which the rhetoricians' theories depend, and in analyzing the specific recommendations that they offer. The attempt is to provide a description

---

[4] Peterson, p. 42.

[5] *Elizabethan and Metaphysical Imagery*, p. 425.

[6] *Ibid.*, p. 110. Miss Tuve explicitly criticizes the attitudes of Clark and C. S. Baldwin (*Elizabethan and Metaphysical Imagery*, p. 413). In a later article, "Ancient Rhetoric and English Renaissance Literature," *Shakespeare Quarterly*, II (1951), 204, Clark acknowledges her criticism, but continues to undervalue the rhetorical influence on the lyric. This influence has since been demonstrated by O. B. Hardison, Jr., *The Enduring Monument: A Study of the Idea of Praise in Renaissance Literary Theory and Practice* (Chapel Hill, N.C., 1962), pp. 25–26, 95–102.

[7] Ong, "Tudor Writings on Rhetoric," *Studies in the Renaissance*, XV (1968), 49; Vickers, *Classical Rhetoric in English Poetry* (London, 1970), p. 119.

of what the poets managed to do with the rhetoric they learned. The significance of rhetoric for literature lies less in the sophistication of the textbooks than in that of the students, less in the intentions of the educators than in the useful tools their books actually contained. It seems therefore irrelevant, in terms of the investigation of literature, to assail the rhetorics because they pervert the purity of Aristotle or appear to have theoretical frameworks that seem to us dogmatic and jejune. Given the emphasis of the English rhetorical tradition on style as ornament, we should rather inquire what these ornaments consisted of, what possibilities of expression they presented to the young men who were drilled in detecting and producing them from grammar school on up to the first or second year of the university.[8]

The third book of Puttenham's *Arte of English Poesie* (more than half the treatise) contains the most extensive and entertaining catalogue of the ornamental figures of speech, including both schemes and tropes. His approach to the subject is traditional, not Ramist, and his book the most frequently used by modern scholars because it is in English, oriented primarily to literature, and readily available in three modern editions. Puttenham is a gentleman, writing for the general edification of "Ladies . . . or idle Courtiers,"[9] a conscious popularizer, not a scholar writing either for his colleagues or his pupils. It is thus all the more interesting that his classification of the figures in a "table" at the end of the book is more elaborate than that of more academic treatises. He divides them first into the "auricular," the "sensable," and the "sententious," according to whether they serve the ear, the "conceit," or both.[10] The first two divisions are further subdivided according to manner (whether they work by "surplusage," by "disorder," etc.) and according to context (whether they function in word, clause, or sentence). Scarcely one-eighth of the total are exclusively aural; almost two-thirds are the sententious (or "rhetorical") figures that alter both sound and sense. The rest, which pertain exclusively to meaning, include what were more commonly known as the tropes: metaphor (in several varieties), metonymy, synecdoche, and so forth.

It is clear that all these do not much resemble what we ordinarily think

---

[8] T. W. Baldwin surveys the views of the major educationists on logic and rhetoric: *William Shakespeare's Small Latine and Lesse Greeke* (Urbana, Ill., 1944), II, ch. XXXI. At Jesus College, Cambridge, which Greville attended from 1568 to 1571, a student was required to spend the whole first year in exclusive study of rhetoric before he could proceed to logic and disputations with upperclassmen in the second and third years: Mark H. Curtis, *Oxford and Cambridge in Transition, 1558–1642* (Oxford, 1959), pp. 87–89.

[9] Ed. Gladys Willcock and Alice Walker (Cambridge, 1936), p. 158 (III.x). All citations of Puttenham will refer to this edition.

[10] *Ibid.*, pp. 159–60.

of as ornament. When a student practiced dialysis, "the dismembrer," he stated a problem and specified its alternative solutions; when he tossed off a procatalepsis, "the presumptuous," he was anticipating objections to his argument. When he came across epanados, merismus, or prolepsis, he was observing different ways of presenting an idea: specifying the terms of a general statement, omitting the general statement and presenting specific details, or illustrating a general statement without reference to its terms. When he indulged in paralipsis or parisia, he was (like his elvish master, Chaucer) pretending to pass over a point in order to emphasize it, or pretending to ask pardon for offensive matter. For polemical purposes, he might insult his adversary in a delightful variety of tones, by using "the drie mock, the bitter taunt, the merry scoffe, the fleering frumpe, the broad floute or the privie nippe."

All this—and there is a great deal more of the same—has been rehearsed as a defense, if not of the theory, certainly of the practice of rhetorical elocutio. Every figure had its purpose, and the purpose of most figures was not to make the composition sound pretty, but to organize its material in a coherent and telling way. Rhetoric may have been largely confined to handbooks of figures, but in the sixteenth century these figures "included a much broader range of stylistic devices than we now associate with the term; . . . some of these devices, such as description, example, allegory, and irony, were of such inclusive and basic character that to discuss them was to discuss the largest considerations relevant to discourse."[11] And to study them was to study a wide range of structural possibilities, selection among which obviously entailed other selections: of subject, tone, and purpose. The great advantage of such a rhetoric for students was precisely its inclusiveness, its presentation of a large number of potential strategies or techniques of expression designed to channel the thought into its most effective order. No one who has ever had to teach writing of any kind would, I think, scorn the assumption operative here: that style ultimately depends on one's awareness of available alternatives. If Renaissance rhetoric has been discredited as literary theory, it has surely endured as pedagogy, for this assumption is that of almost all the anthologies and handbooks produced for the standard freshman composition course in today's colleges. The vocabu-

[11] H. H. Hudson, ed., *Directions for Speech and Style* (Princeton, N.J., 1935), p. xvii. John Hoskins, the author of this treatise, expounded the severely simplified and shortened rhetoric of Ramus and Talon, in which the figures are greatly reduced in number, but are still classified according to purpose: to vary, to amplify, to illustrate. Professor Hudson's general opinion is echoed by Sister Miriam Joseph, who calls the classification of figures "only codified good sense," and sees it as supplying a "coherent functional pattern" which provides "meticulous and comprehensive analysis of thought, emotion, and expression": *Shakespeare's Use of the Arts of Language* (New York, 1947), p. 398.

lary may be different, the method considerably less detailed and rigorous, but the objective is unchanged. We would perhaps be somewhat embarrassed to call what we do when we explicate an essay in the classroom "presenting a model for imitation," but that describes it exactly. For we hope that the student will learn from that example just what young Greville and Sidney learned at Shrewsbury from committing to memory a felicitous orismus or auxesis of Cicero's: how to present ideas in the most fitting, graceful, and persuasive way. We would simply call this using language effectively; Puttenham might have said "gorgeously."

One of the greatest moral truisms of the Renaissance was "That all things are as they are used,"[12] and to this rule its rhetoric was no exception. The boundless admiration of many humanist educators for the sonorous cadences of Cicero no doubt encouraged in young vernacular writers the infatuated exploitation of the figures (mainly the "auricular" schemes) for their own sakes. Although this kind of mannerism takes its name from the popular prose romance of John Lyly, a University Wit, it was hardly confined to prose. The poetical miscellanies are full of it: their numbing alliteration, their overuse of periodic constructions and "over-dependence on balance and antithesis," their general "literary affectation" have been called poetic Euphuism. "Not many years passed before it became antiquated."[13] Indeed, the assault on the nonfunctional, overelaborate abuse of rhetoric was soon mounted on a variety of fronts: the educational, by the simplified rhetoric of Ramus and Talon; the literary, by the revival of the Senecan plain style; the philosophic, by the scientific insistence on empirical utility; and the religious, by the Puritan insistence on the plain and lucid exposition and application of the Word. We have already noticed in another context Greville's and Sidney's objections to the pursuit of ostentatious elegance; we have also noticed that these objections did not preclude either writer from using the "ornaments" of style functionally, as they were intended to be used. Rhetoric itself contained the principle that when properly observed would compel such use: this of course was the principle of decorum.[14]

Decorum in the Renaissance was an enormously flexible notion—often defined as "apt proportion"—that could be applied to virtually anything that men might perceive, produce, or do. It had not yet become solidified into the specific literary rules of later neoclassicism, or thence still further

[12] The title of a proverbial, moralistic poem by George Turberville, *Epitaphes, Epigrams, Songs and Sonets* (London, 1567), p. 102.
[13] Hyder E. Rollins, ed., *The Paradise of Dainty Devices (1576–1606)* (Cambridge, Mass., 1927), p. lxvii; *A Gorgeous Gallery of Gallant Inventions (1576)* (Cambridge, Mass., 1926), p. xxiii.
[14] Miss Tuve offers an illuminating discussion of decorum and the view of reality which underlay it (*Elizabethan and Metaphysical Imagery*, pp. 230–47).

reduced to mean merely the punctilio of the toilet or the tea-table. Puttenham's sequacious exposition of decorum is a good example of the scope
and significance it once had. He concludes his catalogue of the rhetorical
figures by examining the concept that governs them. Decorum, he tells
us, is decency, or "good grace": "every thing which pleaseth the mind or
sences, and the mind by the sences as by means instrumentall, doth it
for some amiable point or qualitie that is in it, which draweth them to
a good liking and contentment with their proper objects."[15] We might
wish there were a better grace in this definition, a lovelier conformity between his pronouns and their antecedents; but what he means is clarified
as he goes along. He seeks, as he always does, a native Saxon term for
the Latin, and comes up with "seemelynesse," whose meaning he is immediately at pains to extend "even to the spirituall objectes of the mynde,
which stand no lesse in the due proportion of reason and discourse than
any other materiall thing doth in his sensible bewtie, proportion and
comelynesse." Puttenham is very careful to include in this aesthetic of
proportion thoughts, feelings, and sensory perceptions: "this lovely
conformitie," he calls it, "betweene the sence and the sensible."

With regard to elocutio, this means that even though "all our figures
be but transgressions of our dayly speach, yet if they fall out decently to
the good liking of the mynde or eare and to the bewtifying of the matter
or language, all is well, if indecently, and to the eares and myndes misliking (be the figure of it selfe never so commendable) all is amisse."
The functionalism of the principle is here explicit: no matter how ingenious the figure, no matter how delightfully full of "artifice," it is in-
decent unless it achieves conformity between mind and ear, creating that
relationship between idea and feeling which is meaning. We can now
understand Puttenham's first confusing remark as a general statement
of this semantic theory: the "good grace" that is decorum is nothing less
than meaning, which is the result of apprehending objects both cognitive-
ly and sensuously or emotionally, in terms of both the thoughts and feelings that are "proper" to them. He further assumes, of course, that this
apprehension produces, finally, in the mind, the pleasure of understanding that is aesthetic pleasure.

There are no formulae for either the creation or the perception of
this meaning, which can indeed be any meaning. To observe decorum
or to recognize its observance requires one to have a practiced facility of
discernment, or educated taste: "the discreetest man . . . of much observation and greatest experience." This obviously follows from the fact that
each particular case has its own particular set of variables, so that decorum "comes to be very much alterable and subject to varietie, in so

---

[15] P. 261 (III.xxiii). The ensuing quotations are from pp. 262–63.

much as our speech asketh one maner of decencie, in respect of the person who speakes: another of his to whom it is spoken: another of whom we speake: another of what we speake, and in what place and time and to what purpose." Puttenham enumerates many examples of this variety, in both speech (of which "writing is no more then the image or character") and behavior.[16] Although the examples of the latter kind consist of the specific recommendations for good manners to which decorum later became wholly confined, those of the former make clear the vital importance of the last variable—purpose—and of the great connotative power of words in realizing it.

As a typical Elizabethan, Puttenham is rather unsystematic, highly anecdotal, and jocular, turgid, witty, fastidious, or obscene by turns. His idiom, the "personalist" vocabulary,[17] is as remote from ours as his belief in the hierarchical view of nature that prescribed the substance of relative proprieties. In spite of all this quintessential "quaintness," we should not conclude too hastily that Puttenham "falls far short of providing anything like an adequate rationale of . . . Renaissance . . . poems of any sort."[18] For his discussion of decorum is not only a blueprint of the "unified sensibility" (one of the lately fashionable rationales for Renaissance verse); it also represents a fundamental insight into the nature of language, distilled from centuries of ancient and medieval thought. And it sees poetry as doing, par excellence, what language itself does—in Bacon's famous phrase, "submitting the shows of things to the desires of the mind," thereby achieving the manufacture of meaning, the interpenetration of fact and value.[19] If, indeed, Puttenham's exposition has a fault, it is just this breadth, which can provide, if not a complete, certainly an accurate rationale for Renaissance poems of *all* sorts. Regarding poetry as the most eminent, heightened, and expressive use of language, the rhetorical principle of decorum sanctioned whatever structures of meaning the poet could present through the senses to the grasp of the

[16] Pp. 263–98 (III.xxiii–xxiv).

[17] That is, applying to things or abstractions words that we should now apply to persons: the "likings" of the mind; "lovely conformity." The idiom is part and parcel of the sensibility he is describing. Walter J. Ong names and analyzes it (*Ramus, Method, and the Decay of Dialogue* [Cambridge, Mass., 1958], pp. 278–79), and concludes: "The mind does not feel the exterior, objective world and the interior, personal world as distinct from one another quite to the extent that we do."

[18] W. K. Wimsatt and Cleanth Brooks, *Literary Criticism: A Short History* (New York, 1957), p. 234.

[19] In our own day, Marshall McLuhan has described the poetic process in precisely this way: "Sight, Sound, and the Fury," *Commonweal*, LX (April, 1954), 7–11. For the basis of such formulations in modern philosophy of language, from which McLuhan's well publicized ideas seem largely to derive, see Susanne Langer, *Philosophy in a New Key* (New York, 1951), ch. V.

intellect. And it gave him, in the figures, hundreds of specific ways to articulate the various meanings that his imagination could contrive. The only unalterable condition was that these meanings be fully articulated, fully realized, so that they might be fully apprehended as conceptual structures by the mind of the reader.

Greville's mastery of decorum is exemplified in the first two poems of *Caelica*.[20] The entire structure of Sonnet 1 is provided by the progressive, suspensive, and summarizing figures of climax, hirmus, and collectour, along with the carefully repeated and varied scheme of asyndeton. The stylistic devices, which include and in part control the prosodic elements of rhythm and assonantal texture, are the felt messengers of the poem's ideas and its purpose—to praise the lady as an embodiment of Neoplatonic harmony. The style is thus a part of the poem's meaning: it partially creates that meaning. In Sonnet 2 the principle is the same, but both style and meaning are very different. The elaborate figures and the balanced schemes have disappeared. The structure of the poem is provided instead by a single metaphor whose selected and developed terms contain both its theme, the suffering of carnal passion, and its purpose, a plea to end that suffering. Throughout our examination of Greville's love poetry we observed his careful adjustment of style to subject, and his skillful manipulation of it in accordance with his ironic purposes. The contemporary principle of decorum was simply a theoretical statement of the practice of all good poets. It encourages us to observe that Greville's style should vary in respect to his themes, that like them—indeed, because of them—it should sound the characteristic notes of both the Elizabethan and Jacobean ages, from mellifluous rhetorical celebration and Petrarchan self-analysis to the harshly logical dispraise of love and the acrid or subtle comparisons of "metaphysical" wit.[21]

Although the traditional rhetorical emphasis on elocutio and its guiding concept of decorum could supply the incipient and discerning poet with a structural and functional style that was a good deal more than window-dressing, rhetoric itself contained other conceptual processes that greatly

[20] These poems were discussed above in some detail, pp. 44–46. In the ensuing analysis of Greville's rhetoric, the names and definitions of the figures are taken from Puttenham, pp. 163–261 (III.xii–xxii). A convenient explanatory list of the principal ones can be found in Veré L. Rubel, *Poetic Diction in the English Renaissance* (New York, 1941), pp. 276–91.

[21] John Buxton (*Elizabethan Taste* [London, 1963], pp. 326–27) emphasizes a point made in different ways by Miss Tuve, *Elizabethan and Metaphysical Imagery*, and by C. S. Lewis (pp. 538–41): that the appeal of these varying styles and attitudes was not at all mutually exclusive. The same audience was reading and appreciating Spenser, Greville, and Donne at the same time—indeed, it had to be well versed in conventional decorum in order to appreciate its conscious reversals.

reinforced such a stylistic ideal. These of course were the processes that rhetoric shared with its sister discipline of logic: inventio and dispositio. Exactly how matter was to be discovered and arranged, and whether these processes were in fact shared by logic and rhetoric but had differing objects in each, or whether they had identical objects and belonged only to logic—the Ramist doctrine—were subjects of considerable confusion and violent controversy in the Renaissance. Partly for this reason the relation of poets and their poetry to Ramism is highly problematic. We should notice in Greville's case that the one time he alludes to Ramism, he does so only to denounce it:

> Indeed to teach they confident pretend
> All generall, uniforme Axioms scientificall
> Of truth, that want beginning, have no end,
> Demonstrative, infallible, onely essentiall.
>
> *(Humane Learning, 22)*

The "generall Axioms" are stock items in the Ramist vocabulary; they have no beginning or end because they are by definition coextensive with objective reality. The last three adjectives most probably refer to the famous three "laws" or "documents": of justice, truth, and wisdom.[22] Greville's derision of these Ramistic pretensions here is a valuable corrective to the unwarranted assumption that because Sidney's circle included some Ramists, Greville was one of them.[23] Evidence for Greville's supposed Ramism is occasionally found in his stress on use or exercise over theory in learning. But this is wholly inadequate: such emphasis was par for humanism; Ascham, an outspoken anti-Ramist, stressed the same thing.

Despite the scholarly and pedagogical furor, however, the disputants all agreed on the broad, humanist conception of logic that made it significant for literature: it was the art of communication. It was a way of ordering the known for systematic presentation; it was not the scientific method of investigating the unknown that Bacon wanted it to be when he gave *invention* its modern meaning, "to discover that we know not."[24] The inventio of traditional logic rather assisted a writer to find out the nature and parts of his subject by viewing it under the various categories contained in (depending on his textbook) the "places" or the "predicaments." The mastery of these categories (which were some

---

[22] For a contemporary exposition of these, see *The Logike of . . . P. Ramus*, trans. [R. MacIlmaine] (London, 1581), pp. 8–11. For excellent criticism of them, see Father Ong, *Ramus, Method, and the Decay of Dialogue*, pp. 252, 258–59.

[23] Buncombe, p. 175.

[24] Quoted by Howell (p. 367) as he discusses this distinction between traditional and modern logic.

version of the Aristotelian dialectic of "substance" and "accidents") was called *dispositio* (or "judgment"—which term in Ramism named a different process and was said to follow inventio) and was of course a prerequisite to their use in inventio. Rhetorical dispositio, in contrast, followed rhetorical inventio, and prescribed ways of ordering the material thereby discovered.[25] Both rhetorical processes presupposed a grasp of their namesakes in logic: one can indeed partly sympathize with Ramus' simplification of the whole business by eliminating the frequent duplication of effort, and with its enthusiastic reception by pedagogues. One of them summed up the situation nicely by remarking that the traditionalists "have taken invention to be a part of Rhetorick, and so judgement, but when they come to explain them, they teach Logick."[26] At any rate, what emerged from the traditional process of inventio, to a greater or lesser degree of complexity and completeness, were the kinds of operations possible to the mind and its language, those, for example, that still appear in textbooks of rhetoric (definition, division, cause and effect, comparison and contrast), along with suggestions of how they might be performed. It should perhaps be reemphasized that this notion of logic is neither scientific nor formally philosophical. It is embedded wholly within the medieval and Renaissance conception of knowledge as disputation and teaching. I use the word *logic* throughout in this general sense, as merely the progressive, conceptual coherence of a discourse.

The poem was thus conceived of, like the oration, as a logical argument having a logical structure. Practice at defining, for example, produced "the form or organization of many short poems, their nature as structural units and their function as wholes. Many lyrics of the period are just such as this section of a logic handbook asks for: they are definitions by praise and dispraise, definitions by differences, definitions by similitudes."[27] Similarly, the "deliberative" lyrics in *Tottel's Miscellany*, which draw their matter from the appropriate "places," have been seen as helping "to develop the potentialities for closely reasoned analysis and argument within the short poem—the kind of analysis and argument present in the sonnets of Sidney and Shakespeare and in the short poems of Greville, Donne, and Jonson."[28] The crucial distinction in this latter account is of course how "closely" the reasoning is pursued, how efficiently the matter gathered from the "places" of invention is put together and organized. It is in terms of this distinction that we may see how Greville, again following Sidney, refines the traditional style into more

---

[25] See Clark, "Ancient Rhetoric and English Renaissance Literature," p. 198, for a succinct general description.

[26] Quoted by Miller, p. 321.

[27] Tuve, *Elizabethan and Metaphysical Imagery*, p. 301.

[28] Peterson, p. 73.

rigorous and dramatic structures that serve more sophisticated rhetorical objectives.

This refinement can be exemplified by comparing Greville's use of one
structural figure with its use in a popular contemporary poem from *The
Paradise of Dainty Devices,* there ascribed to one D. Sand.[29] Called
"Thinke to dye," Sand's poem states in the first stanza the general commonplace that will be specified and amplified (the figure of prolepsis)
in the following six:

> The life is long, whiche lothsomely doeth laste,
> The dolfull daies drawe slowly to their date:
> The present panges, and painful plags forepast,
> Yelds greffe aye grene, to stablishe this estate.
> So that I feele in this greate storme and strife,
> That death is sweete, that shorteneth suche a life.

Specific examples of the sweetness of death are then offered: it is eternal
freedom; it ends a life that is composed of lengthy miseries and brief
joys. The hortatory inference that it should not be feared but welcomed
is drawn and is repeated as a conclusion. The whole poem thus simply
restates, by expansion, the general proposition in stanza one; and the
expansion itself proceeds according to no particular principle. In short,
the idea is repeated, but not developed, so that the poem is "rhetorical" in the worst sense. Its essential lack of progression is interestingly
demonstrated by the fact that three of its identical stanzas (one, three,
and six) constitute a poem attributed to John Harington and called
"Elegy Wrote in the Tower, 1554."[30] The truncation does not harm it in
the least; indeed, a fully comprehensible poem on the same theme might
also be made of stanzas one, four, and seven, or of numerous other com-
binations. The same result would be obtained even if, keeping stanza
seven as the conclusion, we read the other six in exactly reverse order.
There is nothing unique in this; many popular Elizabethan poems were
so treated. Sidney heaps scorn on just this kind of randomly repetitive
composition, which lacks "poetical sinnewes": "For proofe whereof, let
but moste of the Verses bee put in prose, and then aske the meaning, and
it will bee founde, that one Verse did but beget an other, without ordering at the first, what should bee at the last, which becomes a confused
masse of words, with a tingling sound of ryme, barely accompanied with
reason."[31]

But the purpose of such poems was homiletic in the crudest medieval

---

[29] Ed. Rollins, no. 47. The poem was first printed in *Tottel's Miscellany,* 1557.
[30] It is thus reprinted by Norman Ault, ed., *Elizabethan Lyrics* (New York,
1960), p. 27. Rollins (*Paradise,* p. 216) calls the attribution to Harington capricious.
[31] *Works (Defence),* III, 37–38.

way: dogma was stated and restated, hammered into the heads of the hearers by the most obvious schemes of embellishment and the most emphatic, clubbing, monotonous rhythm. The techniques were rhetorically justified by the necessity of talking down to the audience, of implanting a moral cliché in the recalcitrant memories of the ignorant. Like techniques serve like purposes today for preachers, politicians, and advertisers.

Fortunately, the increased sophistication of the purposes would require a commensurate sophistication of technique. When Greville argues with Caelica, it would hardly be decorous for him to shout her down with a homily. Instead, he demolishes her position logically. She advises him to read books,

> The Glasse where Art doth to posterity,
> Shew nature naked unto him that looks,
> > Enriching us, shortning the wayes of wit,
> > Which with experience else deare buyeth it.
> > > > (Sonnet 66)

Very humbly, the poet demurs, not because he thinks he knows everything, but because he believes that books cannot tell him anything worth knowing:

> Books be of men, men but in clouds doe see,
> Of whose embracements Centaures gotten be.

This general proposition—that because books are written by men who perceive but dimly, they contain only chimeras—stated in terms of myth, is specified and amplified (the figure of prolepsis) in the next five stanzas of the poem. In the first place, the knowledge we gain from direct experience is "More lively farre" than that retailed at second hand in "dead Books or Arts." In the second, books can in no way remedy our ignorance and error, "Whose causes are within . . . / For how can that be wise which is not pure?" We must therefore reform our inward spirits, so that reason is freed from the control of the inferior affections, before we can hope to gain knowledge from true arts, which are miracles. The last stanza is the peroration, recapitulating the whole and recalling the terms of the original myth: books, produced by "erring wit," misrepresent truth,

> And so entayle clouds to posterity.
> > Since outward wisdome springs from truth within,
> > Which all men feele, or heare, before they sinne.

Whereas Sand has recourse to the "places" of logic for the matter of individual stanzas, which enumerate the effects and adjuncts of his subject and contrast it to its opposite, Greville connects his stanzas by the logical principle of causation. He amplifies the general statement—that books produce chimeras—by presenting reasons for it on two different grounds: experience and theology. The first argument is a denial of the negative (that books "Show nature"); the second is a syllogism (more accurately, an enthymeme, since the middle term, "men are corrupt," is assumed). The second argument tells us the manner of doing as well as the cause and states the remedy for the condition it describes. Sand uses logic to provide material for amplifying by repetitious illustration; Greville, to provide a structure for amplifying by causal analysis, explanation, and development of implication. (Needless to say, we make hash of Sonnet 66 if we try to read it backwards.) In accordance with his purpose of direct logical refutation, Greville uses none of Sand's obtrusive schemes of sound or syntax; the few figures he employs facilitate the economical expression of the first argument (zeugma and brachylogia, the omission of verbs and conjunctions) and the pointed expression of the second (erotema, the rhetorical question).

We have observed before, incidentally, that this kind of logical rigor is characteristic in less detailed ways of many of the love poems, even of so graceful a song as "Away with these self-loving Lads" (Sonnet 52). It naturally becomes more apparent as Greville gradually shifts his emphasis from figurative and personal celebrations or critiques of love and begins, a little more than halfway through the sequence, to deal more abstractly with somewhat different themes. Sonnet 67, for example, defines and compares fickleness and duplicity. They are defined in separate stanzas on identical bases, manner of doing and ultimate effects, the latter providing the ground for comparison in the final stanza. The brief and compressed analysis in each stanza culminates in terse aphorisms, the first of which is proverbial:

> Time blotting all things out, but evill name.
>
> .    .    .    .    .
>
> Dissemblings then are knowne when they are past.
>
> .    .    .    .    .
>
> Unconstancy and doublenesse depart,
> When man bends his desires to mend his heart.

Greville was of course fond of the traditional habit of "sententious" writing, sprinkling his poems with aphoristic expressions, often in couplets, that his printer signalized by italics. Bacon speaks of this habit with reference to "delivering" scientific knowledge, but his remarks are equally applicable to literature:

the writing in Aphorisms hath many excellent virtues, whereto the writing in Method doth not approach.

For first, it trieth the writer, whether he be superficial or solid: for Aphorisms, except they should be ridiculous, cannot be made but of the pith and heart of sciences; for discourse of illustration is cut off; recitals of examples are cut off; discourse of connexion and order is cut off; descriptions of practice are cut off; so there remaineth nothing to fill the Aphorisms but some good quantity of observation: and therefore no man can suffice, nor in reason will attempt, to write Aphorisms, but he that is sound and grounded.[32]

But no matter how solid the aphorism, how accurate and pithy, a look at a miscellany like *A Gorgeous Gallery of Gallant Inventions* (which never reached a second edition) will demonstrate that random strings of them, sententiousness unrelieved, do not necessarily make poetry. In Greville, they almost invariably serve a logical purpose: to conclude the development of a point by apt summary, to clarify it by comparison, or to draw out its latent implications.

Greville's use of highly variegated logical structures is his main contribution to the historical development of the six-line stanza (in iambic pentameter, riming *a b a b c c*). Probably because this verse form was ubiquitous during the period, it has received, so far as I know, only passing mention from literary historians.[33] It is interesting, however, that its great popularity is confined almost exactly to the reign of Elizabeth. The stanza lacks one line of being rime royal, the form which rivalled it for second place in lyric popularity to the true sonnet. It is also, of course, identical to the sestet of the "Shakespearean" sonnet that Surrey introduced. Wyatt wrote a few poems in tetrameters with the same six-line rime scheme.[34] Whatever or how fortuitous its origins, the six-line stanza first appears in modern English in seven poems from *Tottel's Miscellany*. One is Sand's "The life is long, that lothsumly doth last"; another is a standard blazon; and another is a long political poem, comparing a native, contemporary rebellion to the Trojan wars.[35] The form was thus associated at its beginnings with what the Elizabethans liked best

[32] *Works*, III, 405 (*Advancement*, II). George Williamson has a good brief analysis of Greville's use of *sententia* and antithetic rhetoric to achieve the cynical, epigrammatic "wit of contradiction": *The Proper Wit of Poetry* (London, 1961), pp. 28–31.

[33] Franklin Dickey, "Collections of Songs and Sonnets" (*Elizabethan Poetry*, ed. John Russell Brown and Bernard Harris [London, 1960], pp. 40–45), discusses the prevalence of the six-line stanza in the miscellanies, mentions its use in "extended erotic narrative," presumes that it was "adapted" from rime royal, and ignores Greville entirely.

[34] *Collected Poems*, ed. Kenneth Muir (London, 1949), nos. 186, 187, 190, 192, three of which were printed in Tottel. The tetrameter version also became extremely popular.

[35] Ed. H. E. Rollins (Cambridge, Mass., 1928), nos. 171, 279, 309.

to write: general moralizing, celebrations of love, and political nar-
ratives. Recombination of these topics and treatments would give us
Shakespeare's erotic epyllion and Greville's philosophical treatises.

But before the form was thus extended, it enjoyed a lyric vogue. It is
the most frequent single kind of stanza in *The Paradise of Dainty Devices* (which went through more editions over a longer time than any
other collection, 1576–1606) and in *A Gorgeous Gallery of Gallant Inventions* (1578), where it is, however, greatly outnumbered by poulter's
measure and fourteeners. Spenser used it in the January and December
eclogues of *The Shepheardes Calender*, Sidney in a dozen poems in the
*Arcadia* and *Certain Sonnets*.[36] About half of [Thomas] *Howell His
Devises* (1581) are in the six-line stanza, and almost all the poems in the
first English sonnet-sequence, Watson's *Hekatompathia* (1582), consist
of three six-line stanzas. Almost half the poems in *Brittons Bowre of
Delights* (1591) use the form, which is still the favorite single stanza in
*The Phoenix Nest* (1593), where it greatly outnumbers poulter's measure and the fourteener. Even with increased competition from the bur-
geoning variety of lyric stanzas that poets were creating just before and
after the turn of the century, the six-line stanza manages to hold its own
for a while: it is employed in more than a quarter of the poems in *The
Arbor of Amorous Devices* (1597) and in over 15 percent of the 250
poems in *A Poetical Rhapsody* (1602–1621).[37] It is revealing, however,
that two-thirds of the poems that use the form in the latter anthology are
attributed to the mysterious "Anomos," whose work the compiler,
Francis Davison, tells us was done "almost twentie yeers since, when
Poetry was farre from that perfection, to which it hath now attained."[38]
To Davison, a young man in 1602, the smoothly graceful and conventional performances of the anonymous writer (or writers) seemed old-
fashioned.

If such performances were on their way out by the time of Elizabeth's
death, they were simply not possible at the beginning of her reign. The
six-line stanza thus takes its place as one of the forms in which the syntax
and versification of modern English became sufficiently supple and complex to produce the great age of lyric expression.[39] When the job was
done, when poets had developed a vigorous poetic language and acquired the taste to let it discover new forms, there was no longer any

[36] Ringler lists them, p. 570.
[37] Campion used the form several times—e.g., in the famous "When thou must
home to shades of underground"; Jonson twice—in *Epigrammes* XVII and
CXVIII; Donne once—in "The Expiration"; and Herbert also once—in the long,
directly moralizing introduction to *The Temple*, "The Church-Porch."
[38] Ed. H. E. Rollins (Cambridge, Mass., 1931–32), I, 6.
[39] The general history of versification from Wyatt to Sidney is chronicled by
John Thompson, *The Founding of English Metre* (New York, 1961).

need for the particular advantage that the six-line stanza once provided, and it dropped into disuse.[40]

Exactly what this advantage originally was, for the poets of roughly the latter half of the sixteenth century, may be inferred from a curious, but apparently common, habit of punctuation. In the *Paradise* the terminal punctuation of every line in every poem composed of six-line stanzas (including those in tetrameters) follows a virtually identical pattern ( , : , . , . ). The pattern is maintained, with only occasional exceptions for interrogation marks, even in total defiance of either sense or sound, grammar or rhetoric. The third stanza of Sand's poem is a good example:

> The pleasant yeres that semes so swetely ronne,
> The mery daies to ende, so fast that flete:
> The joyfull nights, of whiche daies dawes so sone,
> The happie howrs, whiche mo doe misse then mete.
> Do all consume as snowe against the Sonne,
> And death maks ende of all that life begonne.

The pattern is clearly the practice of particular printers or compositors, since it is not always maintained in subsequent editions of the *Paradise*. Its continuance in other anthologies, however, over a span of fifteen years, suggests that it was common enough to warrant interpretation. In the *Gorgeous Gallery* the pattern is slightly different ( , ; , ; , . ), but is still almost invariable, and remains so even in the later *Brittons Bowre*.

The persistence of the habit shows that the punctuation was not determined by the particular language of particular poems, but was rather conceived of as an integral part of the stanza itself. So far as I know, no other verse form was singled out for such typographical distinction, which indicates that the six-line stanza was read, felt, and regarded as a way of providing a unique, not to say Procrustean, regularity for poetic expression. It was thus one way of coping with a vernacular which had undergone such change that its earlier poetry would not scan, and to which classical theories of scansion did not readily apply. The whole problem of achieving regularity and smoothness in modern English was of course central to Gascoigne, who was the first theorist to formulate the usefulness of the iambic foot in English, insisting that its metrical stress coincide with the natural stress of the words in their natural order.[41] The relentless regularity, both metrical and syntactical, of much

---

[40] Although not quite into oblivion: the popularity of the *Rhapsody*, as well as the last reprinting of the much inferior *Paradise*, during the reign of James testify to the continued demands of the taste of an older generation.

[41] *Certayne Notes of Instruction in English Verse*, ed. Edward Arber (London, 1868), p. 34. Thompson discusses Gascoigne's "theory of regularity" (pp. 70–75).

miscellany verse is commonplace; but it was a prime contemporary desideratum. Even Puttenham advises it, and argues for the unvarying placement of caesurae in lines of the same length: "it pleaseth the eare better, and sheweth more cunning in the maker by following the rule of his restraint."[42]

The order that the inflexible pattern of punctuation imposed was entirely oral: it insured merely the alternation of brief and extended pauses at the ends of lines, and split the stanza up into two breath-units of quatrain and couplet. At this time punctuation itself was little more than oratorical breathmarks.[43] Though in actual Renaissance practice, punctuation gradually came to be an indication of sense, there were no theoretical principles for its syntactic or logical use. Puttenham still presents the classical-medieval theory of the comma, colon, and period as short, medium, and full pauses that ease the breath. Thomas Howell, in a six-line stanzaic poem from *The Arbor of Amitie* (1568), exemplifies the oratorical practice by indicating his ruthlessly regular caesurae in every line with colons.[44] For poets who had their hands full trying to make English sounds flow in a smooth and orderly way, the conception of the stanza as autonomous breath-unit was a serviceable, if crude, arbitrary, and essentially static notion of poetic structure.

But before the form would become capable of the mellifluous lyrics in the *Rhapsody*, much progress had to be made in versification; and before it could reach what I consider its finest use in Greville's religious lyrics, it had to be enriched by a much more sophisticated kind of oratorical structure, derived not from static prescriptions of oral delivery, but from the progressive and purposeful procedures of logic.

Sidney was of course a pioneer in providing such enrichment "in larger structural patterns which he created by a compact and complex combination of the devices of logic and rhetoric within established or newly invented fixed forms. He prided himself on being 'a peece of a Logician' ... and his poems are notable for the orderly progression of their ideas."[45] One of the established forms was the six-line stanza, to which Sidney brought kinds of logical structure that Greville also made use of. In one poem Sidney secures the "orderly progression" of ideas that express the lover's inevitable suffering by means of a double hypothetical syllogism (*Certain Sonnets* 19). The inferential structure is underlined by the play of anaphora on the key words "if" and "then" in the first two stanzas,

---

[42] Pp. 75–76 (II.iv[v]).

[43] See Walter J. Ong, S.J., "Historical Backgrounds of Elizabethan and Jacobean Punctuation Theory," *PMLA*, LIX (1944), 349–60.

[44] *Poems*, ed. A. B. Grosart (London, 1879), p. 29.

[45] Ringler, p. lvii. He goes on to cite Miss Tuve's work as evidence that in Sidney's verse "the images are controlled by their logical function."

which see the lover's "ease of minde" as the result of two hypothetical
conditions: self-discipline of his thoughts and reciprocation of his love
by the lady. The third stanza denies both, and in the figure of collectour
reaffirms his inevitable passion:

> But since my thoughts in thinking still are spent,
>    With reason's strife, by senses overthrowne,
> You fairer still, and still more cruell bent,
> I loving still a love that loveth none,
>    I yeeld and strive, I kisse and curse the paine:
>    Thought, reason, sense, time, you, and I, maintaine.

The poem's repetitive word-play (ploce and traductio) is copious and
obtrusive, but it is used to point up the paradoxes of the feeling described,
and is not allowed—as it often is in earlier uses of the form—to usurp the
structural function.[46] The figures of omission in the last stanza (zeugma
and brachylogia) not only emphasize the emotional paradoxes but also
compress and tighten the argument.

Sidney's logical structures, however, like Greville's, are seldom quite
so naked and direct. More typical of both writers is the logic implied by
a well-selected or carefully worked-out similitude. Sidney uses the same
two similitudes in a pair of six-line stanzaic poems as an emotional tour
de force (*Old Arcadia* 36, 37). Dorus compares the joy of the merchant
and the farm worker upon reaching the near completion of their respective hopes to his own joy on having gained, through storms and
torments, the favor of his lady. Cleophila (Pyrocles) then uses the same
situations to show that the merchant's, the laborer's, and his own anxiety
and torment are the more increased the closer their several desires approach fulfillment. In this poetic contest, by the way, the two friends of
the *Arcadia* are doing exactly what Sidney and Greville seem to have
done with a common fund of Cupid lore: using the same material for
different purposes. It is a pleasant example of the congruence, the "cross-
fertilization," of life and art.

This method of structuring a poem—by developing one or two similitudes in the quatrains of the stanzas and drawing the significant inferences or applications from them in the couplets—was most convenient
to the verse form itself, and was a favorite with Greville. He uses it in
a great variety of situations and moods: for example, to compare the con-

---

[46] The disciplined use of rhetoric within essentially logical structures in Sidney's
prose is described by P. A. Duhamel, "Sidney's *Arcadia* and Elizabethan Rhetoric,"
*Studies in Philology*, XLV (1948), 134–50. Professor Duhamel shows that Sidney,
unlike Lyly, is more concerned with developing "dialectically probative" material
from inventio than with sheer multiplication of schemes from elocutio. The distinction is ultimately that between a writer who fully understands and observes
decorum, and one who does not.

sequences of infidelity in love with those of the cosmically portentous "Great Year" (Sonnet 69); to compare black magic with the specious honor of nobility as having power to deceive men (Sonnet 92); and more complexly, to contrast and compare malice and love as different in intention but similar in effect (Sonnet 95); and to compare the contrasting effects of youth and age in men with those in states (Sonnet 101). All these poems (cf. also Sonnets 79, 93, 104) vary somewhat in length and complexity, but their structural principle is the same.

*Similitude* is of course a Renaissance term, and I use it advisedly in its Renaissance meaning of "likeness" or "comparison" in the broadest sense. *Simile* is not nearly adequate for the kinds of extended comparison which may be explicit (introduced by *like* or *as*) or implied, and which give shape to whole poems. It is obvious from the above examples that the grounds for such extended comparisons were readily obtained by playing one's mind over the logical places or predicaments. What such exercise produced was training to a high degree of discrimination in the most fundamental operation of the human mind: the perception of likeness or unlikeness.

That such mental facility was a prerequisite for effective writing was certainly not lost on the contemporary theorist. Although most traditional, non-Ramist logics of the period (those that maintained the Aristotelian distinction between scientific demonstration and discourse of opinions), as well as Sidney in the *Defence*, advised against arguing by similitude, or analogy, all poets ignored the advice.[47] And they did so in complete accord with the rhetorics, all of which saw the manipulation of "resemblance" as a primary resource of language. Thomas Wilson, in his vague way, suggests the scope and versatility of similitudes, which "are not onelye used to amplifie a matter, but also to beautifie the same, to delite the hearers, to make the matter playne, and to shew a certaine majestye wyth the reporte of suche resembled things."[48] These things include what we should now call developed metaphors and extended moral fables. Henry Peacham more clearly and explicitly regards similitudes as ministering simultaneously to the dual aim of literature, "yielding . . . profit by their perspicuitie, and pleasure by their proportion. They serve to . . . praise, dispraise, teach, to exhort, move, perswade, and to many other such like effects: of all formes of speech, they are best conceived, most praised, and longest remembered."[49] Puttenham sees the similitude as necessary to beautify, enforce, and enlarge a subject: "I say inforce because no one thing more prevaileth with all ordinary judgements than perswasion by similitude." He goes on to distinguish four

---

[47] Tuve, *Elizabethan and Metaphysical Imagery*, p. 371.
[48] *The Arte of Rhetorique* (London, 1553), fols. 101–101ᵛ.
[49] *The Garden of Eloquence* (London, 1593), p. 159.

subdivisions of this "sententious" figure: omoiosis, comparing by action or manner of doing; icon, comparing by "imagerie"; parabola, or the "parable," comparing by a "dark" metaphorical connection; and paradigma, comparing past actions or judgments with present ones.[50] Such wide-ranging recommendations as these were not merely common-sense formulations of the capabilities of language, but were also potential recipes by means of which a poet might discover logically relevant materials and give them logically coherent form.

Puttenham's treatment of icon is clear justification for Miss Tuve's basic contention that what the readers and writers of the age looked for in images was not physical accuracy, but logical, or qualitative, affinity. Puttenham claims that icon yields a visible representation of the thing described; only his examples make clear that what he means is the visible representation, not of a particular object or person, but rather of that object's or person's qualities: "So we commending her Majestie for wisedome bewtie and magnanimitie likened her to the Serpent, the Lion and the Angell." Similarly, Puttenham adduces a blazon "written of our soveraigne Lady, wherein we resemble every part of her body to some naturall thing of excellent perfection in his kind."[51] Peacham offers the more accurate definition of icon: it paints the image of a thing "by comparing forme with forme, qualitie with qualitie."[52] We have previously observed that Greville uses the imagery of *Caelica* exactly in this way: to suggest not the actual appearance of his mistresses but rather their qualities of power or dignity, and their effects, benevolent or otherwise.

The delight and instruction which the theorists found in similitude clearly consisted in the "nature of the 'affinity' seen."[53] Peacham explicitly cautions that there must be such an "affinity"—a logical ground of comparison—and that it must be neither "strange" nor "unknowne," since "by the one there is an absurditie, by the other obscuritie."[54] Greville did not always succeed in wholly avoiding the latter fault; indeed, almost all his commentators, from Milton's nephew to scholars of the present day, have stressed the obscurity of his writing. A good deal of it, which results from the density of his ideas or from his habit of grammatical ellipsis, will disappear on close examination; what remains can often be traced to his failure to elucidate the exact "affinity" he is after. Sonnet 63 is a typical example: similitudes are used in the last three stanzas as specific support for the generalization offered in the first (the

[50] Pp. 240–46 (III.xix).
[51] Pp. 250–51.
[52] P. 144.
[53] Tuve, *Elizabethan and Metaphysical Imagery*, p. 121.
[54] P. 159.

figure of prolepsis): "No wit can comprehend the wayes of Love." But the precise connection between the compared situations in the quatrains and the couplets that attempt to apply them to love is not quite clear. The general intention is obvious, however: paradoxes in nature are adduced to show that love is fully as incomprehensible; and the implied metaphor of cloud-formation for the frustration of desire is very well realized in the third stanza.[55] But what the "wheeles of high desire" in stanza two have to do with sailing in one direction around the earth, or with the dark complexions of those who live both at the poles and in the tropics we can only guess. We can seek to explain it easily enough: the wheels of love are moved only by "force," and are hence as inexplicable as the natural phenomena described; but it is still bad writing, and bad for just the reason Peacham offers. "Inexplicability" does not provide the specific terms of the comparison with sufficient "affinity"; the exact ground of the comparison is unknown. A similar problem occurs in the final stanza: we can only guess how men's disagreement about the source of magnetic north can produce the final inference that "They once had eyes, that are made blind by love."

The same kind of difficulty is compounded in the third stanza of Sonnet 62 by obscurities of reference: "Mercurists" is vague—Professor Bullough suggests they are politicians, but they might as well be thieves, connycatchers, scholars, or physicians; the context does nothing to tell us which. "Climats" is evidently a corrupt reading (see Bullough's note, I, 260) and makes no sense in context; the MS version, "Chymates," makes no sense at all. But the basis for comparing these two (whoever they are) with the "Masons" of the couplet is impossible to comprehend because the latter are described as doing just the opposite of what the "Mercurists" do. Even the general ground of this comparison is unknown.

Although Greville stumbled occasionally, his average is still very high: even the poems that contain his worst lapses also contain some of his most successful similitudes. What is more, he stumbled in the right direction, toward endowing the six-line stanza with a backbone of close reasoning that would enable it to perform weightier tasks than those imposed by the exclusive and indecorous exploitation of rhetorical schemes. The regular six-line stanza, with its opportunities for neat summary, succinct inference, or liturgical refrain in the couplet, as well

---

[55] Croll comments on the accuracy and plainness of this and other images drawn from common life or familiar learning: Greville makes them "correspond to the exact truth of observation and applies them with ingenious exactness to the truths they illustrate. . . . the effect they are meant to produce is that of the closest possible adherence to reality" (p. 23). Generally, I think, this is true, and it makes his occasional lapses all the more glaring.

as for the more traditional syntactic and rhetorical parallelism, was the verse form most congenial to Greville's habits of thought and feeling. He developed it not only as a tool for extended exposition but also for the analytic presentation of his deepest religious meditations. In *Caelica* this development coincides roughly with the abandonment of Petrarchan themes, and is conducted largely at the expense of the sonnet: sonnets outnumber six-line stanzaic poems three to one in the first half of the sequence, and the proportion, reversed, is over two to one in the last half.

It would perhaps be more accurate to call it simply an increased preference, rather than a development, since from the very beginning Greville could use the six-line stanza for purposes of both rhetorical celebration and logical analysis (as in Sonnets 1 and 9). What developed was his tendency to concentrate (in the lyrics of all forms) more on the latter than on the former. The broad general shift in subject matter and in formal organization is accompanied by a similar shift in the incidence of certain kinds of rhetorical figures. Obtrusive word-figures of repetition that depend on arbitrary placement in the line (anadiplosis, epanalepsis, anaphora) decrease sharply in the second half of the sequence, and virtually disappear in the poems of the last section (after Sonnet 84). The repetitive summary (collectour) and the rhetorical question (erotema) show a similar, though less pronounced, decline. Conversely, figures that facilitate straightforward analysis increase: etiologia (the direct statement of a cause) is used half a dozen times in the last section and once in the first half, and eclipsis (grammatical ellipsis, which Greville uses to compress and tighten his arguments) appears four times as often in the last section of the sequence as it does in the first half. These are merely indications in the large of what can always be seen in specific poems: the conception of style as functional, as varying in accordance with change in subject and in rhetorical objective—the observance, in short, of decorum.

Though Greville eventually came to prefer the six-line stanza as the vehicle of his later purposes, he never gave up the sonnet, which remains the most frequent verse from in *Caelica*. Such structural innovations as he (and Sidney) used to refine the six-line stanza were probably suggested by the extended conceits of Petrarchan sonnets.[56] Greville, as we shall see, was certainly influenced by Sidney's distinctive employment of the sonnet as dramatic, immediate dialogue; but his most characteristic use of the form tends to follow the same lines as his use of the six-line stanza: to present arguments in direct, logical ways or, more frequently, by the implied logical "affinity" of developed similitudes.

[56] In modern English, precedent for logical, analytical structure in the sonnet as well as the song had been provided by Sir Thomas Wyatt: see Peterson's discussion of Wyatt, pp. 104ff.

One of the most successful performances of the latter kind is Sonnet 40:

> The nurse-life Wheat within his greene huske growing,
> Flatters our hope and tickles our desire,
> Natures true riches in sweet beauties shewing,
> Which set all hearts, with labours love, on fire.
>
> No lesse faire is the Wheat when golden eare
> Showes unto hope the joyes of neare enjoying:[57]
> Faire and sweet is the bud, more sweet and faire
> The Rose, which proves that time is not destroying.
>
> Caelica, your youth, the morning of delight,
> Enamel'd o're with beauties white and red,
> All sense and thoughts did to beleefe invite,
> That Love and Glorie there are brought to bed;
>     And your ripe yeeres love-noone (he goes no higher)
>     Turnes all the spirits of Man into desire.

The logical affinity here is of course the idea of the maturing, ripening effect of time: it is used to suggest the exclusively physical, sensual quality of the feelings that Caelica inspires. What is essential to this method of shaping a poem, and a meaning, by comparison is the exact, though figurative, correspondence of its terms—the precise control of diction. The central idea of physical maturation is contained in the original compound adjective in the first line, and is there emphasized, as a process, by alliteration. The verbs in the second line suggest the effects of the process, which are sensual and potentially, perhaps, deceptive. The sensuality is elaborated in the next two lines, which also add a new aesthetic dimension to the process: such natural objects are beautiful, but beautiful in a way that shows us the promise of possession.

The process continues in the second quatrain, with the promise becoming the joy of near fulfillment, and is swiftly recapitulated in terms of another natural object that is a symbol of human love. The recapitulation also provides an opportunity for the direct statement, in the negative, of the idea which is the logical basis of the comparison that follows in the sestet. The terms that describe Caelica's maturation are not those of agricultural harvest and blooming that introduced the process itself, but are borrowed from the metaphor of heat, which has already been used to describe the effects of the process. The morning of her youth is given its conventional aesthetic and philosophical attributes by means of diction and syntax that subtly refuse to commit the poem to the convention and that reinforce the sensual connotations of the octave: the ambiguity

---

[57] The same feeling of pleasant anticipation was expressed in the same terms of harvest (but for a different purpose) by Sidney in *Old Arcadia* 36. The compound adjective in the first line was a favorite device of Sidney's.

of the invitation to belief picks up and echoes the ambiguous suggestion of deception in the flattered hope of the first quatrain; and the phrase describing the conventional union of love and glory is explicitly sexual. The latter connotation thus introduces the noon of her maturity, which vaporizes the earth's moisture, and melts in the heat of passion all the powers of man into a yearning for physical possession. The whole comparative context provides "spirits" with simultaneous exactitude and multiplicity of meaning.

The diction of the poem carefully excludes any suggestion that this desire will be actually realized, and retains to the very end the ironic possibility that the natural hope may be thwarted. This irony is brought into final focus by the negative parenthesis at the end, which implies a qualification of the negative statement of the poem's central idea. The parenthesis reminds Caelica (who is directly addressed in the sestet) that her powers are at their zenith: the metaphor of the sun's daily progress is extended to hint that what time has conferred, he will also take away. Greville thus makes the poem an oblique and subtle plea (in the "Gather ye rosebuds" vein) by ironically qualifying his own theme: "time is not destroying"—*yet*.

The control of rhythm is as masterful and suggestive as that of word and concept. A smooth, sensuous, insinuating flow is secured by intricate patterns of alliteration and assonance on certain kinds of sounds (spirants, nasals, and glides) in the octave. This cumulative effect is maintained in the third quatrain, but is abruptly modulated by the stopped consonants of the wholly masculine rimes (which culminate in the harsh alliteration of "brought to bed"), and is resumed immediately in the couplet by the flowing spirants and glides. Some of this audible virtuosity, which reinforces and in part creates the sensual meaning of the poem, is of course achieved by repetitive word-figures (ploce, traductio, antimetabole). All of it is prevented from becoming cloying or monotonous by frequent metrical substitution, which exquisitely controls the relative speed of the phrasing, and by the skillful variation in placement of caesurae. All these techniques are at work, for example, in the seventh line, which runs on into the emphatic pause after the first foot of the eighth (a favorite device of Milton's). In sum, the poem is a supreme example of the wide emotional resonance and ironic nuance—the complete and complex understanding of an experience—possible to a master of the traditional style disciplined by a precise logical structure.

The developed similitude served Greville as a structural principle in a wide variety of contexts and tones. It could be figurative and serious as in Sonnet 40, or literal and facetious as in Sonnet 49. In the latter princes and Cupid are compared in the octave: both praise what they do not possess, kindness. The poet then contrasts them in the sestet, drawing a personal inference in the couplet:

> Princes wee comprehend, and can delight,
> We praise them for the good they never had;
> But Cupids wayes are farre more infinite,
> Kisses at times, and curt'sies make him glad:
>    Then Myra give me leave for Cupids sake,
>    To kisse thee oft, that I may curt'sie make.

The witty implication is that we can always flatter princes, but that women are too capricious to insure our consistent success in delighting them. By ignoring this implication, the inferential plea to Myra adds the final touch of sophistic wit: that he should kiss her often by no means follows from the logic of the contrast.[58] A similitude might be developed, as here, with a minimum of rhetorical parallelism to underscore it, or, for different purposes, in the elaborately schematic syntax and repeated rimes of Sonnets 16 (quoted above, p. 59) and 86. Both poems depend on the same logical comparison: earth and man fallaciously blame heaven for their own inherent faults. Both then infer from the comparison the remedy of the fallacy: the first by affirming the inviolability of that which man corrupts; the second by suggesting two ways in which man can cope with his corruption. Both poems elucidate the philosophical dualism central to Greville's thought and thus suggest that his structural preference for similitudes employing carefully opposed "Images of Life" was derived from the nature of his ideas.[59]

The traditional conception of the lyric poem (in whatever verse form) as an oration naturally made it seem a kind of monologue: a living voice speaking to move a particular audience to a particular action. It is on this basis that Sidney criticizes, in the *Defence*, those poets who fail to do the job convincingly, who "if I were a mistresse, would never perswade mee they were in love."[60] It is also on this basis that Sidney developed his own distinctive modification of the sonnet sequence in *Astrophil and Stella* by controlling the viewpoint in each poem according to the audience to which it is directed: Stella, his friends, the social and literary

---

[58] Sidney was of course a master of witty sophistry, as in the famous "Grammer" sonnet, *AS* 63.

[59] The congruence of style and idea, theme and technique, is regarded in this chapter as developing through contemporary rhetorical and logical procedures. The next chapter will explore this relation more narrowly, in an attempt to show how Greville's particular ideas shape his particular style and differentiate it from comparable Renaissance writing.

[60] *Works*, III, 41.

circles at court, or Astrophil himself.⁶¹ Sidney, however, does more than merely address poems to this or that audience; often he incorporates the actual or imagined reactions of the particular audience into the poem itself, turning the monologue, in effect, into a dialogue (or into what later came to be called the dramatic monologue). And he does this usually in a vigorous, colloquial style designed to create the "energia," or forceful "sense of vivid dramatic action" that he most prized.⁶² Thus Astrophil argues with his friends who would dissuade him from his passion (*AS* 21); he reports, in order to refute, the false judgments made of him by the social world (*AS* 23, 27, 54); he constantly protests his sincerity as opposed to mere belletristic sophistication (in terms, of course, that only the belletristically sophisticated would appreciate), and he even alludes once or twice to the courtly critical approval of his verse (*AS* 74). Probably the widest scope for dramatic dialogue was provided by Astrophil as his own audience, wrangling with his passions and their obstacles as personified respondents in debate or quarrel: we find him in continual dispute with love, Cupid, virtue, honor, reason, hope, patience, joy, and even as an eavesdropper on a "strife . . . betweene Vertue and Love" (*AS* 52).

The colloquial energy by which all these conflicts was presented was a virtual revolution in English versification alone, and no doubt contributed to the universally high regard in which Sidney was held by his fellow poets at the same time at it established the medium in which they largely worked.⁶³ In *Caelica* Greville exploits this medium with all the techniques and in almost all the situations utilized by his friend (the significant omission being the direct and frequent address to the problem of style per se). We have already seen Greville engaged in some of these various forms of dialogue and drama: addressing his mistress and speculating on the motives implied by her actions (Sonnet 17); reporting and refuting her accusations against him (18, 57) as well as the false judgments of the social world (60); and conversing wittily with ladies of the court (53).

No less did Greville employ the conventions of the inward dialogue to dramatize his own emotional conflicts. Occasionally he speaks with a colloquial immediacy that sounds astonishingly like Sidney:

⁶¹ The multiple audience of *Astrophil and Stella* has been discussed by several critics, among them Hallett Smith, pp. 143–48; and Jean Robertson, "Sir Philip Sidney and His Poetry," *Elizabethan Poetry*, ed. Brown and Harris, p. 120.

⁶² Rudenstine, p. 155.

⁶³ Thompson summarizes Sidney's technical achievement as the importation of drama and wit into poetry by means of his recognition that a metrical pattern could exist, as a norm, within the language of speech—that, in short, inflexible regularity (undeviating coincidence of natural and metrical stress) was unnecessary (p. 140).

> Cupid, my pretty Boy, leave off thy crying,
> Thou shalt have Bells or Apples; be not peevish.
>
> (Sonnet 25)

The calming and cajoling of the petulant child is nicely maintained in a series of rhetorical questions that personify the obstacles to passion, the sources of the conflict:

> Did Reason say that Boyes must be restrained?
> What was it, Tell: hath cruell Honour chidden?
> Or would they have thee from sweet Myra weyned?
> Are her faire brests made dainty to be hidden?

The sestet picks up the sexual connotation in an adroit extension of the domestic situation, suggesting the frustration of natural desire by enforced ceremony:

> Tell me (sweet Boy,) doth Myra's beauty threaten?
> Must you say Grace when you would be a playing?

And it proceeds to develop explicitly the implied notion of child abuse as a condemnation of the lady's coyness, concluding with a desire for reciprocation or revenge:

> Doth she cause thee make faults, to make thee beaten?
> Give me a Bow, let me thy Quiver borrow,
> Is Beauties pride in innocents betraying?
> And she shall play the child with love, or sorrow.

The final point—rather too uncharitable for Sidney, but mild for Greville—emerges wholly from the dramatic situation: the poet is generously taking the child's part against unfair treatment.

Another dialogue with Cupid as mistreated child has Cupid himself recounting his grievances in response to the poet's initial request:

> Cupid, my little Boy, come home againe,
> I doe not blame thee for thy running hence.
>
> (Sonnet 35)

But the child replies, "Alas, I cannot Sir." His "right wing of wanton passion" has become lame by his residence in Myra's eyes, where

> So whip'd and scourg'd with modestie and truth,
> As having lost all hope to scape away,
> I yet take pleasure to 'tice hither youth:
>     That my Schoole-fellowes plagu'd as well as I,
>     May not make merry, when they heare me cry.

Again the dramatic situation produces, this time on a psychological basis, a criticism of the coyness that attracts but does not reward: the boy

wants company in his misery. Greville's most ingenious dialogue with
Cupid portrays him as the poet's vassal, who returns from the wars of
love in despair, defeated by rivals and jealousy, and is peremptorily ar-
raigned for failing to accomplish what he promised: "Find sureties, or
at Honours sessions dye" (Sonnet 71).[64] Cupid defends himself by
pleading the ignorance and inadequacy of faith in winning love, and
begs, as it were, to be reassigned:

> What shall I doe, Sir? doe me Prentice bind,
> To Knowledge, Honour, Fame or Honestie:
> Let me no longer follow Womenkinde,
> Where change doth use all shapes of tyranny;
>     And I no more will stirre this earthly dust,
>     Wherein I lose my name, to take on lust.

Here the dramatic situation restates one of the central themes of the
sequence: that true love seeks worthier objects than women.

Elsewhere, Cupid as the cynical deceiver is rebuked with shocked and
bitter indignation:

> You faithlessse Boy, perswade you me to reason?
> With vertue doe you answere my affection?
>
> (Sonnet 28)

Greville recalls the boy's former assurances that love would overcome
reason and virtue, both of which Cupid is urging on him as consolation
now that Myra no longer loves him. Having inspired her to new con-
quests, Cupid departs, blithely admitting that his former assurances
were based merely on physical enticement, and declaring that

> what is felt with hand, or seene with eye,
> As mortall, must feele sicknesse, age and dye.

In another sonnet on the suddenly altered moods of love, Greville begins
with the exasperated exclamation, "Was ever Man so overmatch't with
Boy?" (Sonnet 26). He goes on to describe Cupid as a willful and irre-
pressible child who cajoles him unwillingly into play and then grows
melancholy and recalcitrant when the poet wishes to continue it. When
scorned for such changeableness, the boy becomes enraged and re-
inflames him with love for Caelica. The child's capriciousness is dryly
identified with that of women in the concluding aphorism:

> If these mad changes doe make children Gods,
> Women, and children are not farre at odds.

[64] This poem is an interesting variation on the sonnet form: it contains one additional quatrain and only four rimes, one of which is repeated in every quatrain.

Using such abrupt colloquial outbursts as the opening lines of these sonnets to plunge us immediately into the middle of a dramatic situation was a technique presumably invented by Sidney and later made famous by Donne. Achieving by this means a vivid impact in the presentation of emotional conflict seems, however, to have interested Greville less than working his way through such a presentation to some general judgment upon the conflict. He thus tends to use even his dramatic structures as vehicles for the logical analysis of an experience. A final example of this is his address to "Patience, weake fortun'd, and weake minded Wit" (Sonnet 46). The octave condemns the advice of Patience to await future satisfaction, since time has only deprived him of his joy, and states the conditions under which such advice would be acceptable:

> Give me sweet Cynthia, with my wonted blisse,
> Disperse the clouds that coffer up my treasure,
> Awake Endymion, with Diana's kisse,
> And then sweet Patience, counsell me to measure.

At this point, the poem has already reached the conclusion of Sidney's sonnet, "Fy, schoole of Patience, Fy" (*AS* 56), to which it invites comparison. The details of the situation in each sonnet indicate the usual difference in theme: Greville's mistress has already been unfaithful; Sidney is merely describing a temporary absence from Stella, who has yet to be persuaded of his love. The language of each poem indicates the usual difference in technique: Sidney's is perfectly conversational, flowing in natural order through no less than five run-on lines; Greville, focusing less on the dramatized presentation of feeling per se, uses more formal diction and rhythm, and permits inversions of normal word order in the second and last lines. The sestet of Greville's poem explains why patience is not applicable to the poet's predicament:

> But while my Love feeles nothing but correction
> While carelessnesse o'reshadowes my devotion,
> While Myra's beams shew rivall-like reflection,
> The life of Patience then must be commotion;
>   Since not to feele what wrong I beare in this,
>   A senselesse state, and no true Patience is.

Greville presents, in other words, logical justification for the epithets applied to patience in the initial outburst: "weake fortun'd" because it accomplishes nothing; "weake minded" because it falsifies the experience of betrayal.

It is evident that Greville and Sidney implemented the rhetorical aim of persuasiveness with regard to a highly sophisticated audience by striving both to present feelings convincingly by dramatic structures, and to judge them convincingly by logical ones. Greville's stress falls more heavily on the latter aim, as, for example, in the reported dialogue of Sonnet 66, where Caelica's suggestion that he read books is an opportunity for the brief but complex exposition of his epistemological theory. In a subsequent pair of sonnets, the dialogue is direct: it takes place within, and gains emotional power from, the personal context of the traditional "answer" to a proposal. Nevertheless, it is not really exploited as drama, but as logical argument and counterargument, both literal and figurative.

In the first of the pair the poet, absent from his mistress, addresses her at the outset and inquires (the figure of anthypophora) "Whence doth the Change, the world thus speakes on, grow?" (Sonnet 72). He then seeks to demonstrate that change in love is an impossibility. His soul admires only her worthiness; his heart desires only her beauty—"What need you new?" The implications of this idea of complete exclusiveness in mutual love are explicitly drawn in the sestet:

> If loving joy of worths beloved be,
> And joyes not simple, but still mutuall,
> Whom can you more love, than you have lov'd me:
> Unlesse in your heart there be more than all;
>     Since Love no doomes-day hath, where bodies change,
>     Why should new be delight, not being strange?

Her love for him is the natural response to his total devotion to her and must also be total, in order to produce the completeness of shared ("not simple") joy that is love itself. They give each other all their devotion, hence she cannot possibly have "more" to give anyone else. The doomsday metaphor asserts that change is pointless because it cannot produce difference: love does not alter with respect to bodies; her experience of it, being perfect with the poet, cannot be more delightful with anyone else. The wit of the metaphor depends on the pun on "change," which means, with respect to doomsday, that bodies are transformed, and with respect to love, that it has found a new object.[65] The ontological subtlety of the metaphor is of course a part of the poem's purpose and meaning: to show that change in love is impossible by conceiving love as a Platonic hypostatization.

It is precisely this conception of love that his mistress refuses to accept in the following sonnet: her reply is exclusively naturalistic.

> Myraphill, 'tis true, I lov'd, and you lov'd me,
> My thoughts as narrow as my heart, then were;

---

[65] Bullough calls this metaphorical argument of the poem "the full Metaphysical manner" (*Poems and Dramas*, I, 265).

> Which made change seeme impossible to be,
> Thinking one place could not two bodies beare.
> This was but earnest Youths simplicitie,
> To fadome Nature within Passions wit,
> Which thinks her earnestnesse eternity,
> Till selfe-delight makes change looke thorough it.
>
> (Sonnet 73)

The permanence of love directed to a single object is for Myra but an illusion of youth, not a philosophical principle. Self-interest cannot be denied; and the sestet describes how she did not deny it:

> You banish'd were, I griev'd, but languish'd not,
> For worth was free and of affection sure;
> So that time must be vaine, or you forgot,
> Nature and Love, no Vacuum can endure;
> I found desert, and to desert am true:
> Still dealing by it, as I dealt by you.

His absence did not devastate her; she knew that she would attract affection from others (indeed, planned to, if her "worth was free"), which would of course be a waste of time unless she forgot about him.[66] The forgetting is simply compelled by his absence, since he created what love cannot tolerate. The pun on "desert," meaning both "desertion" and "deserving," subtly adds to the implication that his departure is responsible for her change: she treats his absence quite as fairly as she treated his presence, by loving whoever admires her. Myra's straightforward naturalistic cynicism is precisely reflected in her metaphors, both of which are drawn from the laws of empirical science and assert a conception of love that is the opposite of Platonic permanence: it is a natural force that brooks no confinement. The metaphors of both sonnets in this dialectical dialogue are thus used to state the central premises of their arguments, which present, through the analysis of a particular experience, general and mutually exclusive definitions of love.

The logical facility, emotional accuracy, and intellectual sophistication in most of Greville's love lyrics show him developing in the general direction of Donne the structures of lyric verse that were prescribed by traditional theory and refined by Sidney. But if Greville, by the importation of drama and close reasoning into lyric forms, can approximate the stylistic practice of both these poets (just as he deals with themes char-

---

[66] Bullough (*ibid.*, I, 265–66) misinterprets, I think, the syntax of her argument by overlooking the figure of zeugma. In the line, "So that time must be vaine, or you forgot," he destroys the antithesis by taking "you" for the active subject instead of the passive subject of "forgot."

acteristic of both), the habitual quality of his language still remains readily distinguishable from theirs. Though Greville could be—whenever the decorum of a given poem demanded it—elaborately rhetorical, conversationally flowing, or metaphorically subtle, he seldom chose to exploit these forms of language very extensively. He preferred a more direct approach and a more formal diction and cadence within regular metrical patterns. Within these patterns his skill at managing versification and sound was consummate.

One innovation in particular, which Greville adapted from Sidney and improved, can partially illuminate some standard assessments of his style. He has been called "slow, archaic, stiff and stately."[67] His ability to "give power to generalizations"[68] has been often praised since Croll analyzed it as follows:

The emotional power of bare unadorned words in expressing intense convictions and deep feeling is one of the secrets of his impressivness, and, like the plainness of his images, his use of such diction is a sign of his effort for incisiveness and expressiveness. . . . It has the effect of keeping his abstract truths . . . alive with the life of the experience in which they were born.[69]

The careful precision of his diction—particularly of his abstract terms—and the exact correspondence of his similitudes, as well as his terse, aphoristic compression, certainly contribute to his expressive power.[70] But this power is also greatly enhanced by that slow and stately movement, which has the effect of pronouncements made only after great deliberation, the final redaction of a great volume of experience.

Greville achieves such solemnity of cadence partly by the way he employs feminine rimes. The historical importance of Sidney's revival of this prosodic resource has been well appreciated by his editor:

His great innovation was to bring feminine rhyme back into English verse and to make it . . . a regularly recurring structural element of his stanzaic patterns. . . . Though feminine rhyme almost never appears in the poetry of the mid-century, by the 1590's, probably in part as a result of Sidney's example, it had become an accepted feature of English verse.[71]

In many of the *Arcadia* poems, however, Sidney is just as interested in the expressive as in the structural use of feminine (and *sdrucciola*) rimes.

---

[67] Odette de Mourgues, *Metaphysical, Baroque and Précieux Poetry* (Oxford, 1953), p. 23.

[68] Thompson, p. 146.

[69] P. 24.

[70] Further striking instances of all these qualities can be found in Sonnet 44, which develops a mythical similitude and applies it to his relationship with Caelica, and Sonnet 81, which praises the queen.

[71] Ringler, p. lvi.

They are of course an integral part of the contest of poetic virtuosity between Lalus and Dorus (*Old Arcadia* 7). But the primary emotional effect for which Sidney used them was that of grief: in lamentations of love (28, 30), in formal pastoral elegy (one of the first in English, 75), and in lamentations of death (76, a riming sestina).[72] Often the multiple rimes are alternated with masculine ones; but Sidney clearly felt that steady streams of falling feminine endings, along with awkward metrical substitution, harsh alliteration, abrupt syntax, and clogged rhythm were expressive of grief. Such passages as this occur at length:

> Justice, justice is now (alas) oppressed:
>    Bountifulnes hath made his last conclusion:
>    Goodnes for best attire in dust is dressed.
> Shepheards bewaile your uttermost confusion;
>    And see by this picture to you presented,
>    Death is our home, life is but a delusion.
> For see alas, who is from you absented.
>
> (*Old Arcadia* 75)

Sidney experiments with feminine rime almost always in extended contexts; he evidently regarded their effect as cumulative, for although he uses them in the songs of *Astrophil and Stella*, he avoids them entirely in those sonnets and generally in the shorter lyric forms.[73] Sidney's practice has been stressed partly as a corrective to the popular modern critical dogma that "Not only is [English] deficient in rhymes, but any attempt at a rhyme of two or more syllables has a weakening, a relaxing, or else an explicitly facetious effect."[74] Both Sidney and Greville held virtually the opposite opinion, the results of which we may perceive by listening carefully to their verse, and by not allowing our view of the English language to be determined by *Hudibras* and *Don Juan*.

But Greville, unlike his friend, was extremely fond of feminine rime in short lyrics, often using it as a regularly recurring structural element.[75] Just as often, in the poems of the first section of the sequence that deal with the sufferings of love, he uses it to express a mournful melancholy or a sense of pain (as in Sonnets 1, 8, 9, 10). But feminine rime is also employed, rather indiscriminately, in other contexts: the development of a cosmic similitude (Sonnet 7), the dramatic dialogue (25), the cyni-

---

[72] Rudenstine offers excellent analyses of the formally evocative multiple rimes in *Old Arcadia* 7 and 30 (pp. 83–90).

[73] Only one sonnet (*Old Arcadia* 69) of all that he ever wrote contains feminine rimes. See Ringler's tables, pp. 569–72.

[74] Harry Levin, "Words in English Poetry," *Contexts of Criticism* (Cambridge, Mass., 1957), p. 223.

[75] Croll first pointed out that his mixture of ten- and eleven-syllable lines made Greville "singular among the sonneteers" (p. 15).

cal redefinition of love (32). Sonnet 19 is the first poem in the sequence to contain no feminine rimes at all; in the first half of *Caelica* more than two-thirds of the poems contain feminine rimes, in the last half, less than half do. Though their use thus becomes less frequent generally, and rather more rigorously confined to structural or affective purposes, they still appear in a variety of contexts. Greville's practice in this regard becomes more moderate, but not really different in kind.[76]

The constant element in this practice seems clearly to be Greville's liking for the richness and density of sound, along with the increased opportunities for patterns of assonance, that feminine rimes could provide. Even a cursory reading of *Caelica* will reveal that his favorite feminine rime sounds are the mouth-filling spirants, nasals, and glides of such word endings as *tion, sion,* and *sure.*[77] Successions of such thick rimes alone or in combination with masculine ones (see Sonnet 46, quoted above), as well as those of lighter sounds (*-ing, -ed*; see 40, quoted above, and 22), were exploited for assonance that lends the verse a density or a smoothness of aural texture.

Fully as important as the quality of the sounds and sound patterns themselves are the rhythmic contexts in which they occur. It was as obvious to the poets of the late Renaissance as it is to us that a series of feminine rimes in a regular (and especially in a light and rapid) meter could easily become singsong and monotonous. In his apparent attempts to avoid these faults, Sidney was forced into awkwardness. Greville seldom was, primarily because of the way he managed meter and sound within the line, not allowing it to rush continually forward to its falling conclusion. This pair of lines can exemplify the practice:

> The nurse-life Wheat within his greene huske growing,
>
> .    .    .    .    .
>
> Natures true riches in sweet beauties shewing.
>
> (Sonnet 40)

The subtle variations in the relative weight of the accents, the juxtaposition of strong accents by metrical inversion and the substitution of spondaic feet, and the juxtaposition of words that end and begin with stopped consonants, which require time to pronounce—all tend to slow down the verse and give it the ponderous deliberative power that is

---

[76] Croll made the erroneous statement—which Bullough (*Poems and Dramas,* I, 37) accepts—that only five poems after Sonnet 72 contain feminine rimes (p. 14). In fact, seventeen of them do; and in eleven of these they play a vital part. Even imperfect *sdrucciola* rime appears in several.

[77] The sound is even fuller when we remember that according to Sidney, words ending in *tion* in which the antepenultimate vowel-sounds are the same constituted *sdrucciola* rimes, the suffix being pronounced in two syllables (*Works,* III, 45).

typical of Greville. Set within such stately rhythms (which are by no means necessarily "stiff"), feminine rimes are neither flaccid nor comic; they are compelled instead to contribute to the somberly evocative cadence and movement of the poetry.

Such movement may be heard giving force to general diction in Sonnet 84, Greville's farewell to love. His performance in this conventional genre of renunciation uses none of the passionate, bitter name-calling rhetoric of his predecessors, Wyatt ("Farewell love") and Sidney ("Thou blind man's marke," *Certain Sonnets* 31). Greville does not see himself as victimized by love; his disillusionment is quieter and more accurate, implying by ironic situation and contrast the judgment of his own folly.

> Farewell sweet Boy, complaine not of my truth;
> Thy Mother lov'd thee not with more devotion;
> For to thy Boyes play I gave all my youth,
> Yong Master, I did hope for your promotion.
>
> While some sought Honours, Princes thoughts observing,
> Many woo'd Fame, the child of paine and anguish,
> Others judg'd inward good a chiefe deserving,
> I in thy wanton Visions joy'd to languish.
>
> I bow'd not to thy image for succession,
> Nor bound thy bow to shoot reformed kindnesse,
> Thy playes of hope and feare were my confession,
> The spectacles to my life was thy blindnesse;
>    But Cupid now farewell, I will goe play me,
>    With thoughts that please me lesse, & lesse betray me.[78]

The smooth, dignified heaviness of the poem's sound is created by intricate patterns of alliteration and assonance, to which the feminine rimes are essential. The assonance can be rather obvious (*ess* and *s* in the sestet) or less so (*ng* in the second quatrain), may be combined with alliteration (*s* in the second quatrain), or doubled in single lines ("hope ... promotion," "my life ... thy blindnesse"). Similarly, the alliteration can be straightforward and self-contained ("bound thy bow"), or can set up a wider resonance by means of rhetorical figure ("bow'd ... bound": prosonomasia) or metrical coincidence ("Farewell sweet Boy ... For to thy Boyes"; "Thy Mother ... Yong Master"). Throughout the poem the prominence of strong accents (achieved by increasing the weight of the stresses in consecutive feet, and by using metrical substitu-

---

[78] This poem inspired Coleridge to the sincerest form of flattery; he wrote a line-by-line imitation of it: *Poems*, ed. E. H. Coleridge (Oxford, 1912), I, 402–03. His version offers a great temptation to invidious comparison, which is best resisted.

tion to juxtapose stresses), together with time-consuming clusters of consonant sounds (see especially lines two, three, seven, and twelve), slow down the verse and emphasize important concepts or contrasts.

The measured and mature tones of Greville's speech make the initial address to Cupid, the posture of self-defense, highly ironic—and ironic at the poet's own expense. A man is serving a boy: and as Greville goes on to avow how scrupulous and loyal this service has been, each specific loyalty becomes a self-condemnation. The poet languished while other men actively strove to be powerful, or famous, or good. The irony is intensified in the sestet by the disavowal of ulterior motive: his service, and hence his folly, was not only complete and exclusive, it was pure. It sought to obtain neither progeny nor reward, but rather a religious subordination of self, which had the natural result of circumscribing the vision of the man by that of the deity he worshipped. The final couplet states the ultimate result of this devotion and leaves no doubt where the blame should fall: he has betrayed himself. And he has done so because it was easy and pleasant—child's play—as opposed to the "paine and anguish" of active accomplishment. Sonnet 84 is a fine summary of Greville's pragmatic view of love as a delightful game which cannot be held responsible for our own willful and lazy overvaluation of it. The ironic situation affirms the acceptance of love as such even as it makes clear its ultimate inadequacy as a substitute for all other human activity. And the renunciation in the last line is the more powerful because it acknowledges this affirmation. It should be noticed, finally, that the progression of the poem is logical: the dramatic irony of "devotion" is established; the nature of the devotion is then stated by exclusion, its motives by negation, its effects by metaphor; and the reiterated "farewell" then passes the judgment that was implicit in the initial irony.[79]

Such is Greville's characteristic achievement in the modes of the traditional style. Within the conception of the lyric as oration, every rhetorical scheme and every prosodic device is disciplined by decorum to furnish the progressive structures of logical argument with the dramatic situation or the emotional resonance which completes their meaning, forming a fully apprehended and coherent view of a particular experience. It is a poetry direct and lucid in outline; exact in diction and structure; complex, subtle, and suggestive in tone, detail, and idea. It is above all a poetry in which every word tells.

[79] William Frost describes this sonnet as "flippancy": *Fulke Greville's "Caelica": An Evaluation* (Brattleboro, Vt., 1942), p. 34. It is witty, to be sure, but it is a less flamboyant version of the so-called "metaphysical" wit that is an instrument of accurate perception and serious judgment. It is difficult to understand how anyone attending to syntax and rhythm could read the poem aloud to make it sound flippant.

# IV  The True Believer

WHEN Greville bids his ironic farewell to Cupid in Sonnet 84, he introduces at the same time the less pleasing, but less betraying, thoughts that will occupy him for the rest of the sequence. In the following sonnet he identifies the object of these thoughts as divine love, which he defines philosophically as the ground of our being ("The first and last in us that is alive"), and describes in terms that provide a diametric opposition to the emotional chaos of earthly desire. True love has "Passed through hope, desire, griefe and feare," to become "A simple Goodnesse in the flesh refin'd." It is

> Constant, because it sees no cause to varie,
> A Quintessence of Passions overthrowne,
> Rais'd above all that change of objects carry,
> A Nature by no other nature knowne:
>   For Glorie's of eternitie a frame,
>   That by all bodies else obscures her name.
>
> (Sonnet 85)

The insights afforded by this Christian perspective of eternity will not result in self-deception, and, if only for that reason, will not be pleasant. Greville's language in both poems implies the two directions that his intense dualism will take: inwardly, a "striving toward God as his proper end"[1] (which necessitates the rigors of repentance), and outwardly, a recognition that the glory of God, far from being manifested in worldly activities and institutions, is merely obscured and travestied by them.

The renunciation of self and the condemnation of society are the themes that Greville develops in the final section of *Caelica*. Although this development is only loosely systematic, it is distinctly progressive. Beginning from the dualistic postulate, he explores the inadequacies of the natural world. His intense inward realization of the process of repentance is achieved in the center (Sonnets 97–99) of this final section; his self-examination is the pivot on which his outward vision turns. It is by means of this inward purgation, this renewed awareness, that Greville subsequently passes final judgment on the natural world, not

---

[1] Peterson, *The English Lyric*, p. 272.

merely in terms of its deceptive effects, but also in the light of the theological reasons for them. The judgments are in part commonplace; but the vision which produces them has been earned. Only by achieving the spiritual discipline of self-renunciation is Greville able to utter the magnificent prayer for doomsday that concludes the sequence and makes clear the ultimate connection between the two themes of the final section. In the opening section of *Caelica* we saw Greville probing the assumptions and examining the consequences of love as a fashionable Petrarchan ideal; here he investigates the nature of love as an immutable Christian ideal. The "heavens" as metaphor for his profane mistresses become the "heavens" as literal, conceptual embodiment of his moral passion.

The quality of this passion is defined by the inferences drawn from the religious doctrines in terms of which the investigation is conducted; it is distinctly Calvinistic. Moreover, it is possible to see how the style and structure of the poems reflect the particular religious sensibility that motivates them. It is also possible to differentiate this sensibility, the ideas upon which it depends, and the modes of expression it compels, from those of other poets who deal with the same experience of repentance, which was central to Protestantism itself.[2]

Greville's exploration of divine love is conducted on the basis of the same metaphysic and in roughly the same way as his exploration of profane love in the opening section of the sequence. The poems of both sections record a developing awareness as they assert the metaphysic and proceed to illustrate it and analyze its logical consequences.

When Greville in Sonnet 85 locates true love in eternity, and sees it as being only "obscured" in "bodies," he echoes the position he reached in Sonnet 10, where he confines ideal love to contemplation,

> Since excellence in other forme enjoyed,
> Is by descending to her Saints destroyed.

He restates this position in Sonnet 16, after having considered in the intervening poems some of the ways that the ideal is destroyed and having attempted to reassert its realization in the flesh. No matter if love can be debased by ingratitude, inconstancy, or lust; no matter if it is doomed, in practice, to result in frustration. If it is thus "obscured," it is by no means invalidated,

---

[2] Peterson discusses the final section of *Caelica* as a series of "penitential lyrics," glossing them with broad distinctions between the Protestant and the Catholic doctrines of repentance, and describing their style in terms of the general historical framework that he seeks to establish (pp. 272–83). The analyses are illuminating on the emotional progress in the poems, but are not designed to explore very fully Greville's individual style.

> Love being plac'd above these middle regions,
> Where every passion warres it selfe with legions.

The same point is made with the same similitude in Sonnet 86. Both poems assert that heaven cannot be blamed for the frailties of earth, either in the macrocosm of time and tempest or in the microcosm of human emotions. The same elaborate parallelism in syntax and diction enforces the argument of both sonnets.[3] In its context, the later poem exemplifies one process by which the heavenly glory of Sonnet 85 is "obscured":

> The Earth with thunder torne, with fire blasted,
> With waters drowned, with windie palsey shaken
> Cannot for this with heaven be distasted,
> Since thunder, raine and winds from earth are taken:
> Man torne with Love, with inward furies blasted,
> Drown'd with despaire, with fleshly lustings shaken,
> Cannot for this with heaven be distasted,
> Love, furie, lustings out of man are taken.[4]

In Sonnet 16 Greville contented himself with isolating the ideal from the real, and falling back on the hope of being able to appreciate it as such, untainted by the shadows of earthly lust. Likewise the third quatrain of Sonnet 86 counsels man to "endure" the inevitable upheavals of passion in his life: "those clouds will vanish." But the concluding couplet offers an alternative that was not present before:

> Or Man, forsake thy selfe, to heaven turne thee,
> Her flames enlighten Nature, never burne thee.

---

[3] They are compared above, p. 97, and Sonnet 16 is discussed in its context, pp. 59–60.

[4] The imagery of this poem is different from the astronomical similitude of Sonnet 16, and was perhaps suggested by Calvin, *Institutes*, I, 233–34 (I.xvii.1): When thick clouds obscure the heavens, and a violent tempest arises, because a gloomy mist is before our eyes, and thunder strikes our ears, and terror stupefies all our faculties, all things seem to us to be blended in confusion; yet during the whole time the heavens remain in the same quiet serenity. So it must be concluded, that while the turbulent state of the world deprives us of our judgment, God, by the pure light of his own righteousness and wisdom, regulates all those commotions in the most exact order, and directs them to their proper end. And certainly the madness of many in this respect is monstrous, who dare to arraign the works of God, to scrutinize his secret councils, and even to pass a precipitate sentence on things unknown, with greater freedom than on the actions of mortal men.
It is additionally suggestive that Calvin's general point here—the castigation of man's pride in seeking to understand the "mysterious judgments" of God—will be elaborated by Greville in Sonnet 88.

The transition from profane to divine love is complete, and it has been made in terms of a paradox that suggests the different effects of each: the flames which provide illumination without harm are the final development of the diametric contrast between the two loves implied by the two preceding poems. The "furie" and "lustings" of love, the "playes of hope and feare" (84), are precisely those burning flames whose effects Greville has analyzed throughout the sequence; they are self-deceptive, giving heat without light, and ironically cannot achieve their ostensible aim of emancipation from self.

Greville underscores the broad thematic progression of *Caelica* by asserting this contrast between the two loves in a sonnet whose idea, structure, and style are virtually identical to those of the earlier sonnet, in which the idea which governs his treatment of the first kind of love is first stated. Having considered the kind of ideal love which cannot be realized in practice, he now turns to the kind which can. From the analysis of the worshipful pose he turns to that of worship itself. The contemplative religious and political poems of the final section are thus neither miscellaneous nor irrelevant to the sequence: they are a literal development of the religious vocabulary and attitudes of love. As such, they exemplify Greville's development of the lyric poem and his enlargement of the scope of the sonnet sequence. We may thus observe in the microcosm of *Caelica* one of the most important general tendencies in the lyric verse of the age, whereby the courtly conventions of praise, petition, and frustration, "which in the beginning had been introduced into the religion of love by the deliberate parody of religious experience are now, some three-and-a-half centuries later, reintroduced as ways of ordering thought and feeling within the very areas of experience from which they originally derived."[5]

Greville has consciously made this transition in Sonnets 84–86 on the basis of his dualistic metaphysic and from the point of view of the effects of the two kinds of love on the individual. The divine can accomplish what the profane cannot: the "forsaking" of self. How this can be accomplished is the subject of the next three poems. The first step is taken in Sonnet 87 with a contemplation of death whose two brief stanzas give powerful expression to man's perversity and impotence when confronted with eternity:[6]

[5] Peterson, p. 175.

[6] The poem, out of context, has been highly and variously praised: Miss de Mourgues (pp. 24–25—the most illuminating discussion of the poem), sees it as a "reflection of the philosophical pessimism of the late Renaissance, centred . . . on the problem of knowledge," presenting a kind of "metaphysical horror" by its skillful "alliance of concrete terms and abstract qualities." Fred Inglis (*English Poetry 1550–1660* [London, 1965], p. 34) includes it with Jonson's "To Heaven" and Herbert's "Church-Monuments" as direct, complex triumphs of "traditional

When as Mans life, the light of humane lust,
In socket of his earthly lanthorne burnes,
That all this glory unto ashes must,
And generation to corruption turnes;
   Then fond desires that onely feare their end,
   Doe vainely wish for life, but to amend.

But when this life is from the body fled,
To see it selfe in that eternall Glasse,
Where time doth end, and thoughts accuse the dead,
Where all to come, is one with all that was;
   Then living men aske how he left his breath,
   That while he lived never thought of death.

Both couplets present reactions which are ironically irrelevant and anti-climactic to the situations described in the quatrains: dying, the unregenerate wish belatedly, out of fear of punishment, for time to reform; when such a one dies, we who remain can only inquire the manner of his departure. As the poem adjures us, in the traditional fashion of the *memento mori*, to consider death, it simultaneously exposes the usual wrong motive for doing so, and implies our epistemological inability to do so directly. The "eternall Glasse" is no peephole into either the torments or the joys of the afterlife; it is rather a mirror that reflects merely our misguided efforts to penetrate it; it is the ultimate mystery, the final paradox, the literally inconceivable point at which time ends and which yet contains all time.

Greville proceeds in the following poem to specify the things we cannot see in that "eternall Glasse," delineating the epistemological boundaries of the finite creature:

Man, dreame no more of curious mysteries,
As what was here before the world was made,
The first Mans life, the state of Paradise,
Where heaven is, or hells eternall shade,
   For Gods works are like him, all infinite;
   And curious search, but craftie sinnes delight.
                                (Sonnet 88)

These sinful speculations, as well as the punishments given or prophesied for them in the Old Testament,

Are nothing to the mans renewed birth;
   First, let the Law plough up thy wicked heart,
   That Christ may come, and all these types depart.

---

moral language." C. S. Lewis (p. 524) remarks that the three lines on death in the second stanza "make most sixteenth-century poetry on that subject seem a little facile and external."

The last stanza summarizes the results of this twofold process of inward regeneration, which is identified as man's sole approach to infinity:

> For Goodnesse onely doth God comprehend,
> Knowes what was first, and what shall be the end.

The careful grammatical ambiguity of "onely" indicates both the error of man's prideful attempts to understand the eternal (only God knows first and last) as well as the moral direction such attempts must properly take (God comprehends only goodness).

The next poem further defines the nature of man's proper approach to divinity by continuing the invidious contrast of knowledge with the experience of contrition, the ploughing up of the wicked heart. Here, however, knowledge is represented not as cosmic speculation, but as accurate comprehension of religious faith. Greville describes the Manichaean heresy as intellectual idolatry and then denies, by irony, that our clearer view of Christ is sufficient for salvation:

> We seeme more inwardly to know the Sonne,
> And see our owne salvation in his blood;
> When this is said, we thinke the worke is done,
> And with the Father hold our portion good:
>   As if true life within these words were laid,
>   For him that in life, never words obey'd.[7]

(Sonnet 89)

In the final stanza, Greville continues to be ironic at the expense of those foolish enough to imagine that "true life" could result from true knowledge that is not truly acted upon:

> If this be safe, it is a pleasant way,
> The Crosse of Christ is very easily borne:
> But six days labour makes the sabboth day,
> The flesh is dead before grace can be borne.
>   The heart must first beare witnesse with the booke,
>   The earth must burne, ere we for Christ can looke.

The carefully orchestrated paradoxes, culminating in the metaphor of doomsday for individual regeneration, develop the widest possible implications of the doctrine of repentance as it was stated in the previous

---

[7] Refuting the Manichaeans' denial of Christ's humanity and asserting the union of the two natures in one person were traditionally orthodox. The doctrine that Christ could not fulfill his function as redeemer of sins unless "He died; die he could not except he were mortal; mortal He could not be except He took our nature on Him," was often preached on Christmas day before the King by Bishop Andrewes (*Ninety-Six Sermons* [Oxford, 1841], I, 10 *et passim*). Calvin asserted it with less rhetorical flourish, but for the same reasons, explicitly scorning the Manichaeans: *Institutes*, I, 518 (II.xiii.1).

poem: the old man must be destroyed by the law and created anew by the gospel, just as the coming of the New Adam redeems the eternal death incurred by the Old. Here the vision is extended to his second coming—with emphasis on the necessary destruction of the world by those flames of heaven which "enlighten Nature"—as emblematic of the heart's experience when grace destroys nature. The imagery of flame has been skillfully ordered first to distinguish the effects of profane from those of divine love (Sonnet 86), and then to suggest the operation of the latter in terms of the vast Christian principle of human moral history: ontogeny recapitulates phylogeny.[8]

It is significant that Greville has begun his contemplation of the love which passeth understanding by insisting precisely on that aspect of it. The forsaking of self as well as the purification of the world demands the destruction of both as they exist in nature. In following this Calvinistic emphasis Greville explicitly short-circuits the traditional approach to self-abnegation in the *memento mori*. For him, the human mind merely boggles at the eternity which unfolds beyond the grave; it cannot lead us out of our chaos of self-preoccupations. Only the experience of Christ can accomplish that. The epistemological perspective of all the treatises is here explicit, as is the rigorous, uncompromising Pauline definition of knowledge as virtue. To know well is to be good; and Greville has at the start of this final section of *Caelica* mapped out the single path to true goodness. It remains for him to travel it, to practice the doctrine he has stated by undergoing, in verse, the experience it requires.

But before Greville proceeds to the inward application of the doctrine of repentance, he prepares for it in the next seven poems by exploring the inadequacies of the natural world. In so doing, he is virtually following his own advice to the "Honorable Lady" to renounce the world, as far as possible, on its own terms, by using the Stoic attitude as a kind of approach to the ultimate Christian renunciation. Although reason cannot of itself discover the right, it can partially detect the wrong, and thereby make a beginning in the vital experience of dying to this world; it can at least show us "Vice, a restlesse infinite" (Sonnet 96). What is judged and found wanting in these poems are those "Rewards of earth" (Sonnet 91) that Greville analyzed extensively in the treatises, plays, and

---

[8] Regarding events in Scripture as representing "facts that recurred in the inner life of man" is cited by Haller as characteristic of "the tradition of Puritan preaching, which . . . wove together out of the scriptures a version of the sacred epic as an image of inner life" (p. 212). The fullest poetic use of this kind of allegory can be seen in *The Faerie Queene*, I.xi, where Red Crosse is Christ harrowing hell at the same time as he is the individual soul combatting its own sins and weaknesses with the aid of the sacraments.

in the first eighty-four poems of *Caelica*: nobility, fame, and pleasure. Morris Croll noticed the parallels in subject and form between the political poems of this last section and the treatises, and suggested that the lyrics were "chips thrown off" in the shaping of the longer works.[9] This is certainly probable; but Croll's metaphor is misleading in its connotations of haphazardness. These chips are cut from the same thematic block, and are here arranged to provide an initial stage in the poet's progress to the realization of divine love in the experience of regeneration.

Sonnets 90–96 all exploit the ironies latent in the perception that our seeming goods are real evils; all devalue what the world most admires, and the world is specifically made to include the heathen and Christian, ancient and modern, so as to become the traditional moral personification of the false and the self-destructive. The initial irony is precisely that the "Christian freedome" of Europe, guaranteed in theory by a system of law, is in fact no different from the absolute despotism of Turkey, which "allowes no Law," and which Christians therefore scorn (Sonnet 90). The reason for the essential similarity is that even Christian law can prove as "crooked as power lists to draw, / The rage or grace that lurkes in Princes brests." Greville further deflates the Christian pretension to political superiority by asserting that both kinds of government are equally successful at satisfying their subjects. The net implication of the poem is that since both governments are equally capricious and equally workable, the distinction between them is irrelevant.

Now Greville had much acquaintance, in life and in art, with various forms of tyranny; the investigation of the uses and abuses of arbitrary power had been his constant study, and it usually led him to maintain the exact distinction that he here denies.[10] But this would be grounds for finding contradictions in his thought only if we wholly ignored the context of this poem, its place here in the final section of the sequence, the thematic perspective of which the poet has so carefully established. From the viewpoint of that divine and perfect love which is offered to man only through Christ, and which demands that "The earth must burne, ere we for Christ can looke" (Sonnet 89), political distinctions are indeed irrelevant. In Sonnet 90 Greville is simply applying to worldly politics the same ironic attitude toward Christian pretension that he applied in the previous poem to salvation. The point of both is to underline the necessity for the heart's experience of conversion: the mere name of Christian does not entitle us to distinguish ourselves either from ancient heretics or modern tyrants.

The next three poems proceed to judge and to reject the worldly

[10] Bullough (*Poems and Dramas*, I, 281) cites his more customary excoriation of Turkish rule by arbitrary will from *Monarchy*, 307–08.

honors of rank and reputation—"To senses Glorie, and to conscience woe" (Sonnet 91). Nobility is but the instrument of power to enslave, to conceal its own capriciousness and evil. It dazzles and attracts the foolish and blinds them to the real nature of its possessors (Sonnet 92).

> Fame, that is but good words of evill deeds,
> Begotten by the harme we have, or doe,
> Greatest farre off, least ever where it breeds,
> We both with dangers and disquiet wooe.
>    And in our flesh (the vanities false glasse)
>    We thus deceav'd adore these Calves of brasse.
>
>                     (Sonnet 91)

The principle stated in the third line of the stanza is exemplified and developed in Sonnet 93 by the Roman "Augurs," who privately scorn the reputation they are careful to cultivate publicly. By thus presenting the actual purposes and effects of nobility and fame, the poet can discredit the viewpoint of the "world," which gives them value—the "fleshly wit" that has banished truth, the "false glasse" of vanity.

Another false value reflected in this glass is our delight in the pleasures of sense, which we are at pains "to multiply" (Sonnet 94). This covetousness, however, leads only to frustration; all such pleasures wither. Greville uses the natural fact as a basis for the customary exhortation ("Fixe then on good desires") from which he draws, however, a striking inference to conclude the poem:

> For lest Man should thinke flesh a seat of blisse,
> God workes that his joy mixt with sorrow is.

Even when taken in and for themselves, the things of the world and the flesh are self-defeating, self-deceiving; that they can provide no lasting satisfaction is apparent even to our carnal understanding. A somewhat specialized and striking example of this principle is offered in Sonnet 95. Greville contrasts the intentions and compares the operation and effects of malice and love:

> The one to hurt it selfe for others good;
> The other, to have good by others spite,
> Both raging most, when they be most withstood;
>    Though enemies, yet doe in this agree,
>    That both still breake the hearts where in they be.

Both worldly passions, even though they are the absolute moral opposites of selfishness and selflessness, end in self-destruction.

The first four stanzas of Sonnet 96 gather together all the subjects of the six preceding poems and restate the conclusion to be drawn from them. The last three stanzas reintroduce the ultimate and only remedy for the debilities thus uncovered—the grace of God. Greville begins this summary of his preparations for repentance by seeing "Pleasure . . . as a Goddesse,"

> Who like an Idoll doth apparel'd sit
> In all the glories of Opinions art;
>     The further off, the greater beauty showing,
>     Lost onely, or made lesse by perfect knowing.

Here Pleasure is far more than merely sensual; she is the personification of all worldly values. Greville picks up an ironic echo in "glories" that is reinforced by the metaphor of worship: he has already described the true object of worship as divine love, the "Goddesse of the minde," the "Glorie" that is of eternity and is obscured "by all bodies else" (Sonnet 85). And the obscuring elements have been shown to be precisely "bodies," that is, all that appeals to the "Sense, Desire and Wit" (Sonnet 96) of the flesh, those "Rewards of earth" which are "To senses Glorie, and to conscience woe" (Sonnet 91).

The ironies that Greville has manipulated in this series of poems by the repetition of these key terms all serve to suggest the profound and intense dualistic otherworldliness of Platonism which lies deeply embedded in his contemporary Calvinism.[11] The language of the poetry is explicitly Christian at the same time as it evokes a wider richness of philosophical conception. And the conception is the same Platonic one that he employed in the first section of the sequence to deny the claims of Neoplatonic love. The world of Greville is the cave of Plato; and his task as a writer is constantly to show how all ideals are there either perverted or false.

Having observed of pleasure, as he did of fame, that her attractiveness depends upon ignorance, Greville justifies the observation by analyzing in the next two stanzas of Sonnet 96 the consequences of her worship. The analysis is begun in a political metaphor: even though she has usurped the place of reason,

> Yet rules she none, but such as will obey,
> And to that end becomes what they aspire;
>     Making that torment, which before was play,

---

[11] C. S. Lewis (p. 386) has succinctly identified the parallel strains. Apropos of *The Faerie Queene* he observes that "few pagan systems adapt themselves so nearly to total depravity and *contemptus mundi* as the Platonic. The emotional overtones of the words 'Renaissance Platonism' perhaps help us to forget that Plato's thought is at bottom otherworldly, pessimistic, and ascetic; far more ascetic than Protestantism. The natural universe is for Plato, a world of shadows . . . the soul has come into it at all only because she lost her wings in a better place . . . and the life of wisdom, while we are here, is a practice or exercise of death."

> Those dewes to kindle, which did quench the fire:
> Now Honours image, now againe like lust,
> But earthly still, and end repenting must.

Her rule is not by force but by deception. Men pursue her in whatever guise their whims dictate and find that these are ever changing and never satisfied, and that to be ruled by them results in the misery that comes from taking seriously what is merely frivolous. The next stanza elaborates on this misery by comparing man with the satyr who is burned kissing the "faire apppearing light" of fire. The image rings another change on the earlier contrast of the burning flames of passion to the illuminating flames of heaven (Sonnet 86). Here it is used to suggest in addition man's obstinacy in acting on his whims, and his perplexity at being harmed by an apparent good. The image of heat is further developed in the second half of the stanza to express the irony that our affections are mutually contradictory: what pleases one irritates another.

Greville's diagnosis thus far has evoked, and depends upon, two moral principles, ultimately derived from Greek philosophy, which were central to the Renaissance: the Platonic idea that the soul becomes what it meditates on, and the Aristotelian idea that pleasure in itself can never be an end of any action. The first results in the debasement of the soul devoted to objects unworthy of it; the second in its confused and frustrated misery. Greville has analyzed both of these consequences at length in the varied and particular situations of *Caelica's* love lyrics; he now summarizes them directly in the fourth stanza of Sonnet 96:

> In which confused sphere Man being plac'd
> With equall prospect over good or ill;
> The one unknowne, the other in distaste,
> Flesh, with her many moulds of Change and Will,
> So his affections carries on, and casts
> In declination to the errour still;
>     As by the truth he gets no other light,
>     But to see Vice, a restlesse infinite.

Bullough's paraphrase (I, 283) is accurate: "When his pleasures turn to pain man is in a confused state, hating the evil but ignorant of good; hence, his flesh still debasing his desires into error, his only glimpse of truth is of the infinite variety of vice." Here, in its most compact and general statement, is Greville's entire epistemology of the sinful, developed (as in the treatises) within a theological perspective by inference from empirical observation.

At this point the poet has followed the great ethical precepts of antiquity as far as they can lead him: the only truth that we are able to perceive in the natural world is how miserable we are in it. "By which

true mappe of his Mortality, / Mans many Idols are at once defaced," so
that "Falne nature" is "Forc'd up to call for grace above her placed."
Man's only way out of the misery of mortality is by "Regeneration," to
which he is compelled by that misery itself, and which will destroy his
vicious and deluded restlessness. The Biblical metaphor for this process
is repeated from Sonnet 89: "His sixe dayes labour" ends in "Sabboths
rest."

> For God comes not till man be overthrowne;
> Peace is the seed of grace, in dead flesh sowne.

Calvin's great English interpreter, William Perkins, is unambiguously
emphatic on this crucial and complete opposition of nature and grace.
Arguing that we are "by nature" prone to all evil, he says, "For I know
by good education, and by grace, it is otherwise: grace rectifieth nature,
but that is no thanks to nature: for it is as evill and corrupt still, being
severed from grace: and therefore nature must be fully abolished, afore
man come to heaven." [12] The final stanza of Sonnet 96 recapitulates the
recalcitrance of the flesh in a series of images which emphasize the necessity of its destruction. It can be disciplined only by "Whips," polished
only by "afflictions." It must be discarded like "Dust," and can grow
only by "selfe-ruine" like the phoenix that springs from its ashes, or the
snake whose birth destroys its parent. The concluding image implies the
ultimate danger of moral shipwreck unless the destruction occurs:
flesh is

> A boat, to which the world it selfe is Sea,
> Wherein the minde sayles on her fatall way.

When at the beginning of this final section of *Caelica* Greville renounced human love for divine love, he presented the realization of the
latter as a process involving two parts: a dying to the world and a dying
to the self. He has now completed the first part as a preparation for the
second. The last seven poems have catalogued the unprofitable uses of
this world with psychological acuity and philosophical sophistication.
Their style exhibits the best features of the language of the treatises: the
compressed epigrammatic force, the closely developed similitudes, the
orderly substantiation of general judgments (in three poems by the
structural figure of epanados), the exact identification of causal relationships (in four poems by the "sententious" figure of etiologia), and above
all the precise and abstract diction. The style likewise employs the functional variation on key metaphors and images that was characteristic of

[12] *Workes* (London, 1612–1613), III, 415. H. C. Porter discusses this aspect of
Perkins' theology: *Reformation and Reaction in Tudor Cambridge* (Cambridge,
1958), pp. 297, 312.

the love lyrics in the opening section. The voice in the poems is wholly impersonal and discursive, shifting occasionally into the imperative mood or the second-person address when the moral analysis gives way to exhortation. Their emotional tone is that of grim, ironic, and traditional pessimism which the poet directs at both himself and the reader by the occasional but consistent use of the first person plural. Greville's basic style—its conceptual density, logical progression, and abstract diction—is firmly established; but we shall perceive within it subtle and profound modifications of tone, voice, and rhythm as he proceeds to apply the principles and doctrines he has thus far stated.

This application is of course the vital experience of regeneration central to Protestantism in general and Calvinism in particular. Accounts of such experience usually formed the central drama in the spiritual autobiography of Puritan diarists; and how to induce the rigorous self-examination it required was a constant concern of the godly minister laboring to instruct his flock. One way to accomplish the latter, according to Richard Rogers (who was both minister and diarist), was by "holy meditations, and such like practices of repentance."[13] For Rogers, meditation was the second private help to devotion (the first was "watchfulness"). Its purpose was to "set our mindes on worke about the cogitation of things heavenly . . . and so debate and reason about the same, that our affections may thereby be moved to love and delight in, or to hate and feare, according to that which we meditate on; so that we may make some good use of it to our selves."[14]

The formula is indeed broad and general enough to encompass most traditional patterns of Christian devotion, and was purposely so: Rogers sneers at Catholic devotional books for overspecifying these patterns—by giving appointed prayers for appointed days—and for idolatrously relating them to physical objects, saints, and so forth. As the formula was developed in English Calvinism it contained three areas of characteristic emphasis. The first lies in conceiving of meditation itself almost ex-

---

[13] *Seven Treatises*, 5th ed. (London, 1630), p. 339. The first edition was published in 1603, making this one of the earliest systematic English books of practical Protestant devotion. It was written, Rogers informs us in the Preface (sig. A7), in response to the Roman Catholic criticism "that wee have nothing set out for the certaine and daily direction of a Christian." The book went through several editions in its original form, and several more, from 1618, in an abbreviated version called by the last part of its original title, *The Practice of Christianity*. Rogers' career as Puritan clergyman—he was an associate of Perkins, Cartwright, and other leaders—and his theological emphasis on personal, introspective piety, are discussed by Patrick Collinson, *The Elizabethan Puritan Movement* (Berkeley, Calif., 1967), pp. 320–21, 381–82, 434–35.

[14] Pp. 311–12.

clusively as an instrument of and stimulus to repentance. Rogers' main argument for the necessity of meditation in our daily lives is that it purges from even the hearts of the faithful the "noysome poisons" of their sundry lusts.[15] The second is that although the function of meditation is to move the "affections," this is to be accomplished by a process of "cogitation." The mind, in other words, is carefully to direct and control the emotions. Rogers stresses this essential control in his first two "rules" for the conduct of meditation: the individual must weigh how "slippery" and "fickle" his heart is, and must "watch over his heart, (having beene so oft deceived by it) thorowout his whole life, and have it in suspition."[16] The suspicion reveals the fundamental ambivalence in the whole Puritan attitude toward emotional experience: not to be trusted, on the one hand, for any secular purpose, but absolutely necessary, on the other, for salvation (though it can easily lead us astray even there). How to assess the validity of the religious intuitions that Protestantism appeared to sanction—with respect to such thorny questions as one's assurance of election, the operation of the inner light, the place of "affections" in worship—was a principal source of disagreement and division.[17]

The third area emphasized is "good use," the personal application of the meditative subject to ourselves. To encourage the individual worshipper to find the subjects most immediate and meaningful to him, Rogers repeatedly lists subjects that are personal and penitential, recommending especially that he consider first "his unworthinesse, vilenesse, and other his severall corruptions, and sinnes. Secondly . . . the greatnesse of Gods bountie in forgiving so many." Rogers also gives his reader explicit direction regarding any and all meditations of which he gives examples: "thou must apply that which is set downe (generally to all Christians) to thy selfe, as if it were spoken only to thee."[18] John Downame, in a later, lengthier, and more elaborately organized book of practical devotion, cites Rogers' treatment of meditation as exemplary, and builds his own upon it. Downame's version is fuller, more detailed—though equally broad and general in approach—and seems written for a slightly more sophisticated audience than Rogers'; but in substance and in emphasis it is the same. Downame insists upon personal "use,"

15 P. 313. This activity, obviously, was both crucial and never-ending. Richard Greenham followed Calvin, as did all Puritans, in preaching that repentance was constant and godly sorrow: "Wherefore as it is requisite continually to till the ground, if we will have fruite, and daily to eate, if we will live; so in spirituall things, we must be humbled with continuall sorow, that we may be refreshed with daily comfort in Christ," *The Workes*, 2d ed. (London, 1599), p. 172.

16 P. 324.
17 See Haller, pp. 193–94 *et passim*.
18 Pp. 317, 325.

asserts that the affections to be aroused must be directed by the understanding, and assumes that meditation is a chief means to repentance.
The extended example of a meditation that he presents has repentance
*per se* as its subject.[19]

Without postulating any specific influence—Greville's spiritual life
was, after all, lived at a higher and more intelligent level than that which,
even in those zealous times, the writers of devotional tracts could assume
of their audience—we may see that the poet's procedure in his contemplative lyrics generally corresponds to these large emphases in English
Calvinist devotion. His initial "meditation" on divine love modulates
immediately into a "practice of repentance" having two parts, which
are taken up separately and developed with logical rigor. Greville's
habitual style, in which emotions are always directed and controlled by
concepts, is also a clear reflection of these devotional attitudes, which
may help to explain why his religious verse is so conspicuously non-
"metaphysical" (in the stylistic sense, although completely "metaphysical" in the real sense), so different from that of his great contemporaries
who dealt with the same experience in terms of some of the same
doctrines.[20]

Since the devotional attitudes are themselves functions of certain leading tonalities in Calvinism, they may also suggest other forms of discourse as models for Greville's typical procedure and style. Chief among
these is certainly the Puritan sermon—that naked and direct exposition
of the Word—which invariably "opened" the text by reducing it to
literal statement, deduced from it the doctrine, gave the reasons for and
implications of the doctrine, and, most importantly, applied it, presenting its uses in practical life.[21] Greville's procedure in both the opening and closing sections of *Caelica* may be described in this way. The
"doctrine" of secular or divine love is initially stated; its implications are
meticulously probed; objections against or reasons for it are weighed;
and what remains is then applied to the relevant situations of life. The
"uses" were conventionally regarded as the most important part of the
process: in the love lyrics these take the form of analyzing the psychological consequences of a love whose ideal qualities are illusory; in the
religious lyrics they take the form of inwardly realizing the consequences

---

[19] *A Guide to Godlynesse* (London, [1622]), pp. 533, 584 ff. (V.xiii.1, xx.6).

[20] Peterson (p. 283) observes that Greville does not use the "meditative exercises" described by Louis Martz in *The Poetry of Meditation* (New Haven, 1954).
How Greville's style differs from Donne's and Herbert's will be discussed below.
By an odd coincidence the first collections of all three poets were printed, all
posthumously, in 1633.

[21] See Miller, p. 326, H. C. Porter, p. 225—or any Puritan sermon. The virtual
opposite of this plain kind of discourse may be seen in the sermons of Andrewes
and Donne.

of a love whose ideal qualities are real. Kenneth Murdock's summary of the preachers' manner of accomplishing the process applies equally well to the poet:

> The Puritan's earthy phrases and images, his restriction of his material to that supplied by the Bible or the everyday life of his audience, his seriousness of purpose, and his willingness to admit only those rhetorical devices and "similitudes" which served to drive home or to make more intelligible what he saw as the truth, were all directly related to his view of God and of man. The realism and concreteness of his work, the firmness of its structure, and its dignity of tone, all reflect the profound conviction from which it came.[22]

Greville begins his personal application of the doctrine in Sonnet 97 with a direct address to that "Eternall Truth, almighty, infinite," which, because it is "Onely exiled from mans fleshly heart," can reveal to our natural understanding only the infinity of vices that have been catalogued in the preceding poems. But when, by the operation of grace, our spirit is humbled by the law to welcome the mercy of faith, we are led to prayer. At this point the poem ceases to address truth and becomes a magnificent analysis of how we pervert faith itself by imagining its obligations are fulfilled in mere external actions and words. We pray as if to something wholly apart from our real selves, as if a moment of religious observance could undo the self-concerns of a lifetime,

> Thinking a wish may weare out vanity,
> Or habits be by miracles defac'd.

The remainder of the poem further identifies our delusion and implies in a Biblical metaphor the method of its correction:

> True words passe out, but have no being within,
> Wee pray to Christ, yet helpe to shed his blood;
>    For while wee say Believe, and feele it not,
> Promise amends, and yet despaire in it,
> Heare Sodom judg'd, and goe not out with Lot,
> Make Law and Gospell riddles of the wit:
>    We with the Jewes even Christ still crucifie,
>    As not yet come to our impiety.

The metaphor of crucifixion is skillfully managed to suggest the full magnitude of the perversion that results from an unfelt belief: doing to Christ what we ought to do to ourselves; refusing to acknowledge his sufferings by undergoing them in our own lives.[23] The language develops and extends the ironies of Sonnet 89, intensifying the insistence

---

[22] *Literature and Theology in Colonial New England* (Cambridge, Mass., 1949), p. 61.
[23] The metaphor is Saint Paul's (Rom. 6:6), and was a favorite with Calvin.

upon "using" the doctrine by bearing "The Crosse of Christ" in the terrible experience of true contrition, which alone will permit us to escape the prison of our selves.

It remains only for Greville to follow his own advice. He has talked about false prayer and the necessity of feeling: in Sonnet 98 he prays for the necessary feeling, for the kind of sorrow proper to the truly repentant. He has talked about repentance by law and by gospel: in Sonnet 99 he demonstrates the effects of both upon himself. Of all twenty-five poems in the final section of *Caelica* these are the only ones that employ the first person singular; and they do so in a peculiarly impersonal manner which, paradoxically, is an integral part of the intensely personal experience they present.

In the first stanza of Sonnet 98 Greville locates himself exactly in that spiritual state whose debilities he has been describing, the natural state where truth can find only the results of sin:

> Wrapt up, O Lord, in mans degeneration;
> The glories of thy truth, thy joyes eternall,
> Reflect upon my soule darke desolation,
> And ugly prospects o're the sprites infernall.
> Lord, I have sinn'd, and mine iniquity,
> Deserves this hell; yet Lord deliver me.

The liturgical refrain is more than confession and plea; it is an acknowledgment of God's absolute justice and power. The second stanza further explores the desolation of the soul by developing the idea of reflection:

> Thy power and mercy never comprehended,
> Rest lively imag'd in my Conscience wounded;
> Mercy to grace, and power to feare extended,
> Both infinite, and I in both confounded;
> Lord, I have sinn'd, and mine iniquity,
> Deserves this hell, yet Lord deliver me.

Perceiving, but being unable to comprehend, the power and mercy of God, the soul experiences grace only as pain and terror. The condition is indeed desolate; it is the uniquely Christian despair that results from a profound conviction of guilt, which is the essential first step toward repentance but which itself can be the ultimate danger to the moral life.[24] The soul which acknowledges itself as justly damned can find only anguish in the power and mercy of God; it is condemned by the first and unworthy of the second.

[24] This kind of despair, resulting not from loss of faith but because of faith, is the final and greatest temptation of Red Crosse (I.ix), to which he easily succumbs, and from which Una must save him.

Greville goes on in the third and final stanza to outline the highly con-
ditional manner by which release from this anguish may be obtained:

> If from this depth of sinne, this hellish grave,
> And fatall absence from my Saviours glory,
> I could implore his mercy, who can save,
> And for my sinnes, not paines of sinne, be sorry:
>     Lord, from this horror of iniquity,
>     And hellish grave, thou wouldst deliver me.

The poet identifies the hell he is suffering as spiritual death, and implies
that it will remain such—will not result in a true dying to the self—
unless the suffering is caused by the proper motive. By insisting that his
sorrow be for sin, for willful offense against God, and not for fear of
punishment, Greville perceives the final deception—masking a self-
concern as a godly sorrow—practiced by the sinful self in its obstinate
struggle to avoid annihilation. The insight was of course provided by
the traditional Christian psychology of repentance, was vastly intensified
by the importance it acquired in the central Protestant doctrine of justification by faith, and was attained in different ways by other devotional
poets of the seventeenth century.[25] Greville attains it here as the last
revelation in an investigation that has peeled away, one by one, the
delusions that the soul is subject to in the exercise of faith, in accepting
God's gift of love. We can mistake an empty form for a real feeling; we
can have a real feeling for the wrong reasons.

The fear and trembling with which the sincere Protestant—and especially the Puritan—searched his heart for the adequate feeling on which
his whole salvation depended (and which could be placed there solely
by God) is legendary. A particularly vivid and homely warning on the
dangers of a "false and hollow-hearted turning" is offered in another
devotional handbook:

> What great need have we then in our Repentance to examine the truth of it,
> least we be deceived: and the rather because most in the world are daily
> couzened with Copper instead of Gold. The Divell like some Couzening
> coiner . . . well he knowes the parts and properties of Repentance, and hath
> gotten the Counterfeit thereof in each particular, as like it as if it were the
> same. Rebeccah did not more cunningly . . . delude old Isaac's sences, then
> he hath a worldly sorrow in true Repentances dresse, to delude the world.[26]

Having detected these delusions in himself, Greville is ready at last to
confront his spiritual condition as it is. He has been building to this
moment ever since he said farewell to the love that pleased but betrayed;
it is the literal and figurative turning point, the climax of the final sec-

[25] Cf. Jonson's "To Heaven" and Herbert's "Affliction (I)."
[26] Nehemiah Rogers, *The True Convert* (London, 1632), p. 251.

tion of *Caelica*—and indeed, considering his dualism, of the whole sequence. There is no irony because there is no discrepancy between appearance and reality; there is no anguished outcry to God because the anguish has been assimilated and transcended; there is no imagery except for the continued development of established metaphors which contain the central concepts; there is no dramatic framework, no dialogue, no similitude. There is simply direct and abstract analysis—the naked statement of a naked soul—magnificent in the precision of its language and the weight of its intelligence. Sonnet 99:

> Downe in the depth of mine iniquity,
> That ugly center of infernall spirits;
> Where each sinne feeles her owne deformity,
> In these peculiar torments she inherits,
>     Depriv'd of humane graces, and divine,
>     Even there appeares this saving God of mine.
>
> And in this fatall mirrour of transgression,
> Shewes man as fruit of his degeneration,
> The errours ugly infinite impression,
> Which beares the faithlesse downe to desperation;
>     Depriv'd of humane graces and divine,
>     Even there appeares this saving God of mine.
>
> In power and truth, Almighty and eternall,
> Which on the sinne reflects strange desolation,
> With glory scourging all the Sprites infernall,
> And uncreated hell with unprivation,
>     Depriv'd of humane graces, not divine,
>     Even there appeares this saving God of mine.
>
> For on this sp'rituall Crosse condemned lying,
> To paines infernall by eternall doome,
> I see my Saviour for the same sinnes dying,
> And from that hell I fear'd, to free me, come;
>     Depriv'd of humane graces, not divine,
>     Thus hath his death rais'd up this soule of mine.[27]

The poem is divided by the negative modulation in the refrain into two halves, the first of which demonstrates the effects of repentance by law,

---

[27] Winters (*Forms of Discovery*, p. 50) clears up some grammatical difficulties in the poem: "The word *depriv'd*, by modern standards, is a dangling participle, for it modifies the understood pronoun *I*, which does not appear until we reach the last stanza. . . . This construction, however, was common among learned writers well into the eighteenth century. . . . The subject of *shows* is *impression*. The remarkable inversion of construction in the first four lines of the second stanza is not due to awkwardness; rather it enables Greville to place the details in order of increasing importance."

the second by gospel. The first line of each stanza states, in a prepositional phrase that gives a spatial location to an idea, the concept whose consequences the stanza will explore.

In the depth of the poet's iniquity the punishment fits the crime; that is, the consciousness of each individual sin is exact and complete. The crime is therefore, in effect, its own punishment. This mental state is identified as hell. The word "deformity" indicates the quality of perversion, of turning away from God, man's proper end, that is common to all sin; the way Greville modifies the word suggests the grotesque lineaments of particular sins. The word "inherits" suggests an awareness of the cause of all sin; but again, the way it is used keeps the focus on the subject, the sins of the poet. The first word of the refrain defines the psychological state as total privation of being.[28] The second line of the refrain comes as a violent contrast to all the foregoing, a stark, paradoxical assertion of faith in the presence of God. The contrast is audibly reinforced by the strong masculine rime and the sudden metrical variation in the line caused by its added initial monosyllable. The word "graces" is explicitly employed on two levels: the divine, where it suggests the only means of release from the state of sin; and the human, where the lack of the aesthetic proportion it connotes combines with the denotations of "ugly deformity" to express the proper attitude of loathing and revulsion toward that state.

Such exquisite control of the meanings of language is characteristic of Greville's best work. The principle upon which it is achieved has been well analyzed by Wesley Trimpi:

---

[28] The ancient Augustinian, ultimately Platonic, definition of evil as the absence of good was current coin in Renaissance Christianity. Greville elaborates the concept elsewhere in speaking of Pluto's kingdom:

> Privation would raigne there, by God not made;
> But creature of uncreated sinne,
> Whose being is all beings to invade,
> To have no ending though it did beginne:
> And so of past, things present, and to come,
> To give depriving, not tormenting doome,
> But horror, in the understanding mixt . . .
> And into reason by our passion brought,
> Here rackt, torne, and exil'd from unitie;
> Though comes from nothing, must for ever be.
>
> (*Alaham*, "Prologus")

The widely diffused literary employment of the idea is traced by James L. Rosier, "The Chain of Sin and Privation in Elizabethan Literature," Ph.D. Diss., Stanford University, 1957. He observes that Greville "seems almost obsessed with the theological definition of privation" and that he offers the most explicit, vigorous, complex, and precise treatment of privative psychology in literature. Rosier also describes how the concept governs the entire action of *Alaham* (pp. 114, 95, 123).

The distinction between the connotative and denotative qualities of language is artificial in so far as each of these qualities can properly be described only in terms of the other; any given statement is made up of both, and the relationship between them is the statement itself. Denotation usually refers to the simple referent of a word, connotation to its context and the qualifications which that context imposes. . . . In the plain style the denotative and the connotative most nearly approach each other in the exclusion of irrelevant associations from the context [and conversely, we may add, in the inclusion of relevant ones]. The denotative statement defines the writer's experience so sharply that it will not admit further qualifications other than his attitude toward the experience, which will itself be the context.[29]

The first stanza of Sonnet 99 not only defines its subject in terms of its psychological and ontological consequences, but also expresses in relation to that subject the theologically necessary feeling that was obliquely prayed for in the last stanza of Sonnet 98.

God may be present even in the depth of man's iniquity, but the effects of his presence, which Greville specifies in the metaphor of the "fatall mirrour," show us that he is present only in terms of his law. The metaphor seems virtually to be a conflation of two images used by Calvin to explain "the office and use" of the moral law:

But when [man] is constrained to examine his life according to the rules of the law, he . . . perceives that he is at an infinite distance from holiness; and also that he abounds with innumerable vices. . . . And it is not without cause that the Apostle says, "I had not known lust except the law had said, Thou shalt not covet"; because, unless it be stripped of its disguises, and brought to light by the law, it destroys the miserable man in so secret a manner, that he does not perceive its fatal dart.

Thus the law is like a mirror, in which we behold, first, our impotence; secondly, our iniquity, which proceeds from it; and lastly, the consequences of both, our obnoxiousness to the curse; just as a mirror represents to us the spots on our face.[30]

Greville uses "mirrour" simultaneously both in its figurative sense (an exemplar) and in its literal meaning. Man sees himself in it as nothing but the product of his hideous and limitless sins. Only the law can reveal our sins, supplying the perception that causes the death of the Old Man. "The law is the ministerie of death and damnation, because it shewes a man his wretched estate, but shewes him no remedie."[31] Hence the

[29] *Ben Jonson's Poems: A Study of the Plain Style* (Stanford, Calif., 1962), p. ix.
[30] *Institutes*, I, 383 (II.vii.6–7).
[31] Perkins, I, 456. He is discussing "the nature and practice of repentance," here describing its first process—"mortification." The danger in the process is described by Downame as "that fearfull gulph of deepe despaire, whereby we shall cast off all hope of Gods mercy, and reject the all-sufficient merits and satisfaction of Jesus Christ, through our incredulity, as though the multitude and hainousnesse of our

despair of "the faithlesse," which Greville very nearly approached in the preceding poem, and from which he here tacitly and grandly dissociates himself. In this context the refrain functions as evidence for his having surmounted despair, and takes on a note of defiant triumph.

The third stanza continues to examine the consequences of privation in terms of the metaphor of reflection. The perception of God's infinite attributes is a constant torment to those in the state of spiritual hell. But the third line of the stanza achieves a complete understanding of this state by implying its origin in man and not in God: man's hell is "uncreated"; he has willed it himself. This understanding is essential to the experience; it states the reason why God's glory causes suffering and embraces that suffering as an effect of his grace (now introduced in the refrain), which can turn evil, the nothing which God has not made, into good.

The means of vouchsafing this grace—the acceptance of the gospel— is specified in the final stanza. The suffering caused by the law is expressed by the Pauline metaphor of crucifixion (which was used in ironic reversal in Sonnets 89 and 97) for the death of the self. Understanding the nature and cause of the suffering has permitted the inward assimilation of its symbol, and has resulted in renewed faith that "the merits and satisfactions of Christ are of infinite value, and an all-sufficient satisfaction for the sinnes of the whole world." [32] The "saving God" of the law has given way to the "Saviour" of the gospel. The fourth and sixth lines of the stanza state the personal acceptance of Christ's sacrifice in the simplest possible language: the words of both lines are all of one syllable. The syntax of the stanza is also far simpler and more direct than that of the preceding three. Greville has emerged from the dense, polysyllabic convolutions of his spiritual agony onto a plane of crystalline assurance whose audible rendering can only be called sublime. The art which animates this poem is not the art that conceals art—for there is nothing to conceal—but rather the art that lies beyond the reach of art, which is made possible only by a mastery of experience.

Douglas Peterson has accurately described Sonnets 97, 98, and 99 as "genuine modes of discovery" of the kinds of feeling "essential to the central Protestant experience," and has called them great poems, as good

---

sinnes, did farre exceed them. And this is the very cut-throat of all piety," p. 809 (VI xii.5).

[32] Downame, p. 810 (VI.xii.5). The entire process is thus summarized by Calvin (*Commentaries*, pp. 155–56): "The law is for us a mirror showing us our own unrighteousness. But the way to obtain righteousness, as taught by Christ, is simply to know him; and this is faith. In faith we lay hold on the benefit of his death and find full rest in him."

as Donne's best religious verse.[33] I think that they are in fact superior to Donne's religious verse, and that this superiority can be measured in terms of their impersonality. Greville rises through the experiences in which Donne is perpetually engaged, the fears of judgment and hypocrisy, the passionate outcries for true contrition, to that experience which Donne, in verse, never reached: the complete renunciation of self.

The habitual mood of Donne's devotion is the imperative pleading of prayer—"Teach mee how to repent"—even in those poems that present his faith in its most fully realized form: "This is my playes last scene," "Goodfriday, 1613," and the two great Hymns to God.[34] Donne demands to be taught precisely what Greville has learned. The contrast is not, however, between a man who doubts he is saved and one who does not. Donne presumably doubted it much of the time: his own spiritual vacillations—"my devout fitts" and "humorous" contrition— are the subject of a Holy Sonnet, "Oh, to vex me, contraryes meete in one." The nature of Greville's style, however, makes it impossible to estimate the relative weight that the doubts or the assurances thereby expressed had in his own life. It is significant that equally thorough Greville scholars reach contradictory conclusions on the question of whether or not he considered himself among the elect.[35] To urge either alternative is both to overlook the ambivalence of the "signs" and to ignore the delicate and paradoxical balance that the radical Protestant was required to maintain in the matter. A potent sense of sin could, for example, be interpreted either way: one might feel damned, and yet take the feeling as the affliction by which God purifies His saints. Haller's summary is apt: "we live in danger, our greatest danger being that we should feel no danger, and our safety lying in the very dread of feeling safe."[36] But most importantly, Greville's language does not give us grounds to infer his biography from his poems: "There is a greater

[33] P. 283.

[34] The quoted line is from "At the round earths imagin'd corners" in *The Divine Poems*, ed. Helen Gardner (Oxford, 1952), p. 8. The page numbers in this edition—from which all Donne's verse will be cited—of the other poems mentioned are, respectively, 3, 30, 50, 51. Miss Gardner's introduction gives a very interesting and very differently valued assessment of the necessary omission of self in devotional poetry (pp. xv–xvii).

[35] Miss Buncombe (pp. 96–99), finding signs of sanctification in the religious lyrics of *Caelica* and in the account of the invisible Church (*Religion* 56–63, 95–105), is sure that he did. Mr. Carter (p. 259), specifying the tension between Greville's practical, opportunistic career and his religious ideals, suggests that he probably did not, that his conscience never left "him at his ease in Zion." Miss Rees distinguishes two classes of the elect—the general believer and the actually saved—and claims Greville for the former but not the latter (pp. 114–15).

[36] Pp. 156–57.

density of intellectual content in his work than in the work of any other poet of the Renaissance.... It is in this concern for his matter and in the corresponding indifference to his own personality that he differs equally from Sidney and from Donne."[37]

The contrast is rather between the poetic styles each man employed to investigate the same body of experience. The so-called metaphysical style has been primarily praised by modern critics as a vehicle for expressing—through the fertile use of catachresis, the ingenious yoking together of heterogeneities—individual idiosyncrasy, for plotting the private and particular course of a "mind in motion."[38] The style is thus preeminently self-interested: not necessarily in the sense of egotism, but in the sense that it tends to focus attention on the vehicle rather than on the tenor, on the witty and startling succession of perceptions and moods, rather than on the subject which motivates them—in short, on the circumstances of an experience rather than on the experience itself. For example, Greville would certainly have accused Donne, even as he obliquely accused himself, of making his subject a "riddle of the wit" in such a poem as "The Crosse," which deals with the Pauline metaphor of crucifixion as necessary affliction: "No Crosse is so extreme, as to have none." The poem is a serious and in part a moving exhortation that takes the "cross" through its various natural appearances (as noun) and its various meanings (as verb). The experience that the metaphor implies is personally invoked in the first four lines and its object is generally summarized in the last four; but it is not realized, not assimilated. To alter the famous formula, the style functions not as a sensuous apprehension of thought or experience, but as a sensuous avoidance of both. Such a style is of course perfectly designed to express a subjective view of reality, upon which it partly depends (and which, I suspect, largely accounts for its modern vogue). But it cannot deal adequately with other kinds of reality, and especially that reality which is assumed in the theology and psychology of redemption.

It seems possible that what Donne's detractors have identified as his neurotic, obsessive-compulsive concern for his own salvation is really a limitation of his style—a defect not in his character but in his literary equipment and its use. The distinction may be a nice one, for we all know that style is the man—but style is also, and was especially so in the Renaissance, any mode of approaching experience which was employed by many men. To distinguish these modes and their uses is essential to an accurate understanding, critical or historical, of literature. For example, of the "metaphysical" poets, George Herbert may indeed be said

[37] Winters, *Forms of Discovery*, p. 52.

[38] Douglas Bush gives an excellent compendium of modern reinterpretations along with some necessary historical correctives, pp. 131–32.

to have dealt adequately with redemptive psychology. But he did so by modifying the "metaphysical" style (even sometimes by abandoning it), by reining in its centrifugal tendencies, by subjecting it to various forms of control—in his use of Christian symbol and ritual, syntax, rhythm, diction—seldom or never exercised by Donne.

What the objective metaphysic of redemption finally requires is the forsaking of self in the operation of the basic Christian paradox that to find life is to lose it. All the individuating desires and fears of the sinful self are to be shuffled off as the soul seeks to accept the divine love of its Creator. The personal use or appplication of this doctrine therefore entails the eradication of personality. The "I" in Sonnets 98 and 99 is consequently wholly impersonal: it is the voice of the universally human sinner examining himself under the microscope of God. It seeks no extenuation, offers no rationalization, and admits of no emotion which is not motivated by the twofold acceptance of grace. No element of style is too humble to embody the essence of this experience: when Greville passes from the prayer of the first poem into the declaration of the second, the obliteration of the self is brilliantly rendered by the very grammar of the poem. The subject "I" of the first three stanzas is unexpressed until the fourth. Both poems are full of sound and resolved fury; they represent the ultimate refinement of the techniques Greville had long since mastered: the thick patterns of alliteration and assonance, the ponderous feminine rimes, the heavy movement, the successive rhythmic, prosodic, and tonal variations in the refrains.

It is unfortunate that the word "metaphysical" is already in literary use; otherwise we could take the contemplative lyrics of *Caelica* as its chief exemplar, and use it to describe poetry that is genuinely philosophical, poetry that presents a logical analysis of its subject exclusively in the light of the (transcendent and objective) reality of which it is a part, and that expresses this reality in terms of its emotional consequences for the subject. Greville's verse (like, perhaps, all successful poetic expression) is precisely a sensuous apprehension of thought; the thought is fuller and more profound, the apprehension more exact and more coherent, than is usual with Donne. Greville's plain style achieves this apprehension "only in the most restrained subtleties of diction and of cadence, but . . . by virtue of those subtleties inspires its universals with their full value as experience."[39] The style, in short, is the meaning of the experience. Puttenham would no doubt have called it simply the observance of decorum. Greville himself might have referred it to his own didactic theory, which defined the true art of eloquence as "formes of speech,"

[39] Winters, *Forms of Discovery*, p. 4.

> Such as from living wisdomes doe proceed;
> Whose ends are not to flatter, or beseech,
> Insinuate, or perswade, but to declare
> What things in Nature good, or evill are.
> (*Humane Learning*, 110)

Thus far we have observed in Greville's religious verse the progress of its general Christian and philosophical themes, examining as well the style in which they are developed, and glancing briefly at the extent to which both seem to reflect general procedures in English Calvinist devotion and discourse. Taking a hint from the poet's own conception of style, we shall now look at the more specific "living wisdom" which finds a voice in the "formes of speech" we have discussed.

We shall find that Greville hews very closely to Calvin's doctrine of repentance, which is itself largely traditional but which also contains certain implications and emphases that distinguish it from the Anglican doctrine. After enumerating some historical interpretations of the doctrine, Calvin offers his own summary and redefinition:

The Hebrew word for repentance denotes conversion or return. The Greek word signifies change of mind and intention. Repentance itself corresponds very well with both etymologies, for it comprehends these two things—that, forsaking ourselves, we should turn to God, and laying aside our old mind, should assume a new one. Wherefore I conceive it may be justly defined to be "a true conversion of our life to God, proceeding from a sincere and serious fear of God, and consisting in the mortification of our flesh and of the old man, and in the vivification of the Spirit."[40]

The terms *mortification* and *vivification* are also traditional, and they imply the same human reactions that *repentance by law* and *repentance by gospel* do. In the first case, fear of judgment stimulates contrition; in the second, faith in Christ's sacrifice results in consolation.[41] The basic doctrinal substance, then, is by no means revolutionary.

What might be considered the "reformed" elements in Calvin's view of repentance occur as he elaborates the traditional terms to make them conform to other cardinal principles in his doctrine. *Mortification* is thus expanded from a mere "laying aside" of the old mind to indicate the death of the flesh, the total "destruction of our common nature," which is made necessary by the complete enmity of flesh and spirit, the absolute opposition of nature and grace.[42] *Vivification* is likewise expanded from

[40] *Institutes*, I, 653–54 (III.iii.5).

[41] Calvin analyzes both pairs of terms and acknowledges their effects in his summary of historical views on repentance: *ibid.*, I, 651–53 (III.iii.3–4).

[42] *Ibid.*, I, 657 (III.iii.8). This stringent dichotomy has been previously mentioned as constituting in itself a primary distinction between strict Calvinism and

mere "consolation" to include regeneration, "the restoration of the Divine image within us," so that we are enabled to go forth into the "warfare" of the Christian life, to run the "race of repentance" which God imposes as a lifetime obligation upon the faithful.[43] Throughout this examination, Calvin's emphasis is on the intense and continual inner activity that repentance requires, the proper emotional content of which is specified as "godly sorrow when we not only dread punishment, but hate and abhor sin itself from a knowledge that it is displeasing to God."[44] Nowhere does he conceive of repentance in any institutional form; it is accomplished entirely within the soul of the believer as, alone, he contemplates his God.

But the most significant and distinctive feature in Calvin's doctrine of repentance is his view of the redemption, which underlies it. The paramount function and importance of Christ for Calvin is as a Redeemer, "that by this intercessor [God's] wrath has been appeased; that this is the foundation of peace between God and men."[45] The focus is on the act of Christ's sacrifice as the evidence of God's love for man. And although this love does not depend upon the Atonement for its existence, the only way that men can partake of God's love is through that Atonement,

since it is impossible for the life which is presented by the mercy of God, to be embraced by our hearts with sufficient ardour, or received with becoming gratitude, unless we have been previously terrified and distressed with the fear of the Divine wrath, and the horror of eternal death, we are instructed by the sacred doctrine, that irrespective of Christ we may contemplate God as in some measure incensed against us, and his hand armed for our destruction, and that we may embrace his benevolence and paternal love only in Christ.[46]

Calvin never tires of insisting that "God, in a certain ineffable manner, at the same time that he loved us, was nevertheless angry with us, till he was reconciled in Christ," or of repeating "that Christ is the only

---

Anglicanism: see ch. I, p. 12, n. 23, and above, p. 120, n. 12. Perkins insists on "the combat of the flesh and spirit" and defines flesh as the natural corruption of mind, will, and affections, including that of "naturall reason" which can only "serve to make a man without excuse," I, 469.

[43] *Institutes*, I, 658 (III.iii.9).

[44] *Ibid.*, I, 656 (III.iii.7).

[45] *Ibid.*, I, 533 (II.xvi.2). Helen C. White, in her survey, *English Devotional Literature 1600–1640* (Madison, Wis., 1931, p. 195), sees as one of its "controlling ideas" precisely "this concentration on the redemptive aspect of Christ's life in this world," which "inevitably resulted in more attention being paid to his official role than to his personality."

[46] *Institutes*, I, 553–54 (II.xvi.2).

pledge of his love, without whom the tokens of his hatred and wrath are manifest both above and below."[47]

On the basis of this view of the redemption, Calvin erects an ontology: "It is Christ alone who joins heaven to earth. He alone is Mediator, reaching from heaven to the earth. He it is through whom the fullness of all heavenly gifts flows down to us and through whom we on our part may ascend to God"; and draws its epistemological consequences: "Christ . . . was always the link joining men to God, and God did not reveal himself otherwise than through him."[48] These consequences are succinctly summarized by his modern editors: "there is no knowledge of God's goodness except in the knowledge of the crucified and risen Christ."[49]

And this latter kind of moral knowledge leads us directly back to the critical experience which alone can produce it, the working of the true and inward spirit of repentance. The importance of this experience as man's sole avenue of approach to God is clear; equally apparent is that in Calvin's view God's love is itself subordinate to the sole means of its manifestation. It should be no less apparent that Greville's treatment of these subjects in the final section of *Caelica* is founded wholly on Calvin's development of and emphases upon them. From the first introduction of divine love as his subject in Sonnet 85—in terms that simply distinguish it from mortal passion—Greville never describes it or seeks to approach it directly (which is, for Calvin, not possible), but only through its manifestation in Christ's passion and Atonement. And to assimilate this manifestation is to have the experience which Greville so carefully prepares for and so thoroughly undergoes, an experience exclusively internal, a drama entirely enacted on the stage of the heart. Moreover, a part of the preparation for the experience has consisted in asserting, according to Calvin's epistemology, that nothing less will serve: castigating man's pride in thinking to know God by other means—by dreaming of "curious mysteries," or by contemplating death.

Since the very beginning of *Caelica* we have noticed how keenly Greville, like all great Renaissance poets, understood the principle of decorum, which insured that his "formes of speech" would be exact embodiments of the ideas and attitudes they contained. In his best religious poems, the forms of language and structure we have examined may thus

---

[47] *Ibid.*, I, 580 (II.xvii.2); I, 604 (III.ii.7).

[48] *Commentaries*, pp. 147–48.

[49] *Ibid.*, p. 45, where they also quote from a commentary which they do not print, in which Calvin concludes that "all cogitation on God apart from Christ is an immense abyss which immediately swallows up our whole mind." He wished to be perfectly clear on the point: "God is apprehended in Christ, and in him alone," *Institutes*, I, 374 (II.vi.4).

be seen as functions of this distinctively Calvinist view of repentance and redemption. His whole temper of philosophical abstraction, with its concomitant solemn grandeur of tone, generality of diction, and neglect of concrete sensory details and images, reflects the effort to achieve the most direct possible contact of man with God through Christ, a contact made entirely within a human consciousness, unadorned by objects or ceremonies, unmediated by persons or institutions. His Calvinist bias also generates his repeated and varied use of the Pauline metaphor of crucifixion for both the suffering that the experience involves and the avoidance of that suffering. It results further in the syllabic density and rhythmic heaviness which apprehend that suffering and make it audible. The thickness of aural texture is also a partial rendering of God as the "fatall mirrour of transgression," the hostile Calvinist Almighty—impenetrable, majestic, opaque. To contemplate this God is to scourge our fallen humanity:

if we once elevate our thoughts to God, and consider his nature, and the consummate perfection of his righteousness, wisdom, and strength, to which we ought to be conformed, —what before charmed us in ourselves under the false pretext of righteousness, will soon be loathed as the greatest iniquity; what strangely deceived us under the title of wisdom, will be despised as extreme folly; and what wore the appearance of strength, will be proved to be most wretched impotence.[50]

Finally, the rigorous logical structure of the poems (combined, in Sonnet 99, with spatial organization) serves to isolate each successive reflection in that fatal mirror in order to comprehend most fully its nature, its causes and effects. Greville's plain style thus endows a universal Christian experience with the meaning—the tone, the structure, and the somber power—it acquired from the "living wisdom" of John Calvin.

The same experience, developed in a different theology, will acquire a different meaning, which will in turn require a different poetic style. Richard Hooker shares Calvin's basic view of repentance as a gift of God, an effect of divine grace, initially stimulated by fear of judgment. He also agrees with Calvin about the office of repentance, the satisfaction of God's wrath toward men through Christ as Mediator.[51] But his development of these shared doctrines proceeds along lines very different from those taken by Calvin.

First, Hooker distinguishes between the "virtue" and "discipline" of repentance. The first of these terms corresponds to Calvin's entire treatment of the subject as the inward conversion of the individual soul. Second, Hooker enlarges on the motive of this experience as follows:

[50] *Institutes*, I, 49 (I.i.2).
[51] *Works*, III, 7–8, 56–58 (*Laws* VI.iii.2, v.2–3).

as we never decay in love till we sin, in like sort neither can we possibly forsake sin, unless we first begin again to love. What is love towards God, but a desire of union with God? And shall we imagine a sinner converting himself to God, in whom there is no desire of union with God presupposed? I therefore conclude, that fear worketh no man's inclination to repentance, till somewhat else have wrought in us love also. Our love and desire of union with God ariseth from the strong conceit which we have of his admirable goodness. The goodness of God which particularly moveth unto repentance, is his mercy towards mankind, notwithstanding sin: for let it once sink deeply into the mind of man, that howsoever we have injuried God, his very nature is averse from revenge, except unto sin we add obstinacy; otherwise always ready to accept our submission as a full discharge or recompense for all wrongs; and can we choose but begin to love him whom we have offended? or can we but begin to grieve that we have offended him whom we now love? [52]

Hooker revalues the whole psychology of the experience: he does not divide it into law and gospel and confine God to the terrible effects of the former; our perception of God's "admirable goodness" does not, for Hooker, result straightaway in terror and despair, but rather compels us to love him for his mercy. This psychology is in fact an implicit denial of Calvin's compartmentalization of the experience: Hooker is saying in effect that law and gospel must work together and that both are subsumed by God's mercy.

Hooker goes on to describe the "just sorrow" of contrition hereby stimulated and then to explain in the remaining nine-tenths of Book VI of the *Laws of Ecclesiastical Polity* how this inward conversion is fulfilled in the institutional "discipline" of repentance, the offices and sacraments of the Church. The net effect of all the ceremonies and works of repentance is to prevent the solitary torments that Calvin so strenuously insists upon, to come between the sinner and his sense of guilt. Hooker's psychology is extremely acute. Here, for example, is his justification of public confession and penance:

Furthermore, because the knowledge how to handle our own sores is no vulgar and common art, but we either carry towards ourselves for the most part an over-soft and gentle hand, fearful of touching too near the quick; or else, endeavouring not to be partial, we fall into timorous scrupulosities, and sometimes into those extreme discomforts of mind, from which we hardly do ever lift up our heads again; men thought it the safest way to disclose their secret faults, and to crave imposition of penance from them whom our Lord Jesus Christ hath left in his Church to be spiritual and ghostly physicians, the guides and pastors of redeemed souls, whose office doth not only consist

[52] *Ibid.*, III, 9 (*Laws* VI.iii.3).

in general persuasions unto amendment of life, but also in the private particular cure of diseased minds.[53]

The continual implicit thrust of Hooker's argument is virtually the opposite of Calvin's: what one seeks privately to break down into particular and successive parts the other seeks to bring together in a wider and more public context; where one sees the experience primarily as process, and concentrates upon its progression of paradoxical dichotomies, the other sees the experience primarily as end, and concentrates upon the unity and poise of its dichotomies in what is at once their source and resolution. Calvin's sense of God is that of a just and malevolent punisher; Hooker's, that of a merciful and benign forgiver. Hooker of course never insists as Calvin does on the total opposition of flesh and spirit, and the consequent necessity for the destruction of nature. As a result his doctrine of the redemption is not nearly so narrowly developed as Calvin's—since he does not need to stress God's hatred of men apart from Christ—and merely exemplifies the Anglican doctrine of repentance instead of being a basis for its promulgation. Indeed, Hooker nowhere treats redemption per se in the *Laws*. For Calvin, God's love is available to men, and perceivable by them, only in the Atonement; for Hooker, it is everywhere.

The poetry which most directly echoes these tonal emphases in Anglican theology is of course that of George Herbert, whose sense of the omnipresent divine benevolence is evident even in the way he develops the implications of his title. *The Temple* is that place wherein the spirit of God dwells: it is the mind, heart, and language of man, the edifice of the Church, the whole frame of creation. The characteristic style which proceeds from and embodies this religious sensibility may be seen most clearly in one of Herbert's most famous penitential lyrics, "Love (III)," and may be contrasted at every point with Greville's practice in Sonnet 99. Both poems deal with the same Christian experience, and both share the same doctrinal skeleton: the sinner, being fully conscious of his own guilt, feels unworthy of salvation until he becomes aware of the efficacy of Christ's sacrifice. But where Greville's God demands the exact scrutiny and anguished mortification of the guilty self, Herbert's is full of radiant assurance and kindly invitation.

"Love (III)" is a dramatic dialogue between the sinful self and personified divine love, developed in the implied metaphorical situation of hospitality.[54] The diction throughout is extremely simple, homely, and

---

[53] *Ibid.*, III, 31 (*Laws* VI.iv.7).
[54] The poem may be found in *The Works of George Herbert*, ed. F. E. Hutchinson (Oxford, 1941)—to which all subsequent citations of Herbert refer—p. 188.

colloquial; the tone one of quiet intimacy. When the poet, feeling guilty of "dust" (as tenor, the frailty of mortal men; as vehicle, the dust of the road, which itself suggests the additional tenor of the Christian journey through life), is reluctant to enter the abode of love,

> quick-ey'd Love, observing me grow slack
>              From my first entrance in,
> Drew nearer to me, sweetly questioning,
>              If I lack'd any thing.

The language portrays divine love as a kind of friendly innkeeper, fearful of losing a guest, whose speech (which suggests the peddler's cry, "What d'ye lack?") is that of a solicitous tradesman. Greville's God has, of course, a considerably more elevated sense of his social position. Herbert's homely situation, which could so easily become ludicrous, is handled with his customary exquisite tact, in that it remains entirely a matter of implication, a subtle but complete establishment of the vehicle, after which the dialogue is concerned wholly with the concepts of the tenor. It is by such discipline and control—the limitation of the possible connotations of the vehicle as such, the refusal to allow it to run away with the poem—that Herbert's style differs typically from Donne's.

The attitude of solicitation in "Love (III)," combined with the everyday, domestic familiarity of the atmosphere, suggests both the accessibility of God's love and his eagerness to dispense it. The latter is made additionally clear by the whole antithetical movement of the dialogue—reinforced by the alternation of pentameter and trimeter lines—in which the "Lord" disposes of all the objections the poet can raise. The action that suddenly resolves the argument and concludes the metaphor of hospitality, when the poet sits and eats, is narrated in language which brilliantly evokes the ritualistic symbol of the Eucharist, the institutional ceremony which is the outward and visible sign of the inward and spiritual process of repentance in all its parts: confession, contrition, expiation in the passion of Christ, and rededication of the soul to God. And the repeated narrative rubrics of the final stanza, highly colloquial in their use of the present tense in a context of past narration ("sayes Love"), keep the focus of attention on the final cause of both process and ceremony: God's merciful affection for his creatures.

Herbert's employment of the dramatic narrative structure, the concrete and homely dialogue and metaphor, the intimate tone, result from his profound apprehension of a God whose "very nature is averse from revenge." His extension of the metaphor to suggest the Church ritual that commemorates the experience he is describing is an admirable rendering of the "virtue" of repentance being fulfilled in its ceremonial and symbolic "discipline." Other conspicuous examples of both the intimate dramatic dialogue and the metaphorical extension occur in "The Collar" which "expresses rebellion and atonement in the same vocabulary," again by suggesting the Eucharist.[55] This poem is the best example of the famous rhetorical strategy in "Love (III)"—and to lesser and varying degrees in "The Pearl" and "Redemption"—of dramatizing some inner conflict at length, and resolving it in a quick, sudden, but inevitable conclusion. The effect of the strategy is further to enhance the ease and amplitude of God's all-forgiving love. The two latter poems also employ concrete and homely metaphors of bargaining. "The Pearl" and "Man" are Herbert's clearest statements of the blessedness of creation and the appeal of worldly activities: nature for him is far from the limitless corruption that it is for Greville; he seeks God not because of its inherent evil, but in spite of its indisputable value—because God's love simply overwhelms all else.

The whole strategy of *The Temple* is to present the physical and sacramental body of the Church as the repository of divine love, as yet another of the many ways in which man is invited to climb to his Creator. For Greville, the many ways do not exist; hence the narrower range, the tremendous austerity, of his style. If Herbert can indulge all manner of stylistic audacities to experience the meaning of repentance as a multi-faceted acceptance of God's all-searching and all-forgiving love, Greville can only state the rigorous terms and uncompromising consequences of God's all-judging and all-destroying law. Within the techniques requisite to their themes and purposes, both poets are of course masters of rhythm and sound. In "Love (III)" the luminous simplicity of the diction and the extreme lightness of aural texture produce an effect of syllabic transparency which is the exact opposite of the density of Sonnet 99. Each effect serves its respective theological function: in Greville's case, to focus the fatal mirror on earth; in Herbert's, to look through it and perceive the glory of heaven beyond. Herbert prays in "The Elixir" for the ability to do just this—to see God in all things—using the same metaphor in a way that succinctly contrasts the object of his vision to Greville's:

> A man that looks on glasse,
> On it may stay his eye;
> Or if he pleaseth, through it passe,
> And then the heav'n espie.[56]

---

[55] Jeffrey Hart, "Herbert's 'The Collar' Re-Read," *Boston University Studies in English*, V(1961), 66–68.

[56] Hutchinson, p. 184. It should perhaps be emphasized that both writers share equally didactic intentions. Greville's have been discussed in ch. I, and Herbert's are well known from the "Jordan" poems (Hutchinson, pp. 56, 102) and from his dying injunction to his friend Ferrar (see Walton's *Life*, ed. George Saintsbury

Ultimately, Hooker and Herbert stipulate what Calvin and Greville dwell upon: man's total degeneration, the consequent intense inward purgatives essential to his salvation, and the stringent dualism which postulates, in all human experience other than this purgation, implacable hostility between the temporal and the spiritual. When Greville develops the traditional theme of *sic transit gloria mundi*, he concludes: "For lest Man should thinke flesh a seat of blisse, / God workes that his joy mixt with sorrow is" (Sonnet 94). In "The Pulley" Herbert portrays God as bestowing all possible worldly blessings on man, except the divine blessing of "rest," and concluding: "If goodnesse leade him not, yet wearinesse / May tosse him to my breast."[57] Greville's God sees to it that everything man may engage in is tainted; Herbert's God goes out of his way to provide man with a pleasant earthly stay, and to ensure his entrance into heaven even if he is beguiled by worldly delights. As Helen White has said, "The most distinctive thing about Herbert's God . . . is his yearning for man."[58] And this yearning can indicate as well the basic difference between Calvin's and Hooker's Gods, between a God who strenuously upholds the letter of the law and one who subsumes the letter of this law in the benevolence of its spirit.

Having undergone the experience of repentance, which in his epistemology is the only pathway to truth, Greville proceeds in the last ten poems of *Caelica* to turn the inward vision outward, to judge the world from the viewpoint his repentance has afforded him. Half of the poems are primarily political, offering trenchant and concise analysis of the selfish corruption of consolidated power (Sonnet 101), of the world's hatred of justice (Sonnet 106), and of war as producing effects which, though ostensibly superior to those of peace, are nonetheless vain and empty (Sonnet 108). Two of them recapitulate earlier themes: the blind vanity, the "gilded curb," of nobility (Sonnet 107), and the false idols of friends, fame, and fortune, which are rejected with the final comment, "Divels, there many be, and Gods but one" (Sonnet 105). The other five poems are psychological and religious, displaying most directly the consequences of the inward vision as they examine human experience in terms of its theology, from what might be called the perspective of the "regenerated."

Perhaps the most obvious of these consequences is a renewed hatred of sin. Just as Calvinism laid principal stress on the proper motives in the

---

[London, 1927], pp. 314–15). Both men consciously disciplined their poetry to express their different kinds of piety.

[57] Hutchinson, p. 160.

[58] *The Metaphysical Poets: A Study in Religious Experience* (New York, 1936), p. 181.

process of repentance, it similarly emphasized proper motives as the result of that process. "In one word, repentance is not a bare leaving of sinne, but an utter condemning and misliking of that sin which we have left."[59] Greville's condemnation of sin takes the form of arriving at a more comprehensive understanding of it by exploring further the idea of privation that provided him with the crucial insight of Sonnet 99.

Sonnet 100, probably the best of the five regular sonnets in the final section, is the highly compressed development of an implied similitude between man's confused imaginings of fearful things by night and the warp in his perceptions which results from his sinful state. The physical and psychological description is acute and exact throughout, focusing attention wholly on the depraved faculties of man:

> In Night when colours all to blacke are cast,
> Distinction lost, or gone downe with the light;
> The eye a watch to inward senses plac'd,
> Not seeing, yet still having power of sight,
>
> Gives vaine Alarums to the inward sense,
> Where feare stirr'd up with witty tyranny,
> Confounds all powers, and thorough selfe-offence,
> Doth forge and raise impossibility:
>
> Such as in thicke depriving darkenesses,
> Proper reflections of the errour be,
> And images of selfe-confusednesses,
> Which hurt imaginations onely see;
>    And from this nothing seene, tels newes of devils,
>    Which but expressions be of inward evils.

The watching eye is prevented from exercising its power by "thicke depriving" darkness. The epithets affixed to the physical terms of the similitude transform them into the Calvinistic concepts of reason and sin respectively. In the absence of light the eye conjures up terrifying figments which are "nothing" but reflections of internal error. Thus the reason can perceive only the nothingness of evil, the fact of its own depravity—which, however, it does not recognize as such, but objectifies as "devils." The insight that we give the "evils" outward form instead of acknowledging them as our own (what a modern psychologist would call "projection") is brilliant. The diction and structure of the poem express it by endowing each part of the perceptual process with its definite and precise theological meaning. The careful correspondence of the

---

[59] Greenham, p. 171. Nehemiah Rogers (pp. 252–54) insists at length that merely mourning, grieving, confessing, and even departing from our sins, do not constitute true repentance unless these are accompanied by the proper motive of hatred and loathing for sin per se.

terms of the similitude, the perfect selection and adjustment of vehicle and tenor, achieves a complete epistemological awareness of the human condition of sin.

Herbert's "Sinne (II)" offers a striking parallel in material, and a striking contrast in meaning, to Sonnet 100. The same idea of privation and the same comparison of visual apparitions to our own sins are used to show that "God more care of us hath had."[60] Herbert begins by exclaiming, "O that I could a sinne once see," and then explains why he cannot. This kind of argumentative structure—making a wish or a vow only to deny it on further examination—is a frequent technique of Herbert's for expressing the chastening of pride, the humble submission of self to God's will and wisdom. His argument in "Sinne (II)" is that God, by depriving sin of all "being," has specifically prevented us from seeing what could make us "grow mad." He permits us only to see "devils," which are but the distorted (by implication, the softened and reduced) picture of our sins. What for Greville is the effect of man's psychological contumacy is for Herbert the effect of God's merciful affection. Greville's point-by-point exposition confines the meaning to the exact terms of the similitude—to the functional analysis of man's mental depravity. There is no such confinement (nor precision) in Herbert's poem, which employs the similitude in the broader context of a dialogue with himself to suggest that the cause of his inability to see sin is God's loving care for man. Thus the style and structure of the two poems are again designed, in the first case, to delineate the reflection in the fatal mirror; and in the second, to see beyond it. No more concise an example could be found of the tonal differences, and their stylistic consequences, in the two strains of Protestantism we have reviewed.

Sonnet 102 (whose thirteen six-line stanzas make it the longest poem in the final section, and one of the longest in the sequence) is a direct analysis of the nature of sin in terms of a meditation upon its causes and effects. Both are introduced in the first two stanzas: the former as man's foolish desire to "know more than hee was created to"; the latter as the immediate change of "his being to privation . . . / Whereby immortall life" has become "the hell of flesh and blood." The third and fourth stanzas enlarge upon these consequences by explicitly asserting the viewpoint that was more or less tacitly assumed in several of the earlier lyrics:

> But grant that there were no eternity,
> That life were all, and Pleasure life of it,
> In sinnes excesse there yet confusions be,
> Which spoyle his peace, and passionate his wit.

[60] Hutchinson, p. 63.

. . . . .

> And as Hell fires, not wanting heat, want light;
> So these strange witchcrafts, which like Pleasure be,
> Not wanting faire inticements, want delight.

As is his constant practice, Greville defines the theological state in moral and psychological terms, here frankly hypothesizing that the temporal world alone provides sufficient evidence of sin in the destructive and unilluminating flames of apparent pleasure.

Having thus established the reality of the fall in terms of its effects, Greville returns in the next four stanzas to contemplate the astonishing wonder of its cause, wrestling with the fundamental Christian paradox of a perfect Creator and an imperfect creation. He suggests reasons why the fall seems inconceivable: man's total innocence ("All things uncurst") in the state of rectitude; man's creation in the image of God, his profound alliance ("Eternity was object to his passion") with omnipotence. Consideration of the latter ("So as, against his will no power could take, / A Creature from him") of course implicates God in the fall and diminishes his goodness, which Greville immediately denies:

> And yet who thinks he marr'd, that made us good,
> As well may think God lesse than flesh and blood.

But the problem of the origin of privation remains. Since nothing in God or in man can account for it, it is found in "the Angels," whose "discreation" proves that "no being was secure, / But that transcendent Goodnesse" which is God himself.

The next three stanzas describe this ontological process of the fall as resulting from the natures of the agents and the acted upon. The already fallen spirits, "Refined by their high places in creation, / To adde more craft and malice to temptation," were able to work with great "force upon these middle spheares, / Of Probable, and Possibility," where there is no certitude, no fixed boundary. The point is that earth is ontologically distinct from heaven: paradise was potentially mutable, and the state of innocence provided no way of knowing that any change would be for the worse. Hence the ease with which the tempters could raise our aspirations

> onely by our will;
> Perswading, like it, all was to it free,
> Since where no sinne was, there no law could be.

The last two stanzas summarize the ambivalent motives of original sin. In their carefully orchestrated stress upon the paradoxically reversed limitations of man's knowledge before and after the fall, in their compressed lucidity of language, in their compendious and precise management of complex ideas, they constitute an exact and powerfully moving statement of the uniquely human tragedy of sin:

> And as all finite things seeke infinite,
> From thence deriving what beyond them is;
> So man was led by charmes of this darke sp'rit,
> Which hee could not know till hee did amisse;
>> To trust those Serpents, who learn'd since they fell,
>> Knew more than we did; even their own made hell.

> Which crafty oddes made us those clouds imbrace,[61]
> Where sinne in ambush lay to overthrow
> Nature, (that would presume to fadome Grace)
> Or could beleeve what God said was not so:
>> Sin, then we knew theee not, and could not hate,
>> And now we know thee, now it is too late.

The poem is Greville's justification of the ways of God to men. It is of course wholly nondramatic, but it might almost serve as a conceptual blueprint for *Paradise Lost*. Significantly, though, there is nothing at all *felix* about the *culpa* as Greville describes it; the point from which he views sin even after the experience of repentance is still exclusively earth-bound, still in terms of its consequences as we perceive them here. And in these terms, the emotional tone is still one of grim lamentation, anguish, and sorrow, although it is no longer personally directed, but is now the result of a wider and more general understanding. It is the kind of feeling proper to the regenerate sinner as he labors to comprehend the full extent of the world's corruption.

Greville enlarges this comprehension in the next poem by transferring his hatred for the incredible privation of sin to these ontologically "middle" spheres that make sin possible. "O false and treacherous Probability," he cries out, "Enemy of truth, and friend to wickednesse" (Sonnet 103). There is no certainty in this world, only opinion, which misleads humanity, loses "obedience in the pride of wit," and dares to judge and mold "the Deity" according to human reason. The sestet of the sonnet maintains that God will remain a "riddle" to "Vaine thought" until "the vayles be rent, the flesh newborne."[62] The concluding couplet emphasizes the consequent folly of probing his secrets:

[61] The allusion is to the myth of Ixion, Greville's favorite figurative expression for various kinds of self-deception—see ch. 1, p. 14. Here of course it suggests the original self-deception which begot all the others.

[62] The rending of the veil of the Temple (which signified the revelation of divine mysteries) at the moment of Christ's death on the cross is described in Matt. 27:51, Mark 15:38, and Luke 23:45. An accompanying omen, the opening of graves to release the bodies of the saints, is described in Matt. 27:52, and is cited

> Who therefore censures God with fleshly sprite,
> As well in time may wrap up infinite.

In the course of redirecting his emotion from sin itself to the milieu of sin, Greville condemns the latter on the standard epistemological grounds, but with two interesting twists. First, the kind of Biblical language which has before been used metaphorically to locate the epistemological remedy in the experience of conversion is here used literally to locate that remedy only in the actual and future event of the body's resurrection on the day of judgment. The implication is that even the experience of Christ, as undergone by the truly repentant sinner, can provide mortality with no real knowledge of religious truth. Second, this implication, along with the tenor of the whole criticism—judging the Deity, censuring God—invites us to read the sonnet as a self-rebuke for the searching examination that God's decrees were subjected to in the previous poem.

Although Greville was very careful in Sonnet 102 not to blame God for sin (denying in stanza seven the *unstated* implication that would do so) and to assign it explicitly to the serpent's deceit and man's presumption, his nostalgia for lost innocence was possibly too great, his sense of its moral ignorance possibly too keen, his amazed inquiry into God's justice possibly too persistent, his explanatory sympathy with man's predicament both before and after the fall possibly excessive. Perhaps the whole tone of the poem is an implicit censuring of God, an obstinate expression of painful dissatisfaction with the conditions under which he has decreed we must live. Certainly its anguished tone recalls that of Greville's most famous utterance:

> Oh wearisome Condition of Humanity!
> Borne under one Law, to another bound:
> Vainely begot, and yet forbidden vanity,
> Created sicke, commanded to be sound.
>                 (*Mustapha*, "Chorus Sacerdotum")

Such passionate laments may issue without rebuke from the dramatic personae of heathen priests; but they may indeed be impious in the mouth of a true believer. It should be stressed that Greville's understanding of sin is impeccable. What is in question are the delicate and subtle adjustments of conscience, the proper emotional responses, to that understanding: the requisite hatred for the nature, causes, and effects of sin cannot become so agonized as to constitute even an implicit grudging

---

by Calvin as "an earnest, of the final resurrection, which we expect," *Institutes*, II, 256 (III.xxv.7). In this context "the flesh newborne" clearly looks forward to that literal event.

against the divine wisdom that allowed it to occur. Greville's awareness of this fact reflects the intense and incessant obsession with motive characteristic of Calvinism. His expression of it is achieved by his habitual mastery of language and genre, in which the individual images and poems form a continuously developing examination of experience, subtly modifying what has gone before and foreshadowing what is to come.

Sonnet 103 has indeed foreshadowed the conclusion of the whole sequence, the final solution, as it were, of the human problem. God's providence remains a riddle to mortal minds, ultimately impervious even to the sincerely faithful, whose task is simply to accept his mysterious decrees and to believe that they will be revealed only on that day when he will be known even as he knows. And in this world even this faith "every where findes scorne." Greville proceeds in Sonnet 104 to exemplify the consequences of these ideas for religious institutions. He contrasts the worldly lust of Islam for conquest to the lesser and apparently otherworldly lusts of monasticism and draws the ironic inference in the concluding couplet:

> Now if of God, both these have but the name,
> What mortall Idoll then, can equall Fame?

Greville's conviction that all earthly churches are godless is familiar from the treatises.[63] He restates it here as a consequence of God's ultimate mystery, and in language that reemphasizes the foolishness of imagining that any institution—from the most world-seeking to the most world-renouncing—is capable of containing it.

The introduction of "Fame" makes the transition to the next four poems, which are the final catalogue of "mortal idols," some of which Greville has rejected before as a part of his preparation for repentance. Here they are rejected anew as a part of his preparation for realizing the ultimate object of that repentance. As the metaphorical death of the flesh required a preliminary metaphorical dying to the world, so the literal resurrection of the flesh requires the literal death of the world. The connection is made clear by the last poem in the sequence, a somber and magnificent prayer for doomsday, which is the inevitable logical and emotional conclusion of the rigorous spiritual discipline achieved through all the poems of the final section. Sonnet 109:

[63] Croll sums it up as follows: "Religion, he believed, was purely an aspiration of the individual souls of the elect, and could not be expressed in an institution" (p. 29). Bullough sees even the dramas as extending the point by showing the futility of all human institutions, from which individuals must seek to free themselves by means of grace: "Sénèque, Greville et le jeune Shakespeare," in *Les tragédies de Sénèque et le théâtre de la Renaissance*, ed. Jean Jacquot (Paris, 1964), p. 195.

Syon lyes waste, and thy Jerusalem,
O Lord, is falne to utter desolation,
Against thy Prophets, and thy holy men,
The sinne hath wrought a fatall combination,
    Prophan'd thy name, thy worship overthrowne,
    And made thee living Lord, a God unknowne.

Thy powerfull lawes, thy wonders of creation,
Thy Word incarnate, glorious heaven, darke hell,
Lye shadowed under Mans degeneration,
Thy Christ still crucifi'd for doing well,
    Impiety, O Lord, sits on thy throne,
    Which makes thee living Light, A God unknown.

Mans superstition hath thy truths entomb'd,
His Atheisme againe her pomps defaceth,
That sensuall unsatiable vaste wombe
Of thy seene Church, thy unseene Church disgraceth;
    There lives no truth with them that seem thine own,
    Which makes thee living Lord, a God unknowne.

Yet unto thee, Lord, (mirrour of transgression)
Wee, who for earthly Idols, have forsaken
Thy heavenly Image (sinless pure impression)
And so in nets of vanity lye taken,
    All desolate implore that to thine owne,
    Lord, thou no longer live a God unknowne.

Yet Lord let Israels plagues not be eternall,
Nor sinne for ever cloud thy sacred Mountaines,
Nor with false flames spirituall but infernall,
Dry up thy mercies ever springing fountaines,
    Rather, sweet Jesus, fill up time and come,
    To yeeld the sinne her everlasting doome.

The poem is Greville's final indictment of human society. The stark, terrifying plea for annihilation is made possible only by the complete renunciation of self, which results in complete comprehension of sin and acceptance of God's justice in destroying it—an acceptance (on faith alone, for God is beyond understanding) so complete that this very justice is seen as mercy. This attitude is the last refuge of the true believer: "To desire and love Christs comming, and the day of judgement, that an end may be made to the daies of sinne." [64] The yearning for apocalypse was regarded in Protestant theology as one of the chief effects and signs of sanctification. As such, it is the appropriate culmination of the whole conceptual and emotional movement of the final section of *Caelica*. The

[64] Perkins, I, 113.

honest passion of the poem is unquestionable, although I do not think it permits us to make any statement whatever on whether Greville actually considered himself elected. He is apprehending the meaning of what it feels like to be saved; he is writing about this experience, not about himself. What is achieved in this kind of art—the highest kind—is not transferable to biography. We know what Greville believed about life, as we know some of what Shakespeare believed; we do not know what either believed about himself. As subject matter for art, the latter sort of belief was probably regarded by both men as not worth the attention of posterity.

Although the feeling was a prime desideratum in Calvinist devotion, Greville expresses it in terms that once again out-Calvin Calvin. Neither the founder of Genevan theocracy nor his great English disciple, William Perkins, would have permitted the logical extension of the effects of sin so far into the visible Church. Greville, assuming the profoundly Hebraic tone so congenial to Puritanism, relentlessly calls down the wrath of God upon all institutional religion which has mocked his truth with superstition, unbelief, and venality. At the end of his long and disillusioning battle in the wars of truth, Milton reached the same position. The archangel Michael makes all these points as he finishes his survey of human history for Adam (*Paradise Lost*, XII.508–50), concluding:

> so shall the World go on,
> To good malignant, to bad men benign,
> Under her own weight groaning, till the day
> Appear of respiration to the just,
> And vengeance to the wicked, at return
> Of him
>
>                    .        .        .        .        .
>
>                                        thy Saviour and thy Lord,
> Last in the Clouds from Heav'n to be reveal'd
> In glory of the Father, to dissolve
> Satan with his perverted world.

Milton of course went on to emphasize the eternal bliss attainable by the individual soul; Greville did not.

The rhetorical procedure of Sonnet 109 is customarily direct, logical, and orderly. The poem recapitulates in microcosm the general procedure of the entire final section as broadly corresponding to that of Calvinist meditation and sermon. A general assertion—that holiness is profaned—is made in stanza one, substantiated in stanzas two and three (thus far the figure of prolepsis),[65] and its consequences applied, by means of con-

---

[65] In addition to this structural figure, the poem employs six other figures of both sound and sense: epimone, asyndeton, paroemion, ploce, traductio, antonomasia.

fession and prayer, in stanzas four and five. Each step in the procedure is both reinforced and connected by the careful modulations of tense and image in the liturgical refrain. The imagery of the poem similarly recapitulates and ties together the recurrent themes it has previously contained. "Thy Christ still crucifi'd" echoes back through the whole experience of repentance which the crucifixion has symbolized, to evoke the irony and perversion of unfelt and unacted belief which it expressed in Sonnets 89 and 97. The "mirrour of transgression" summons up the Old Testament God of law, whose divine perfection is human agony, and adds powerful resonance to the "living Lord" of the refrain, into whose hands it is a terrible thing to fall. The steady beat of the last phrase in the refrain (the only one that is repeated without alteration) is a solemn and constant reminder that knowledge of God is impossible in this sinful world. The "false flames spirituall but infernall" recall all the consequences of sin: self-deception and self-defeat when it is not recognized, and self-torment even to despair when it is.

The language of the poem is of surpassing power and brilliance. The whole atmosphere of sexual corruption and death suggested by the diction of the third stanza is made audible by its patterns of alliteration and assonance and by the literally shocking metrical variations in its third and fourth lines. And the immediate contrast with the entirely regular meter of the heavy, slow-moving monosyllables of the fifth line has the effect of assimilating the shock, of acknowledging a truth the horror of which is perfectly apprehended. It is by such supreme skill at managing sound and rhythm that Greville is able "to insist on the personal grief behind the public utterance,"[66] to state an idea at the same time as he expresses the emotional reaction to it. The style makes thought and feeling coextensive and inseparable. Such a precise yet subtle, complex yet lucid, grasp of experience is what makes lyric poetry great. "Syon lyes waste" is probably the best poem in the collection; it is one of the greatest poems in the period, and in the language.

One of Greville's latest critics, himself a poet, has offered a perceptive but limited evaluation of his achievement in religious verse:

In the last poems of *Caelica*, much of the greatness lies in the clarity and strength of the poignancy he gives to the despair that can be cured only by the end of life. And in these poems, too, the body cries out in pain at the rejections it is being forced to make, and in the note of the cry we recognize the very humanity it is a cry against.[67]

What Gunn calls "despair" here is not the ultimate Christian temptation to disbelieve in one's own salvation because of a profound sense of guilt,

---

[66] Thom Gunn, p. 40.
[67] *Ibid.*, p. 41.

which Greville dealt with in Sonnets 98 and 99. What Gunn means is simply Greville's total emotional absorption in "the idea that life is vanity," and his "holding out for an abstraction of complete purity which can never be possessed on earth"—a "despair," in other words, that human life can ever be anything but sin. Greville's unconditional rejection of the temporal world is unacceptable to Gunn, so he praises Greville for the pain it cost him to arrive at and express it. The praise is accurate as far as it goes, and Gunn keenly appreciates how the hard-won expression can make even an unacceptable conviction into a living experience.

Perhaps this is the best that modern criticism can do for Greville, to recognize the poetic power of the experiences he describes while scorning the ideas that motivated and shaped those experiences. And this is perhaps not inconsiderable: it reflects, after all, the exercise of the enlightened historical imagination; it represents a great advance over the cultural myopia of the turn of the century, which sought a complete bifurcation of "dead" ideas and poetic style. But as criticism, it is still, I think, neither necessary nor sufficient.[68]

The conviction that defines the world we live in as totally depraved is probably unacceptable to most people today. I should like therefore to say something in its defense. It proceeds of course from the great Christian myth of original sin; it was a fundamental and universal assumption in the Renaissance; it provided the subject for the greatest epic poem in English; and its implications were consistently and logically extended by Greville far beyond the limits imposed on them by contemporary theologians. The farthest and most sophisticated extension is found in "Syon lyes waste." There Greville sees human society as being merely the sum of the degeneration of its members, of their alienation from God. The principle is that every individual is radically corrupt, and that therefore all conventionally accepted aspirations and social institutions are ultimately the products of this corruption. It provided Greville with the impulse, tone, and style of most of his greatest verse. In this view man is not seen as the noble romantic soul victimized by cruel social, economic, or intellectual systems, but as the creator of those systems. He is his own victim; he has built his own prison, and his only hope of real life is to get out of it.

This diagnosis of the human condition should certainly seem neither eccentric nor contemptible to a generation that has grown up imbibing

---

[68] Miss Rees offers a few general critical observations which are both more sufficient and more sympathetic. She quotes the great religious poems (Sonnets 98, 99, 109), praises their sound, structure, and thought, and concludes that the entire sequence "is one of the most varied, accomplished, dynamic and deeply interesting pieces of writing which the whole of the period produced" (pp. 111–18).

the psychology of Freud—as Greville did the faculty psychology of his day—with the very air it breathed. For it is the same diagnosis: man is a disease and his society an epidemic.[69] From its first major statement in Western thought in the epistles of St. Paul, it has appealed for its validity less to any doctrinal system than to the experience of all men, to one's moral self-awareness. Perkins stated it dogmatically: "leave every man to his nature, we should see that every man would practise any sinne in the world: yea, even the greatest sinnes that ever we heard to be done in the world. All men which know themselves, know this to be true."[70] Thoreau personally: "I never dreamed of any enormity greater than I have committed. I never knew, and never shall know, a worse man than myself."[71]

The social and historical consequences of this ethical insight have been most fully faced by radical Protestantism and by Freudian psychology. The religion developed as its central doctrine St. Paul's interpretation of the Hebrew etiology of evil in order to explain, to make at least comprehensible in terms of human history, the painful mystery of the insight, "the good that I would I do not: but the evil which I would not, that I do" (Rom. 7:19). The science developed as its central doctrine the theory of repression in order to explain the same mystery in the same terms. Both philosophies see man as *unconsciously* driven—in the one case through phylogenetic inheritance, in the other through ontogenetic training—to inward misery and outward misbehavior by failing to understand his own nature, by denying his true being and alienating himself from its source. Now the philosophies obviously present diametrically opposed definitions of this true being: the intangible soul versus the tangible sense. Where the one describes the mechanics of man's dilemma as reason's failure to repress the appetite, the other describes them as the superego's success at repressing the id. But the dilemma and its consequences are the same: man is trapped both by his inner contradictions and by their outward institutional forms. Also the same is the prescribed, socially pessimistic solution for it: salvation must begin with the individual; the world in the sense of the conventionally acceptable must be rejected; institutional reform is meaningless, if not impossible, without individual regeneration. It is additionally suggestive that both Protestantism and Freudianism conceive of this regeneration as resulting in the transfiguration of the body[72]—in the hereafter versus the here and now—

[69] This is precisely the thesis of Freud's most provocative modern interpreter, Norman O. Brown, in *Life against Death: The Psychoanalytical Meaning of History* (Middletown, Conn., 1959).

[70] *Workes*, III, 415.

[71] *Walden*, ch. I (Signet Classics, New York, 1960), p. 57.

[72] The point is made by Norman O. Brown (pp. 308–09); his analysis of the

and that both deny the agency of the intellect in bringing it about. The Calvinist tyranny of wit is the Freudian death instinct.

Our giving full credence to the literary presentation of this vision of reality does not, of course, depend on our wholehearted assent to either set of its literal terms. We do not have to accept either the Christian or the Freudian eschatology as literal truth; we may doubt equally whether the body is resurrected after death, or whether it can be resurrected in life by the recovery of infantile polymorphous perversity. But we ought not to feel it necessary to reject the vision that sees the body in need of resurrection. That the vision is contained both in the Christian doctrine of the fall and in the scientific and speculative thought of one of the greatest minds of the twentieth century should permit us to accept it as mythical truth, that is, as one enduring possible model of human experience, as one profoundly significant way of understanding life as we live it.

A sufficient criticism must, I think, accept it as such, if criticism is to account at all for its literary impact. How can we apprehend the effects of a style if we deny the vision which has formed the style? How can we appreciate the experience a poet describes, or the way in which he understands it, if we cannot share it, or if we cannot to some extent understand it in the same way? We do not, finally, read Greville—or any great poet —because he gives powerful expression to his own feelings for reasons we can ignore; we read him because he enables us to comprehend, for reasons that we might not otherwise perceive, feelings that are ours.

---

insights which the psychology and the religion share (pp. 231–33) is useful and acute.

# V   Critical Perspectives

THE history of Fulke Greville's reputation as a poet may be regarded virtually as a belated footnote to that of John Donne. Critical respect in the poets' own age was shortly followed by almost total neglect. Although Greville passed unnoticed in Dr. Johnson's criticism of "metaphysical" excesses, he shared in the romantic revival of interest in the quaint authors of the Renaissance. By 1870 he was sufficiently identified with the "metaphysical school," then in general disfavor, for his editor to protest the abusive use of the term.[1] But in the ensuing flurry of scholarly activity on both sides of the Atlantic from about 1890 to 1920 Greville's position became more ambiguous. Most of the ambiguity resulted from using romantic canons of taste in judging him, but some of it proceeded from the revaluation of the metaphysicals and an uncertainty as to whether Greville belonged in their category or not. The definitive direction that the revaluation eventually took—in Eliot's famous review of Grierson's anthology—pretty much ensured that he did not, with the result that scholarship then tended to consider him in the context of its growing historical interest in the Elizabethan sonneteers. Eliot himself once remarked apropos of the dramas that Greville had "never received quite his due."[2]

With respect to the lyrics, his due was a long time coming, and is arriving in our own time as the result of yet another revaluation of Renaissance literary history largely expounded for the last thirty years in the work of Yvor Winters.[3] Much of the value and the growing influence of Winters' theory of the plain style lies in its (at the time pioneer) approach to the Renaissance lyric in terms of the rhetoric of the period, which scholars have since become willing to take seriously. The theory

[1] Grosart is attempting to praise Greville's "thought," though what he is really praising is his piety, and feels it necessary to score off the prevailing contempt for "intellectual" poetry: "Your stupid critic mutters 'metaphysical School,' and so there's an end on 't'" (II, xix).

[2] *Elizabethan Essays* (London, 1934), p. 195.

[3] The seminal essay is "The 16th Century Lyric in England," *Poetry*, LIII (Feb., Mar., 1939), 258–72, 320–35; LIV (Apr., 1939), 35–51. It is reprinted and enlarged, with a much fuller treatment of Greville, as the first chapter in his last book, *Forms of Discovery*.

thus aims to provide an accurate historical understanding of what Renaissance poets were consciously attempting, while furnishing critical standards to judge those attempts in the poetry with which it is concerned. Ironically, however, the theory has been subsequently developed in a way that undervalues, when it does not ignore, certain kinds of lyric performance at which most Renaissance poets excelled. Despite this deficiency, the theory has ultimately widened our perception of the Renaissance lyric in general, and has raised broader critical questions of considerable importance for Greville in particular.

As a gentleman, for whom publication was improper, and as a courtier, for whom it could be dangerous, Greville published nothing in his lifetime.[4] The lack was mildly lamented in the first critical notice we have of him in 1589 by Puttenham, who catalogued with taste and comprehensiveness the "crew of Courtly makers Noble men and Gentlemen of her Majesties owne servauntes, who have written excellently well as it would appeare if their doings could be found out and made publicke with the rest." Puttenham, a firm believer in hierarchical degree, lists them in order not of literary merit but of social rank, being careful to supply the titles of those still living. He begins with the Earl of Oxford and includes, among others, "Sir Philip Sydney, Sir Walter Rawleigh, Master Edward Dyar, Maister Fulke Grevell."[5] Although seventeen of the *Caelica* lyrics were set to music between 1597 and 1630 by Cavendish, Dowland, and Peerson, only a few of them found their way into the manuscript collections of the day.[6]

It is hard to believe that this relative scarcity (when compared to the many surviving versions of Sidney's and Donne's poems) does not at least in part result from the prudence of the cautious statesman exercised throughout his long life. A man who burned a play of his lest it offend the queen (*Life of Sidney*, pp. 155–157) would surely be unlikely to allow copies of anything but the more harmless amorous poems to circulate widely, or even to circulate at all. The situation grew even touchier after Elizabeth's death, when Greville was reduced to writing toadying letters to Cecil for preferment. A man who sought service with James and his favorites would hardly have wished to be known as the author of "Syon lyes waste," not to mention the treatises.[7]

---

[4] A pirated edition of *Mustapha* appeared in 1609.

[5] P. 61 (I.xxxi).

[6] This is the opinion of Bullough (*Poems and Dramas*, I, 38), whose notes identify which lyrics are used in which songbooks.

[7] The publication of *Religion* was in fact prevented in 1633, and when it finally appeared with *Monarchy* in 1670, Richard Baxter expressed astonishment as "a Poem lately Printed for Subjects Liberty, which I greatly wonder this Age would bear," quoted in Wilkes, p. vii.

Where Puttenham's list aimed at inclusiveness, another contemporary mentioned Greville in a more exclusive company who were explicitly representative of a certain taste, a company "whose English hath in my Conceit most propriety, and is nearest to the Phrase of Court, and to the Speech used among the noble, and among the better sort in London." The language of Raleigh and Donne, among others, "but especially of Sir Foulk Grevile" is cited as preliminary to the final panegyric: "I never tasted English more to my liking, nor more smart, and put to the height of Use in Poetry, then in that vital, judicious, and most practicable Language of Benjamin Jonson's Poems."[8] A sometime member of the court, Sir Thomas Smith, while telling an exciting tale about some iniquitous Russian emperor, wished "for some excellent pen-man," like Sidney, to render it in poetry, "or in an Earth-deploring, sententious, high rapt tragedie with the noble Foulk-Grevill."[9]

Taken together, these contemporary notices suggest that in the educated literary opinion of his time Greville was regarded as a conscientious craftsman whose use of language was succinct and socially elevated. That his diction was praised for its "propriety" should be remembered, since what seemed elegant and proper to the standards of 1620 was to be generally scorned by the changing taste of the Restoration. The preference for the pellucid politeness of Waller and Denham became the dominant fashion that consigned Greville, along with all the other more demanding poets of the earlier seventeenth century, to virtual oblivion. In this literary context William Winstanley listed Greville's works, omitting *Caelica*, and quoted the judgment of Milton's nephew, Edward Phillips, upon them: "in all which is observable a close mysterious and sententious way of Writing, without much regard to Elegancy of Stile, or smoothness of Verse."[10] In substance, this judgment remained final, and was constantly quoted for over two hundred years.[11]

[8] Edmund Bolton, *Hypercritica*, ed. Anthony Hall (Oxford, 1722), pp. 235, 237. The book is a treatise on historiography and was presumably written between 1610 and 1621. The passage is quoted by Thomas Warton in *The History of English Poetry*, ed. W. C. Hazlitt (London, 1871), IV, 206. It is also quoted by Trimpi, who takes it as an identification of plain-style poets (p. 115).

[9] *Sir Thomas Smithes Voyage and Entertainment in Rushia* (London, 1605), Sig. Kl^v.

[10] *The Lives of the Most Famous English Poets* (London, 1687), p. 87. Phillips' book, almost all of which Winstanley borrowed, was *Theatrum Poetarum* (London, 1675). Phillips' condescending comment on all of Sidney's verse—made after treating him largely as a pattern of chivalry—is further evidence of Restoration taste: "having, if I mistake not, a greater Spirit of Poetry, then to be altogether disesteem'd" (Sig. Gg4^v).

[11] Other discussions of Greville which maintain this viewpoint in effect or in citation are: [Elizabeth Cooper, ed.], *The Muses' Library* (London, 1737), I, 216–17, who is quoted by Southey, *Select Works of the British Poets from Chaucer to*

The supposedly abstruse mysteries that the neoclassical age detested were of course just what delighted the romantics. Hazlitt found that Greville alone could surpass Chapman "in gravity and mystery," and wrote a pleasant account of Lamb's desire to call up the ghosts of Greville and Sir Thomas Browne to unravel the "dark hints and doubtful oracles" in their writings.[12] But if the romantic taste for the quaintness of "these old crabbed authors" resulted in little penetrating criticism, it at least acknowledged that the poetry had some kind of power and appeal, and brought it back into public view. The romantic appreciation of Greville, however, was necessarily limited by what it regarded as the tyranny of mind in his verse. Although Lamb found in the dramas "the finest movements of the human heart, the utmost grandeur of which the soul is capable," his general judgment, echoed in most subsequent scholarship, was that "whether we look into his plays or his most passionate love-poems, we shall find all frozen and made rigid with intellect."[13] In addition, Greville's work as biographer made it easy to patronize him, an attitude also echoed in subsequent scholarship. Landor remarked that he "had the virtue and good-sense to found his chief distinction" on his friendship with Sidney.[14]

The romantic dislike of the rational combined with the romantic perception of poetic power established the ambivalent tone of most Victorian criticism, which is generally characterized by assertions of distaste and grudging admissions of value. Gosse saw Greville as a "solitary phenomenon . . . a kind of marsupial in our poetical zoology," and called his verse "unsympathetic and unattractive, yet far too original and well-sustained to be overlooked."[15] Saintsbury was more severe on "the strangely repellent character of Brooke's thought," but later acknowledged the technical achievement of *Caelica's* metrics, and credited Gre-

---

*Jonson* (London, 1831), p. 515, and by Grosart, II, vi–vii; Horace Walpole, *A Catalogue of the Royal and Noble Authors of England, Scotland, and Ireland . . . Enlarged and Continued . . . by Thomas Park* (London, 1806), pp. 220–21, 230–31; Charles Lamb, *Specimens of the English Dramatic Poets* (London, 1808), p. 296, who is quoted by Grosart, II, xvii, by Hugh de Sélincourt in *The Cambridge History of English Literature* (London, 1909), IV, 160, and approved by Saintsbury in *A History of Elizabethan Literature* (London, 1887), p. 99. Both Lamb and Phillips are quoted with approval by Edmund Gosse, *The Jacobean Poets* (New York, 1894), pp. 195, 198.

[12] *The Complete Works,* ed. P. P. Howe (London, 1931), VI, 231; XVII, 123–24.

[13] Lamb, p. 296.

[14] *The Works and Life of Walter Savage Landor* (London, 1876), IV, 3.

[15] Pp. 194–95. W. J. Courthope, on the contrary, was quite able to overlook Greville's verse entirely in his very influential *History of English Poetry,* II (London, 1897).

ville with "central poetic heat."[16] Mrs. Ward was impressed by his "sheer power of mind," denied that either his subjects or his manner were those of "true poetry," and then admitted that "yet at bottom Lord Brooke had many of the poet's gifts."[17]

Since the turn of the century we have of course witnessed the numerous, but usually partial, movements of critical taste away from the romantic position that took the expression of "repellent" notions in rigorously logical structures to be unforgivably unpoetical. Such reaction was an obvious precondition for the popular revival of the metaphysicals. Long before Eliot, however, scholars were appreciating the intricate thought and the mockery of amorous convention in both Greville and Donne.[18] Croll's study, *The Works of Fulke Greville*, published in 1903, was the first attempt at a thorough understanding of the poet, an understanding which is reflected by Felix Schelling's later treatment of him in *English Literature during the Lifetime of Shakespeare* (1910).[19] Although today the realization that "many later sixteenth-century poets wrote some more or less metaphysical poetry"[20] is commonplace, the vogue for the metaphysicals has continued to focus more on those facets of the style that distinguish it from, rather than on those that link it to, the earlier poetry in the plain style.

But despite this distinction, Greville, like the metaphysicals, now enjoys a higher reputation than he has in any period since his own age. The changing taste that has placed him there may be gauged by comparing the extent and nature of his representation in two British anthologies typical of their respective periods. In *A Pageant of Elizabethan Poetry*, compiled by Arthur Symons in 1906, the lyrics of Campion and Herrick greatly outnumber those of any other poet. Three well-selected lyrics from *Caelica* are included (Sonnets 4, 52, 22), all of which employ the ornate style, two of them with varying degrees of irony. In *English Poetry 1550–1660*, edited by Fred Inglis in 1965, the lyrics of Greville outnumber those of Campion and Herrick put together. None of his ornate poems is included; instead the emphasis is on the great religious lyrics and the more ironic, bitter, and cynical secular ones. The nature and extent of this representation is approximately the same in a recent

---

[16] *A History of Elizabethan Literature*, p. 99; *A History of English Prosody*, II, 91–92.

[17] *The English Poets*, ed. Thomas H. Ward (New York, 1906), I, 365–66.

[18] See Joseph E. Duncan, *The Revival of Metaphysical Poetry* (Minneapolis, 1959), pp. 113–15.

[19] Pp. 125, 305. William Frost's *Fulke Greville's "Caelica": An Evaluation* (1942) deserves credit as a sympathetic appreciation designed to get Greville out from under the shadow of the romantically viewed Sidney.

[20] Duncan, p. 6, where he specifically mentions Greville's resemblance to Donne.

American collection, *English Renaissance Poetry* (1963), edited by John Williams.

The editors of both these recent anthologies specifically acknowledge their debt to the criticism of Winters. Douglas Peterson, a former student of Winters, whose book is an attempt to trace in detail the consequences of his theories for literary history, concisely summarizes the revaluation that has brought Greville into greater prominence:

> Recognition of the *plain* and *eloquent* traditions makes possible a more comprehensive and . . . a more accurate account of the evolution of the short poem, or lyric, in the sixteenth century than any previously proposed. It makes clear . . . that the domestication of the sonnet and English Petrarchism, which the standard literary histories have always stressed as being of central importance, are only minor events within a larger context of developments, and that the grouping of Tudor poets by Lewis into a "Drab" and a "Golden" school is arbitrary and at the expense of major continuities. Furthermore, it locates precedents for Donne's anti-Petrarchan sentiments that qualify his position as an innovator and identify him with an anti-courtly movement that is nearly a century old.[21]

This revaluation, while having its own drawbacks (which will be discussed below), has nonetheless suggested lines of inquiry that seem important to pursue. And if Greville is not yet as well known as he perhaps deserves to be, the critical framework Winters outlined has at least provided a context in which Greville's claims to attention may be seriously considered. Most importantly, perhaps, the context has facilitated such consideration by stimulating the reprinting of Greville's text, making *Caelica* in its entirety now fully available in the general market.[22] I have tried to treat the lyrics throughout this study in such a way as to demonstrate the dimension and the resonance they gain by being read as a sequence, as a collection for whose arrangement the poet was himself responsible.

The adequate appreciation of Greville's achievement requires the discussion of three critical problems: two arise from the Wintersian revaluation, the other from the nature of Greville's writing.

The first is the least troublesome, and is the obvious and natural result of a polemical view that seeks to expose what it regards as error. In order to cry up the plain style, it was necessary both to cry down the ornate, labeling it decorative and trivial, and at the same time to acknowledge

---

[21] P. 349.

[22] In *Selected Poems of Fulke Greville*, ed. Thom Gunn, who was also a sometime student of Winters; and in *Five Courtier Poets of the English Renaissance*, ed. Robert M. Bender (New York, 1967), who places many of Greville's lyrics with "the finest Elizabethan poetry" (p. 479).

the technical resources that its experiments made available to the plain. But since the prime object of the argument was to establish the superiority of the plain style, the functional potentialities of the ornate per se were ruled out and its contribution minimized. The ironic result of the polemic for Greville is that it underestimates his range and flexibility, in not allowing for a full awareness of his manipulation of the structures and diction of the ornate style.[23] Winters' polemic, however, has gradually come to be employed in scholarship—in conjunction with an increased sophistication in matters of Renaissance rhetoric and literary theory—as an exploratory tool rather than as an argumentative weapon. So used, it has revealed the depth and variety of purposes in the ornate style, and made it possible to perceive the interaction (and not merely the opposition) of both styles in the work of individual poets.[24] For example, one recent critic uses Winters' and Peterson's approach not "to assert the superiority of the plain style to the eloquent style," since "each has its own virtues and corresponding defects," but rather to point out that if Greville's best lyrics are not like those of Sidney or Spenser, "in their own stark fashion they are *as* good as the most eloquent products of his contemporaries."[25]

If the polemical revaluation furnishes one perspective that requires a correction for its narrowness, it also offers another that requires the same correction for its breadth. This is the whole conception of the plain style as a historically changing, but always distinct, phenomenon. It is much more visible in Peterson's development of Winters' theory than in Winters' own exposition of it. The latter, although it took a historical approach and was intended as a historical corrective, was primarily critical; the historical correction was offered in terms of the critical values by which Winters defined the plain style. Having defined it thus, Winters could freely juxtapose Greville with Wallace Stevens or Robert Bridges, as well as with Jonson or Herbert, to argue for the merits of the style and for the reorganization of literary history on its terms. He did not therefore necessarily have to assert it as a historical continuity; it was treated, in short, more as value than as fact.

Peterson, however, wants to have the plain style equally as fact and value, as a single identifiable attitude toward experience that can be

[23] This kind of underestimation is apparent in the otherwise laudatory view of Greville taken by a British Wintersian, Fred Inglis: *The Elizabethan Poets: The Making of English Poetry from Wyatt to Ben Jonson* (London, 1969), pp. 101–12.

[24] Montgomery credits Winters' historical approach and uses it to demonstrate that Sidney's style is far from dysfunctional. Rudenstine uses it to show that Sidney employed both styles, each of which can only be understood in relation to the other.

[25] Peter Heidtmann, "The Lyrics of Fulke Greville," *Ohio University Review*, X(1968), 41.

traced from the Middle Ages up to Donne, and even beyond. So far as this attitude can be demonstrated, Peterson demonstrates it well, but he extends it to the point where it becomes both historically inaccurate and critically untenable. By the time the native medieval plain style emerges from its modification by the continental ornate, he must admit that "stylistically, the contemplative or noncourtly tradition is no longer so easily identified."[26] Indeed it is not: we are hard put to detect lines of historical development that can connect the *styles* of Donne and, say, Barnabe Googe. When the historical interaction of the plain and ornate styles thus erases the individual continuity of the former, Peterson, seeking to preserve it, is forced to appeal to ever more generalized criteria. Two of these are: the examination of feelings in terms of their motives, and the use of logical exposition; and it is on these grounds that he asks us to see Greville using the same "methods of approaching religious experience" as Donne, Herbert, Vaughan, and Crashaw.[27] First, it is doubtful that the latter two poets used these "methods" to any great extent; second, even if they all did, the "methods" are so broad that to say so is to tell us very little about the poetry under consideration, and to ignore all the other palpable differences in its movement and effect. The criteria Peterson adduces here may be critical—they might serve to argue that all these men wrote good poems—but they are not historical: their application results in fact in a total obliteration of historical distinctions. The criteria that he implies elsewhere are not even critical. As he passes beyond the point where real historical discrimination between the styles is possible, he insistently repeats such expansive key terms as "honest," "plain" (now wholly cut loose from its moorings in some single and specific style), "serious," and "the idiom of integrity." In so doing, he comes perilously close to the old notion of "sincerity," partly as a test of literary merit, and partly as glue to hold the splintering plain style together. The terms seem to slide from describing the poems to making dubious postulations about the poets' actual motives, curiously perpetuating the Victorian hostility to literary artifice in the quest for personal biography.[28]

The overexpanded view of the plain style thus ironically prevents us from making the kinds of discriminations that the original conception of it made possible, discriminations that are essential if we are to arrive at an accurate historical understanding of a poet's manner of writing. The general historical development of the sixteenth-century English

[26] P. 355.

[27] P. 283.

[28] See, for example, his apparent acceptance of Sidney's claims to plainness and honesty (p. 354), and his assertion of the "social" significance of the plain style (pp. 356–57).

lyric reveals a mixture and a modification of both the plain and the ornate styles—a mixture determined in each particular case by whatever reasons a poet may have had for employing either or both. To see Greville as a plain stylist is incomplete insofar as that perspective neglects his use of the ornate style and fails to provide some account of how and why his use of both styles differs from that of other poets.[29]

I have sought to give such an account by investigating his lyrics in terms of what J. V. Cunningham has called "principles of order," that is, "schemes which direct the production of works." Although these include specifically literary conventions, they also derive from theology, logic, rhetoric, or psychology, and consist of abstractions

which belong as abstractions to the province of philosophy and in exemplification to the province of fiction. But all these, though they may be regarded as material or conclusions in other branches of endeavor, are for the man who writes primarily the methods by which he both finds what he has to say and says it in succession and with appropriate emphasis and development.

On this basis, Cunningham defines "the structure of a poem" as "the principles of order that determine it and their inter-relationships with each other."[30] Poetic structure thus becomes a series of selective limitations, of choices among the principles—which include modes of technical presentation—current in a given tradition. To describe structure in this sense is to consider both the principles which are selected (taking notice of those which are not) and the way in which, in the course of the poem, they are related to each other. Criticism in this sense I take to be an evaluation of the appropriateness of these relationships, an attempt to determine how fine an adjustment exists between the selected principles, or between what I have more loosely called themes and techniques.

The advantage of such an approach is that it compels simultaneous consideration both of what a poet works with and of how he works with it, and thus describes how he is distinguished from the given traditions of his age as well as how he is related to them. Applied to Greville, it shows us his mastery of the traditional style in both its ornate and plain forms, and explains his particular preference for the latter in terms of his refinement of rhetorical, logical, and prosodic principles which were basically grounded in a conception of experience provided by religious ones. The approach also demonstrates that he was frequently capable of writing great poems, whose ordering principles are so exactly adjusted

[29] Trimpi supplies just such an account for Jonson in terms of Renaissance interpretations of classical rhetoric, and can therefore differentiate Jonson's use of the plain style from that of Raleigh, Greville, and Donne: *Ben Jonson's Poems*, ch. VI.

[30] *Tradition and Poetic Structure* (Denver, 1960), pp. 19–21.

as to provide a precise, complex, and moving apprehension of experience
—to provide, in other words, the full meaning that results from the careful observance of decorum. But this statement, which is wholly valid
within the context of the approach, where the historical interpretation of
meaning is coextensive with aesthetic appreciation of it,[31] raises the third
and final problem, which is simply that of appreciating the *kind* of apprehension Greville offers, of taking pleasure in the operation of principles of order which are so remote from the traditions of our own time.

Part of the problem has been touched upon before. The relevance of
this part (which concerns the nonliterary principles of order per se) to
criticism has been identified by R. S. Crane:

> The difference between a tragedy or . . . comedy or novel or lyric poem and a
> merely sensational, melodramatic, sentimental, or fanciful work is more than
> a difference in form and technique. It is a difference we cannot very well state
> without bringing in distinctions between true, comprehensive, or at least
> mature conceptions of things and false, partial, arbitrary, or simple-minded
> conceptions; and it is in terms of precisely such distinctions, of course, that
> we tend to differentiate among . . . constructions in philosophy, distinct as
> these are from literary constructions in method and intent.[32]

It is inevitable that literary criticism, in seeking to judge a fiction which
is constructed partly on nonfictional principles, should at some point
consider the intrinsic value of those principles. Certainly our opinion
(whether we consider it or not) of their value will color our literary
judgment of the fiction: the history of criticism itself is ample evidence
of this natural—conscious or unconscious—operation of human prejudice.

Despite its obviousness, this fact has been faced by few modern critics;
indeed, there is a tendency in much modern critical theory to deny that
it exists.[33] We are presumably intended to rise above our prejudices
simply by forgetting about them and by ignoring those aspects of a work
of literature which call them into play. We are invited to regard literature as existing in a vacuum, as operating within a closed system according to self-generated and self-sustaining principles. It is perhaps
possible that some literature does; it is unquestionable that Renaissance
literature does not. More generally, however, to bar criticism from con-

[31] I am not at all sure that, as Cunningham impressively argues (pp. 263–70),
these are always and necessarily identical.

[32] "Literature, Philosophy and the History of Ideas," *Modern Philology*, LII
(1954), 82.

[33] Winters faced it directly and dogmatically, which accounts in large part for
the general unpopularity, until recently, of his views. The whole tradition that
sees the ethical and aesthetic judgments as inseparable has been defended by Keith
F. McKean, *The Moral Measure of Literature* (Denver, 1961), in which he gives
a useful discussion of Winters, both comparing him to and distinguishing him
from the neo-Humanists Irving Babbitt and P. E. More.

sidering the problem as stated by Crane is to blur and curtail one of its principal functions, which is evaluation. It is to refuse criticism its most direct and efficient means of saying why some poems are better than others, or why some should be anthologized or taught before others. For example, I have tried to demonstrate that Greville was a consummate master of the formal and technical skills of his craft; so were Campion and Herrick. But even the most copious of purely "literary" arguments could hardly justify the change of taste in the last sixty years that has given the religious lyrics of Greville an implicitly higher place than the exquisite performances of the other two poets. It can be justified most precisely by an appeal to the "conceptions of things" that Greville offers, to the intrinsic worth of those conceptions in terms of depth, complexity, maturity, comprehensiveness, accuracy, or whatever.

I have of course assumed this worth, and have from time to time suggested what I conceive it to be. It was certainly axiomatic for Greville, who believed with his friend Daniel that only "matter" could satisfy the "judicious." It is not my place, nor within my competence, to defend the "matter" in detail; the reader will judge it for himself. I wish merely to urge that such a judgment of the value of extraliterary propositions should be made, that it is to some extent a critical judgment, and that it be recognized as such.

There is, however, another part of the problem which is really antecedent to this judgment, and which has to do with the way in which the extraliterary propositions are presented and perceived in the work of literature. Before we can judge them with any degree of fairness, we must be willing to entertain them; the work, in other words, must allow for a kind of suspension of disbelief in propositions whose extraliterary statement might permit us to ignore them. In the Aristotelian terms of the Renaissance, the commonplace must be given moving power by its form. The point is nicely illustrated by an anecdote concerning Oliver Wendell Holmes. The great jurist, a notorious agnostic and freethinker, was teased by his wife when she saw him reading a volume of Dante. "Why, Wendell," she said, "how can you read about heaven and hell? I thought you didn't *believe* in heaven and hell." "My dear," he replied, "I do when I read Dante."

The question becomes, then, how can the compressed abstractions of Greville's best lyrics secure the same imaginative assent that generations of cultivated readers have granted to the much broader epic narrations of Dante or of Milton? One way that they can do so, as I have been concerned to point out, is by being examined largely in terms of their emotional consequences, by being employed to judge experience that is universally accessible. Another way is simply that which has been universally acknowledged, even by those critics who do not much like it:

by the "sheer power of mind" which distinguishes their presentation.

To argue for the poetic value of direct intellectual effort, of rational discourse proceeding by logic, is still unfashionable; but it has been ventured on by one eminent modern critic as follows:

I do not doubt that the language of poetry is very largely that of indirection and symbolism. But it is not only that. Poetry is closer to rhetoric than we today are willing to admit; syntax plays a greater part in it than our current theory grants, and syntax connects poetry with rational thought, for, as Hegel says, "grammar, in its extended and consistent form"—by which he means syntax—"is the work of thought, which makes its categories distinctly visible therein." And those poets of our time who make the greatest impress upon us are those who are most aware of rhetoric, which is to say, of the intellectual content of their work.[34]

The ground of the argument is the conceptual nature of language itself, a recognition that the use of language, even in its most poetic indirection, is fundamentally the use of the mind.[35] What this leads to, for Trilling, is a response to "intellectual cogency," whether in poetry or in "ideas" per se, which constitutes an aesthetic pleasure. He further defines this pleasure as "enjoying the power of grace of a mind without admitting the rightness of its intention or conclusion."[36] For appreciation, this is all that is required; for criticism, we need also to see that "delight comes from the wisdom expressed as well as from the expression of wisdom."[37] This kind of delight may be rare enough, but we have all surely been rewarded by it from time to time as we have actively followed the exertions in language of a serious thinker. It depends precisely on the notion of "cogency": we delight not merely in the mind moving, but in its getting somewhere; not merely in its adroit manipulation of masses of recalcitrant or conflicting material, but in its manipulating them into some mentally coherent shape. We feel not only exhilarated by the effort, but illuminated by its result. If it is not a feeling that we commonly associate with poetry, that is, as Trilling suggests, our loss as well as poetry's.

Greville's lyrics can offer us the pleasures of cogency in a direct and

[34] Lionel Trilling, *The Liberal Imagination* (London, 1951), p. 290. The poets he has in mind are Yeats and Eliot.

[35] This recognition was of course taken for granted by the Renaissance as a part of its classical heritage. It was tirelessly insisted upon by Winters, and is indeed the central principle in his theory. From it he deduced the corollary that since "a poem is a statement in language about a human experience . . . this statement will be more or less rational or at least apprehensible in rational terms, or else the medium will be violated," *Forms of Discovery*, p. xvii.

[36] P. 291.

[37] Norman Foerster, "The Esthetic and Ethical Judgments," in *The Intent of the Critic*, ed. Donald A. Stauffer (Princeton, N. J., 1941), p. 75.

highly pressurized form. To appreciate them we have only to allow poetry a resource possible to any use of language, and to see this resource not as frozen rigidity but as potential liberation, as one of the few and fallible means we have to explore the inner spaces of our nature. For what these pleasures finally imply involves yet another principle of Renaissance orthodoxy and modern heresy: they imply that we delight in learning and that poetry can teach.

This ancient conviction has received a restatement for modern taste from Edmund Wilson, who applies it specifically to lyric poetry, which he defines as "a pattern imposed on the expression of a feeling." The effect of the pattern is to reduce the chaos of actual experience "to something orderly, symmetrical and pleasing. . . . And this control of his emotion by the poet has the effect at second hand of making it easier for the reader to manage his own emotions." To be cured of an "ache of disorder," to be relieved "of some oppressive burden of uncomprehended events," is what satisfies us in each "victory of the human intellect"—in philosophy or in poetry.[38]

What, therefore, the poet communicates, and what we perceive with aesthetic pleasure, is nothing more nor less than an understanding of experience and of ourselves. There are to be sure many ways of understanding, just as there are many kinds of poetry, many kinds of order that can be imposed. Greville's is one kind; indeed, it is the most obvious kind, and for this reason possibly the most efficient. For to express emotions as they emerge from a chain of reasoning is not only to discipline and comprehend those that we may share, but also to enable us to become aware of those that we may not. Our own feelings are often sufficiently baffling; those of others which do not coincide with our own, which are elicited by different objects and formed by different experiences, are wholly so, unless their motives are communicated to us by some mental process which is mutually known or knowable. And to obtain pleasure in the process as it unfolds in a poem is one way by which we may be led to an awareness of what is beyond the narrow limits of our actual experience, or indeed of what is within it had we only noticed. The effect of such poetry is to get us out of ourselves, to enlarge our perception of the world by providing through the understanding not only an understanding but a full, sympathetic, and disinterested contact with other human beings. In whatever guise it presents itself, this is a precious gift: it is the gift of civilization, and we cannot afford to refuse it.

[38] "The Historical Interpretation of Literature," in *The Intent of the Critic*, pp. 60–61.

# Bibliography

I. Works by and about Greville

A. Works by Greville

Greville, Sir Fulke, first Baron Brooke. *Life of Sir Philip Sidney*. Ed. Nowell Smith. Oxford, 1907.
———. *Poems and Dramas*. Ed. Geoffrey Bullough. 2 vols. New York, 1945.
———. *The Remains: Being Poems of Monarchy and Religion*. Ed. G. A. Wilkes. Oxford, 1965.
———. *The Works in Verse and Prose Complete*. Ed. A. B. Grosart. 4 vols. London, 1870.

B. Works about Greville

Bender, Robert M., ed. *Five Courtier Poets of the English Renaissance*. New York, 1967.
*Biographia Britannica*. Vol. III. London, 1750.
Bolton, Edmund. *Hypercritica*. Ed. Anthony Hall. Oxford, 1722.
Bullough, Geoffrey. "Fulke Greville, First Lord Brooke." *Modern Language Review*, XXVIII (1933), 1–20.
———. *Mirror of Minds: Changing Psychological Beliefs in English Poetry*. London, 1962.
———. "Sénèque, Greville et le jeune Shakespeare." In *Les Tragédies de Sénèque et le Théatre de la Renaissance*. Ed. Jean Jacquot. Paris, 1964.
Buncombe, Marie Helen. "Fulke Greville's *A Treatie of Humane Learning*: A Critical Analysis." Ph. D. dissertation, Stanford University, 1966.
Buxton, John. *Sir Philip Sidney and the English Renaissance*. London and New York, 1954.
*Cambridge History of English Literature, The*. Ed. A. W. Ward and A. R. Waller. Vols. III and IV. Cambridge, 1909.
Campbell, Thomas, ed. *Specimens of the British Poets*. Philadelphia, 1853.
Carter, Burnham, Jr. "The Intellectual Background of Fulke Greville." Ph.D. dissertation, Stanford University, 1955.

Coleridge, Samuel Taylor. *Coleridge's Miscellaneous Criticism*. Ed. T. M. Raysor. London, 1936.

———. *The Poems*. Ed. Ernest Hartley Coleridge. Vol. I. Oxford, 1912.

[Cooper, Elizabeth, ed.] *The Muses Library*. Vol. I. London, 1737.

Croll, Morris W. *The Works of Fulke Greville*. Philadelphia, 1903.

Daiches, David. *A Crucial History of English Literature*. 2 vols. London, 1960.

Davie, Donald. *Purity of Diction in English Verse*. London, 1952.

Duncan, Joseph E. *The Revival of Metaphysical Poetry*. Minneapolis, 1959.

Elton, Oliver. *The English Muse*. London, 1933.

Farmer, Norman, Jr. "Fulke Greville and the Poetic of the Plain Style." *Texas Studies in Literature and Language*, XI (1969), 657–71.

Frost, William. *Fulke Greville's "Caelica": An Evaluation*. Brattleboro, Vt., 1942.

"Fulke Greville, Lord Brooke," *Times Literary Supplement*, August 30, 1928, pp. 609–10.

Gosse, Edmund. *The Jacobean Poets*. New York, 1894.

Greg, W. W. "Notes on Old Books." *The Library*, VII (1922), 217–19.

Gunn, Thom, ed. *Selected Poems of Fulke Greville*. London, 1968.

Hazlitt, William. *The Complete Works*. Ed. P. P. Howe. Vols. VI and XVII. London, 1931.

Heidtmann, Peter. "The Lyrics of Fulke Greville." *Ohio University Review*, X (1968), 28–41.

Inglis, Fred. *The Elizabethan Poets: The Making of English Poetry from Wyatt to Ben Jonson*. London, 1969.

———, ed. *English Poetry 1550–1660*. London, 1965.

Jacquot, Jean. "Religion et raison d'état dans l'oeuvre de Fulke Greville." *Etudes Anglaises*, V (1952), 211–22.

John, Lisle Cecil. *The Elizabethan Sonnet Sequences: Studies in Conventional Conceits*. New York, 1938.

Kocher, Paul H. *Science and Religion in Elizabethan England*. San Marino, Calif., 1953.

Lamb, Charles, ed. *Specimens of the English Dramatic Poets*. London, 1808.

Landor, Walter Savage. *The Works and Life*. Vol. IV. London, 1876.

Langbaine, Gerard. *An Account of the English Dramatic Poets*. Oxford, 1691.

[Lloyd, David.] *State-worthies; or, The Statesmen and Favourites of England since the Reformation*. 2d ed. London, 1670.

Maclean, Hugh N. "Fulke Greville and E. K." *English Language Notes*, I (1963), 90–100.

———. "Fulke Greville on War." *Huntington Library Quarterly*, XXI (1958), 95–109.

———. "Greville's 'Poetic.' " *Studies in Philology*, LXI (1964), 170–91.

Mahoney, John L. "Donne and Greville: Two Christian Attitudes toward the Renaissance Idea of Mutability and Decay." *College Language Association Journal*, V (1962), 203–12.

Morris, Ivor. "The Tragic Vision of Fulke Greville." *Shakespeare Survey*, XIV (1961), 66–75.

Mourgues, Odette de. *Metaphysical, Baroque and Précieux Poetry*. Oxford, 1953.

Newman, Franklin B. "Sir Fulke Greville and Giordano Bruno: A Possible Echo." *Philological Quarterly*, XXIX (1950), 367–74.

O'Brien, Gordon Worth. *Renaissance Poetics and the Problem of Power*. Chicago, 1956.

Orsini, Napoleone. *Fulke Greville tra il Mondo e Dio*. Milan, 1941.

Peterson, Douglas L. *The English Lyric from Wyatt to Donne*. Princeton, N.J., 1967.

Phillips, Edward. *Theatrum Poetarum*. London, 1675.

Praz, Mario. Review of Orsini, *Fulke Greville*, and Utz, *Anschauungen*. *English Studies*, XXX (1949), 270–73.

Rees, Joan. *Fulke Greville, Lord Brooke, 1554–1628: A Critical Biography*. Berkeley, 1971.

Reeves, James, and Seymour-Smith, Martin, eds. *A New Canon of English Poetry*. New York, 1969.

Rosier, James L. "The Chain of Sin and Privation in Elizabethan Literature." Ph.D. dissertation, Stanford University, 1957.

Saintsbury, George. *A History of Elizabethan Literature*. London, 1887.

———. *A History of English Prosody*. Vol. II. London, 1908.

"Samuel Daniel and Fulke Greville." *Times Literary Supplement*, June 5, 1930, p. 475.

Schelling, Felix E. *English Literature during the Lifetime of Shakespeare*. New York, 1910.

Scholes, Kenneth Andre. "The Elizabethan Devotional Lyric." Ph.D. dissertation, University of California, Berkeley, 1956.

Schultz, Howard. *Milton and Forbidden Knowledge*. New York, 1955.

Sells, A. Lytton. *The Italian Influence in English Poetry, from Chaucer to Southwell*. Bloomington, Ind., 1955.

Smith, Sir Thomas. *Sir Thomas Smithes Voyage and Entertainment in Rushia*. London, 1605.

Southey, Robert, ed. *Select Works of the British Poets from Chaucer to Jonson*. London, 1831.

Symons, Arthur, ed. *A Pageant of Elizabethan Poetry*. London, 1906.

Trimpi, Wesley. *Ben Jonson's Poems: A Study of the Plain Style*. Stanford, Calif., 1962.

Utz, Hans Werner. *Die Anschauungen über Wissenschaft und Religion im Werke Fulke Grevilles*. Bern, 1948.

Walpole, Horace. *A Catalogue of the Royal and Noble Authors of England, Scotland, and Ireland . . . Enlarged and Continued . . . by Thomas Park*. 2d ed., 1759; rpt. London, 1806.

Ward, Thomas Humphry, ed. *The English Poets*. Vol. I. New York, 1906.

Warton, Thomas. *The History of English Poetry*. Ed. W. C. Hazlitt. Vol. IV. London, 1871.

Whitaker, Virgil K. *Francis Bacon's Intellectual Milieu*. Los Angeles, 1962.

Wilkes, G. A. "The Sequence of Writings of Fulke Greville, Lord Brooke." *Studies in Philology*, LVI (1959), 489–503.

Williams, John, ed. *English Renaissance Poetry*. New York, 1963.

Williamson, George. *The Proper Wit of Poetry*. London, 1961.

Wilson, Elkin Calhoun. *England's Eliza*. Cambridge, Mass., 1939.

Winstanley, William. *The Lives of the Most Famous English Poets*. London, 1687.

Winters, Yvor. *Forms of Discovery: Critical and Historical Essays on the Forms of the Short Poem in English*. Chicago, 1967.

——. "The 16th Century Lyric in England." *Poetry*, LIII (Feb., Mar., 1939), 258–72, 320–25; LIV (Apr., 1939), 35–51.

Yates, Frances A. *John Florio*. Cambridge, 1934.

——. Letter to *Times Literary Supplement*. August 7, 1937, p. 576.

II. Other Contemporary Sources

A. Religious Texts

Andrewes, Lancelot. *Ninety-Six Sermons*. Vol. I. Oxford, 1841.

Calvin, John. *Commentaries*. Trans. and ed. Joseph Haroutunian and Louise P. Smith. Philadelphia, 1958.

——. *Institutes of the Christian Religion*. Trans. John Allen. Ed. Benjamin B. Warfield. 2 vols. Philadelphia, 1936.

Coverdale, Myles. *Remains*. Ed. George Pearson. Cambridge, 1846.

Downame, John. *A Guide to Godlynesse*. London, [1622.]

Greenham, Richard. *The Workes*. 2d ed., London, 1599.

Hooker, Richard. *The Works*. Ed. John Keble. 3 vols. Oxford, 1845.

More, Thomas. *A Dialogue of Comfort against Tribulation*. Ed. Leland Miles. Bloomington and London, 1965.

Perkins, William. *The Workes*. 3 vols. London, 1612–13.

Rogers, Nehemiah. *The True Convert*. London, 1632.

Rogers, Richard. *Seven Treatises*. 5th ed., London, 1630.

Rogers, Richard, and Samuel Ward. *Two Elizabethan Puritan Diaries.* Ed. M. M. Knappen. Chicago, 1933.


B. Rhetorical, Literary, and Other Texts

Agrippa, Henrie Cornelius. *Of the Vanitie and Uncertaintie of Artes and Sciences.* Trans. Ja[mes] San[dford]. London, 1569.

*Arbor of Amorous Devices, 1597, The.* Ed. Hyder Edward Rollins. Cambridge, Mass., 1936.

Ascham, Roger. *The Whole Works.* Ed. J. A. Giles. 3 vols. London, 1864–65.

Bacon, Francis. *The Works.* Ed. James Spedding, Robert Leslie Ellis, and Douglas Denon Heath. 14 vols. London, 1857–74.

*Brittons Bowre of Delights, 1591.* Ed. Hyder Edward Rollins. Cambridge, Mass., 1933.

Browne, Sir Thomas. *Religio Medici and Other Works.* Ed. L. C. Martin. Oxford, 1964.

Davies, Sir John. *The Poems.* Facsimile rpt. Ed. Clare Howard. New York, 1941.

Donne, John. *The Divine Poems.* Ed. Helen Gardner. Oxford, 1952.

*Elizabethan Lyrics,* Ed. Norman Ault. 2d. ed., 1949, rpt. Capricorn Books, New York, 1960.

Fraunce, Abraham. *The Arcadian Rhetorike.* Ed. Ethel Seaton. Oxford, 1950.

Gascoigne, George. *Certayne Notes of Instruction in English Verse.* Ed. Edward Arber. London, 1868.

*Gorgeous Gallery of Gallant Inventions (1578), A.* Ed. Hyder E. Rollins. Cambridge, Mass., 1926.

Herbert, George. *The Works.* Ed. F. E. Hutchinson. Oxford, 1941.

Hoskins, John. *Directions for Speech and Style.* Ed. Hoyt H. Hudson. Princeton, N. J., 1935.

Howell, Thomas. *Poems.* Ed. A. B. Grosart. London, 1879.

Moffet, Thomas. *Nobilis; or, A View of the Life and Death of a Sidney.* Ed. and trans. Virgil B. Heltzel and Hoyt H. Hudson. San Marino, 1940.

Montaigne, Michel de. *The Essayes.* Trans. John Florio. Modern Library. New York, n. d.

*Paradise of Dainty Devices (1576–1606), The.* Ed. Hyder Edward Rollins. Cambridge, Mass., 1927.

Peacham, Henry. *The Garden of Eloquence (1593).* Facsimile rpt. Ed. William G. Crane. Gainesville, Fla., 1954.

*Phoenix Nest, 1593, The.* Ed. Hyder Edward Rollins. Cambridge, Mass., 1931.

*Poetical Rhapsody, 1602–1621, A.* 2 vols. Ed. Hyder Edward Rollins. Cambridge, Mass., 1931–32.

Puttenham, George. *The Arte of English Poesie*. Ed. Gladys Doidge Will-cock and Alice Walker. Cambridge, 1936.

Rainolds, John. *Oratio in Laudem Artis Poeticae*. Ed. and trans. William Ringler and Walter Allen, Jr. Princeton, N.J., 1940.

Ramus, Peter. *The Logike*. Trans. [Roland MacIlmaine]. London, 1581.

Sextus Empiricus. *Outlines of Pyrrhonism*. Vol. I. Trans. R. G. Bury. Loeb Classical Library. London, 1933.

Sidney, Sir Philip. *The Complete Works*. Ed. Albert Feuillerat. 4 vols. Cambridge, 1922–26.

———. *The Poems*. Ed. William A. Ringler, Jr. Oxford, 1962.

*Tottel's Miscellany (1557–1587)*. Ed. Hyder Edward Rollins. 2 vols. Cambridge, Mass., 1928.

Turberville, George. *Epitaphes, Epigrams, Songs and Sonets*. London, 1567.

Walton, Isaac. *Lives*. Ed. George Saintsbury. London, 1927.

Watson, Thomas. *The Hekatompathia (1582)*. Facsimile rpt. Ed. S. K. Heninger, Jr. Gainesville, Fla., 1964.

Wilson, Thomas. *The Arte of Rhetorique (1553)*. Facsimile rpt. Ed. Robert Hood Bowers. Gainesville, Fla., 1962.

Wyatt, Sir Thomas. *Collected Poems*. Ed. Kenneth Muir. London, 1949.


III. Secondary Sources


A. Literary History and Criticism


Adams, Robert P. "Bald Bawdry and Open Manslaughter: The English New Humanist Attack on Medieval Romance." *Huntington Library Quarterly*, XXIII (1959), 33–48.

Atkins, J. W. H. *English Literary Criticism: The Renascence*. 2d ed. London, 1951.

Baldwin, C. S. *Renaissance Literary Theory and Practice*. New York, 1939.

Baldwin, T. W. *William Shakespere's Small Latine and Lesse Greeke*. 2 vols. Urbana, Ill., 1944.

Briggs, W. D. "Political Ideas in Sidney's *Arcadia*." *Studies in Philology*, XXVIII (1931), 137–61.

Bush, Douglas. *English Literature in the Earlier Seventeenth Century*. 2d ed. New York, 1962.

Buxton, John. *Elizabethan Taste*. London, 1963.

Clark, Donald Lemen. "Ancient Rhetoric and English Renaissance Literature." *Shakespeare Quarterly*, II (1951), 195–204.

———. *Rhetoric and Poetry in the Renaissance*. New York, 1922.

Courthope, W. J. *A History of English Poetry*. Vol. II. London, 1897.

Crane, R. S. *The Languages of Criticism and the Structure of Poetry.* Toronto, 1953.

———. "Literature, Philosophy and the History of Ideas." *Modern Philology,* LII (1954), 76–83.

Cunningham, J. V. "Logic and Lyric." *Modern Philology,* LI (1953), 33–41.

———. *Tradition and Poetic Structure.* Denver, 1960.

Cruttwell, Patrick. *The Shakespearean Moment.* London, 1954.

Dickey, Franklin. "Collections of Songs and Sonnets." *Elizabethan Poetry.* Ed. John Russell Brown and Bernard Harris. London, 1960.

Duhamel, P. Albert. "Sidney's *Arcadia* and Elizabethan Rhetoric." *Studies in Philology,* XLV (1948), 134–50.

Eliot, T. S. *Elizabethan Essays.* London, 1934.

Ellis-Fermor, U. M. *The Jacobean Drama.* London, 1936.

Esch, Arno. *Englische Religiöse Lyrik des 17. Jahrhunderts.* Tübingen, 1955.

Foerster, Norman. "The Esthetic and Ethical Judgments." In *The Intent of the Critic.* Ed. Donald A. Stauffer. Princeton, N. J., 1941.

Forcione, Alban K. *Cervantes, Aristotle, and the "Persiles."* Princeton, N. J., 1970.

Forest, Louise C. Turner. "A Caveat for Critics against Invoking Elizabethan Psychology." *PMLA,* LXI (1946), 651–72.

Frye, Northrop. *Fables of Identity.* New York, 1963.

Guss, Donald L. *John Donne, Petrarchist.* Detroit, 1966.

Hamilton, A. C. "Sidney and Agrippa." *Review of English Studies,* VII (1956), 151–57.

Hardison, O. B., Jr. *The Enduring Monument: A Study of the Idea of Praise in Renaissance Literary Theory and Practice.* Chapel Hill, N. C., 1962.

Hart, Jeffrey. "Herbert's 'The Collar' Re-Read." *Boston University Studies in English,* V (1961), 65–73.

Howell, Wilbur Samuel. *Logic and Rhetoric in England, 1500–1700.* Princeton, N. J., 1956.

Kalstone, David. *Sidney's Poetry: Contexts and Interpretations.* Cambridge, Mass., 1965.

Levin, Harry. *Contexts of Criticism.* Cambridge, Mass., 1957.

Levy, F. J. "Sir Philip Sidney and the Idea of History." *Bibliothèque d'Humanisme et Renaissance,* XXVI (1964), 608–17.

Lewis, C. S. *English Literature in the Sixteenth Century.* New York, 1954.

McKean, Keith F. *The Moral Measure of Literature.* Denver, 1961.

McLuhan, Marshall. "Sight, Sound, and the Fury." *Commonweal,* LX (April, 1954), 7–11.

Martz, Louis L. *The Poetry of Meditation.* New Haven, 1954.

Miriam Joseph, Sister, C.S.C. *Shakespeare's Use of the Arts of Language.* New York, 1947.

Montgomery, Robert L., Jr. *Symmetry and Sense: The Poetry of Sir Philip Sidney*. Austin, Tex., 1961.

Murdock, Kenneth B. *Literature and Theology in Colonial New England*. Cambridge, Mass., 1949.

Nelson, Norman E. "Peter Ramus and the Confusion of Logic, Rhetoric, and Poetry." *University of Michigan Contributions in Modern Philology*, No. 2 (April, 1947).

Nicholson, Marjorie Hope. *The Breaking of the Circle: Studies in the Effect of the "New Science" upon Seventeenth-Century Poetry*. Rev. ed. New York, 1960.

Ong, Walter J., S. J. "Historical Backgrounds of Elizabethan and Jacobean Punctuation Theory." *PMLA*, LXIX (1944), 349–60.

——. "Tudor Writings on Rhetoric." *Studies in the Renaissance*, XV (1968), 39–69.

Robertson, Jean. "Sir Philip Sidney and His Poetry." *Elizabethan Poetry*. Ed. John Russell Brown and Bernard Harris. London, 1960.

Rubel, Veré L. *Poetic Diction in the English Renaissance*. New York, 1941.

Rudenstine, Neil L. *Sidney's Poetic Development*. Cambridge, Mass., 1967.

Sasek, Lawrence A. *The Literary Temper of the English Puritans*. Baton Rouge, La., 1961.

Scott, Janet G. *Les Sonnets Élisabéthains*. Paris, 1929.

Smith, A. J. "An Examination of Some Claims for Ramism." *Review of English Studies*, VII (1956), 349–59.

Smith, Hallett. *Elizabethan Poetry: A Study in Convention, Meaning, and Expression*. Cambridge, Mass., 1952.

Summers, Joseph. *George Herbert: His Religion and Art*. Cambridge, Mass., 1954.

Tayler, Edward William. *Nature and Art in Renaissance Literature*. London, 1964.

Thompson, John. *The Founding of English Metre*. New York and London, 1961.

Thorne, J. P. "A Ramistical Commentary on Sidney's *An Apologie for Poetrie*." *Modern Philology*, LIV (1957), 158–64.

Trilling, Lionel. *The Liberal Imagination*. London, 1951.

Tuve, Rosemond. *Elizabethan and Metaphysical Imagery*. Chicago, 1947.

——. *A Reading of George Herbert*. Chicago, 1952.

Vickers, Brian. *Classical Rhetoric in English Poetry*. London, 1970.

Watson, George. "Ramus, Miss Tuve, and the New Petromachia." *Modern Philology*, LV (1958), 259–62.

Wellek, René, and Austin Warren. *Theory of Literature*. 3d ed. New York, 1956.

White, Helen C. *English Devotional Literature [Prose], 1600–1640*. Madison, Wis., 1931.

——. *The Metaphysical Poets: A Study in Religious Experience*. New York, 1936.

Wilson, Edmund. "The Historical Interpretation of Literature." In *The Intent of the Critic*. Ed. Donald A. Stauffer. Princeton, N. J., 1941.

Wimsatt, William K., Jr., and Cleanth Brooks. *Literary Criticism: A Short History*. New York, 1957.

Wyld, Henry Cecil. *Studies in English Rhymes from Surrey to Pope*. London, 1923.


B. Intellectual History and Miscellaneous


Baker, Herschel. *The Wars of Truth*. Cambridge, Mass., 1952.

Bethell, S. L. *The Cultural Revolution in the Seventeenth Century*. London, 1951.

Brown, Norman O. *Life against Death: The Psychoanalytical Meaning of History*. Middletown, Conn., 1959.

Collinson, Patrick. *The Elizabethan Puritan Movement*. Berkeley and Los Angeles, 1967.

Curtis, Mark H. *Oxford and Cambridge in Transition, 1558–1642*. Oxford, 1959.

Daniels, George H., Jr. "Knowledge and Faith in the Thought of Cornelius Agrippa." *Bibliothèque d'Humanisme et Renaissance*, XXVI (1964), 326–40.

George, Charles H., and Katherine George. *The Protestant Mind of the English Reformation 1570–1640*. Princeton, N. J., 1961.

Haller, William. *The Rise of Puritanism*. New York, 1938.

Hill, Christopher. *Intellectual Origins of the English Revolution*. Oxford, 1965.

——. *Society and Puritanism in Pre-Revolutionary England*. London, 1964.

Hoopes, Robert. *Right Reason in the English Renaissance*. Cambridge, Mass., 1962.

Knappen, M. M. *Tudor Puritanism: A Chapter in the History of Idealism*. Chicago, 1957 (1st ed., 1939).

Langer, Susanne K. *Philosophy in a New Key*. 2d ed. Mentor Books. New York, 1951.

Macklem, Michael. *The Anatomy of the World: Relations between Natural and Moral Law from Donne to Pope*. Minneapolis, 1958.

Miller, Perry. *The New England Mind: The Seventeenth Century*. Cambridge, Mass., 1939.

Neale, J. E. *The Elizabethan House of Commons*. London, 1949.

——. *Queen Elizabeth I*. London, 1934.

New, John F. H. *Anglican and Puritan: The Basis of Their Opposition, 1558–1640*. London, 1964.

Niebuhr, Reinhold. *An Interpretation of Christian Ethics*. New York, 1935.

Ong, Walter J., S. J. *Ramus and Talon Inventory*. Cambridge, Mass., 1958.

——. *Ramus, Method, and the Decay of Dialogue*. Cambridge, Mass., 1958.

Popkin, Richard H. *The History of Skepticism from Erasmus to Descartes*. New York, 1964.

Porter, H. C. *Reformation and Reaction in Tudor Cambridge*. Cambridge, 1958.

Thoreau, Henry David. *Walden; or, Life in the Woods*. Signet Classics. New York, 1960.

# Index

Material in the footnotes is not included. Individual poems are indexed under their authors only where they receive more than passing mention.

# REPORTS ON TAXATION I

*Papers Relating to the United Kingdom*

## NICHOLAS KALDOR

HOLMES & MEIER PUBLISHERS, INC.
New York

First published in the United States of America 1980 by
Holmes & Meier Publishers, Inc.
30 Irving Place, New York, N.Y. 10003

**Library of Congress Cataloging in Publication Data**
Kaldor, Nicholas, 1908–
  Reports on taxation.

  (His Collected economic essays ; v. 7–8)
    CONTENTS: v. 1. Papers relating to the United
Kingdom.—v. 2. Papers relating to foreign governments.
    1. Taxation—Great Britain—Collected works.
    2. Taxation—Collected works. I. Title. II. Series.
  HJ2600.K34    1980      336.2′00941      78–31926

ISBN 0–8419–0296–8

Printed in Great Britain

# CONTENTS

# INTRODUCTION

The papers collected in this and the following volume relate to a distinct branch of my activities which occurred largely (though not wholly) in consequence of my appointment by Hugh Gaitskell (then Chancellor of the Exchequer) to be a member of the Royal Commission on the Taxation of Profits and Income in 1950. It was as a result of my work on this Commission that I acquired a certain fame (some would say, notoriety) as a tax expert and thus received numerous invitations – more than I could accept – to examine the system of taxation of various countries and make recommendations for reform: coupled with a request, in some cases, to suggest new ways of raising revenue. The latter, however, was an aspect which I regarded as subsidiary to the review of existing tax systems from the point of view of equity, impartiality (or even-handedness) and efficiency, both from an administrative point of view and in regard to its general economic effects.

Any "expertise" that I could genuinely claim in this field was largely the result of the education acquired during four years' work on the Royal Commission as a result of the thoroughness with which the multitudinous aspects of the problems of taxation were reviewed by that body. This, I think, was partly due to Lord Radcliffe, a man of exceptional intellectual powers, who became full-time Chairman of the Commission (after the resignation of its first Chairman, Lord Cohen) and who personally drafted both its interim and its final Reports; and partly to the numerous memoranda (some 400 in all) prepared for the Commission by the Board of Inland Revenue which provided first-rate analyses and summaries of the existing law and practice and of possible alternatives for improvement.[1]

The really important and intriguing problem, as I gradually discovered, concerned the question of how to ensure equality of treatment between taxpayers drawing their income from widely different sources. Most British economists writing on public finance had assumed, almost as a matter of course, that income tax is the best form of taxation (just as free trade was universally regarded as the best commercial policy) and that the British type income tax, which aggregated income from all sources, levied tax on the imputed income of householders, and gave preferential treatment to earned income, was the best form of income tax. There were differences of opinion on the rate of progression of taxation and how far a progressive system could be justified on "scientific" principles. But the more basic problem raised by the meaning of "income" and its definition for tax purposes was one which British writers on public finance – in contrast to German, Italian and American writers – had failed to consider in any depth.[2]

As a result of the consideration of particular issues concerning business profits and irregular receipts from property, I became aware that "taxable income" had a very different significance as between one kind of taxpayer and another – in the words of the minority report, "neither the public, nor the legislature, nor the Courts, are conscious of the extent to which the tax system, behind a façade of formal equity, metes out unequal treatment to different classes of the taxpaying community".

[1] The Board of Inland Revenue was not directly represented on the Commission, as it had been on the 1920 Royal Commission on the Income Tax, but it provided its Secretaries and background information in the form of special memoranda on each issue. Members of the Board were also available for questioning when necessary. It is a matter for regret that these memoranda were not published with the Final Report (with the exception of the memorandum on Capital Gains which was appended to the minority report) though they were made available to various libraries.

[2] Addison's famous Income Tax Act of 1803 (which remains up to the present the basis of British income taxation) did not provide any general definition of income for tax purposes but proceeded by the method of enumerating all the different kinds of receipts which constitute "income" or "gain" for tax purposes. However, the Act also included a final "sweeping-up" clause (the famous Clause VI of Schedule D) which made "any annual profit or gain" liable to tax which was not explicitly mentioned under any previous section of the Act. This procedure left the question whether a particular receipt was taxable or not a matter for the interpretation of the Courts, and over a century and a half a body of case law has been built up which has never been comprehensively codified.

It was in the course of grappling with the problem of finding the definition of income which is fair to all taxpayers that I came to the conclusion that the "ideal" definition of income presents some insoluble problems, most of which are connected with the measurement of net savings as a component of income; so that a tax which uses personal expenditure as a yardstick would secure a more equitable base for personal taxation than an income tax, however comprehensively income is defined for tax purposes. I put these ideas to my fellow members in a series of memoranda, and while the idea of a tax based on expenditure had a certain intrinsic appeal, the majority of the Commissioners (composed of businessmen, lawyers, accountants as well as some conservatively-minded economists) shied away from it when they got a clearer grasp of its implications; while the Chairman felt he would require further guidance on the terms of reference before he could allow any formal consideration of the issue. By that time, a Conservative Government had replaced the Labour Government, and the new Chancellor Mr. (now Lord) Butler felt that the consideration of a tax based on personal expenditure would widen the scope of the inquiry too much. I, therefore, decided to develop my ideas independently in a book written simultaneously with the report of the Commission so as to be able to publish it soon after the Commission completed its work.[1]

The remarkable feature of the work of the Commission was that, mainly as a result of the exemplary manner in which the Chairman conducted the discussions, the basic differences between those who wanted a fundamental clean-up of the tax system and those who preferred to leave things as they were, did not emerge until the final stages of the proceedings, so that the Commission was able to work as a team in reasonable harmony in consideration of a large number of complicated matters, the solution of which did not raise important issues of politics or class interest.

However, in the final stages of the discussion when the Report

---

[1] *An Expenditure Tax*, London, Allen & Unwin, 1955. As I explained in the Preface of that book, for administrative reasons I could only recommend the introduction of an expenditure tax as a replacement for surtax (i.e. the higher-rate bands of income tax), so that the recommendations made in the book and in the minority report of the Royal Commission should be regarded as complementary to each other and not as alternatives.

was largely in draft, I found myself in a position of near-isolation on all the major issues on which the great majority of the Commission took a negative stand despite the fact that earlier discussions established a clear presumption in favour of reform. The most important of these issues was the taxation of capital gains, but there were a host of others—such as the difference in treatment of expenses as between Schedule D and E taxpayers, the rules concerning aggregation of family income, or the alienation of income by covenants—in respect of all of which the existing system contained anomalous features which favoured property owners as against other taxpayers.

On all these matters I could only count on the support of two trade unionist members, George Woodcock who was then the Assistant General Secretary of the T.U.C., and H. L. Bullock. I was disappointed that Mrs. Vera Anstey, who shared my views on most matters (and who signed the minority reservation on an earlier interim report), did not in the end join the dissenting minority. I realised, of course, that refusal to sign the report was a serious matter that could only be justified by a document that set out the requirements of an equitable system of taxation on fairly fundamental lines, and which gave a convincing account of the basic shortcomings of the existing system.

On Woodcock's suggestion, the preparation of the minority report (formally called a *Memorandum of Dissent* since it had only three signatories) was left to me; he accepted my draft on behalf of himself and Bullock with a few minor changes in wording. Its preparation involved three months of continuous effort and it ran to some 45,000 words. It is reproduced here in full, omitting only the Board's memorandum on capital gains (written by the then Head of the Intelligence Section at Somerset House, the present Lord Cockfield) which was annexed to it.

The appearance of the minority report created a considerable stir, chiefly among Labour M.P.s Many of its recommendations were novel in the sense that they did not figure in party programmes—as for example the tax on capital gains, the idea of which, for reasons that I never understood, was opposed by the Webbs and by Hugh Dalton, who was for many years the guiding spirit of the Labour Party on fiscal matters.[1,2] But with Hugh Gaitskell as Chancellor (later Shadow Chancellor and then Party Leader) a new generation took over who had a far clearer grasp of the deficiencies of the existing tax system. He was strongly in favour both of the main reforms advocated in the minority report and also of the idea of replacing surtax by a supplemental expenditure tax; and it was mainly due to him that at least two of the major recommendations of the minority report—the taxation of capital gains and the separation of personal and company taxation—were adopted as official party programme before the 1959 elections.

Sometime before that election, Hugh Gaitskell asked me to assist the Government in carrying out a comprehensive scheme of tax reform if Labour were returned to power, and after his death this offer was renewed by Mr. Callaghan when he became Shadow Chancellor. I thus became the Chancellor's Special Adviser following the 1964 election, attached to the Treasury but seconded to the Inland Revenue in preparation for the April budget. The main provision of that Budget (announced in advance in the "interim" budget of November 1964) included provision for a long-term capital gains tax, a new Corporation tax, as well as a number of other reforms of a minor character, i.e. on convenants, business expenses and the abolition of the special status of overseas trade corporations.

The detailed work on that Budget brought me in close contact with the leading officials of Somerset House, some of whom I knew from the time of the Royal Commission ten years earlier. In the meantime, the Board had done a great deal of preparatory work on both the capital gains tax and the corporation tax, though the final shape and structure of these were left open for Ministerial decisions. The amount of work involved in settling the precise form of either tax and the necessary provisions in relation to the other taxes, the treatment of non-residents, the position under

[1] The traditional view of the British Labour Party on tax matters can I think only be understood by reference to the influence of Henry George on English socialist thinkers of the late nineteenth century.

[2] Hugh Dalton, in a long article in the *New Statesman* (July 2, 1955) reviewing the Final Report of the Commission, said that having read it all he was "still unconvinced" of the case for a capital gains tax. "It might easily turn out to be another case of much cry and little wool."

double tax treaties, etc., proved much greater than anticipated. But Somerset House, under the remarkable leadership of its then Chairman, Sir Alexander Johnston, proved fully capable of coping with the work—indeed this provided a challenge which, according to hearsay, strengthened the morale and improved the spirits of the Department considerably. There were regular weekly meetings with the Chancellor between November and April at which the outstanding issues were thrashed out and finally decided upon by the Chancellor—who, on the few occasions where my view differed from that of the Department, generally followed the official advice.

Nevertheless, the final shape of the two main taxes did not differ too greatly from the recommendations of the minority report published ten years earlier. This was true of the capital gains tax, except that a short-term tax previously introduced by the Conservatives (which made short-term gains liable to both income tax and surtax) had to be retained,[1] while long-term gains were made chargeable at the maximum rate of 30 per cent. instead of at the standard rate of income tax (which was then 41·75 per cent.). And it was also true of the new Corporation Tax which levied tax at a uniform rate on the whole profit of companies (it followed the so-called "classical" system) while income tax was separately deducted at the standard rate from all interest and dividend payments.

The Budget speech of 1965 envisaged that these proposals represented a first stage, to be followed by further major reforms in subsequent years. In fact the Finance Bill, as originally presented to Parliament in 1965, turned out to be the "high point" reached towards getting an impartial and just system of taxation adopted —from then on progress was mainly backwards. In the course of the debates on the Finance Bill, Treasury Ministers were subjected to extreme pressure (not confined to the Opposition benches) for special concessions of the most variegated kind—for farmers, for small businesses, for the holders of gilt-edged, for multi-national companies, and other groups too numerous to mention, who could

---

[1] It was subsequently abolished in the Budget of 1971 after the Conservatives returned to power, a simplification that was well justified by the fact that, in contrast to the long-term tax, it yielded very little.

put up some sort of case of being harshly treated under the new tax regime. The Government resisted where it could; but, after a time, more often gave way by introducing numerous special provisions. By the time the Finance Bill reached the Statute Book the original proposals were truncated at numerous points, giving rise to capricious though unobtrusive shifts in the burden of taxation; and these also re-introduced the complications resulting from numerous special provisions, so that one of the main objectives of the reform, the simplication of the system, was effectively abandoned and the momentum of the reforming zeal was lost— the Chancellor and other members of the Government were no longer in the mood to contemplate the further stages of reform which they so confidently foreshadowed in April.

After the return of the Conservatives, Mr. Barber, as Chancellor, further emasculated both the Capital Gains Tax and the Corporation Tax—the former by introducing the famous "death loophole" (which had plagued the U.S. tax from its inception and had been carefully avoided in the 1965 legislation) and by loosening the tax in numerous other ways. In the case of the Company taxation the essential features of the pre-1965 system were reintroduced—with the important difference that tax, which in the pre-1965 system was deemed to be deducted from dividends and for which a "dividend voucher" was issued entitling the exempt holder to tax repayment, had, under the new system, actually to be paid over to the Revenue (in the form of "advance corporation tax") irrespective of the total tax liability of the company.[1] With the exception of the long-term Capital Gains Tax (which remained in a truncated form) very little of the 1965 reforms was left on the Statute Book, even before the advent of the new Conservative Government in May, 1979.

The long-term Capital Gains Tax has not yet been abolished (at the time of writing) but its survival is under threat, given the hostile attitude of the present Conservative Government to any form of taxation of capital or of the benefits derived from the

---

[1] Before 1965, the tax which was deemed to have been deducted on the dividend was not actually paid to the Revenue in cases where the company's U.K. liability was reduced by credit for foreign taxation and/or in cases where the company had not fully exhausted capital and investment allowances which extinguished its actual liability.

ownership of property—aided by the argument that capital gains during an inflation are illusory and the tax is a haphazard levy on capital.

Yet on closer inspection the argument that inflation invalidates the case for a Capital Gains Tax turns out to be a weak one. It is true that in times of inflation a tax on capital gains becomes, to a greater or lesser degree (depending on the size of the gains and the period over which they occurred), a tax on capital. But there is nothing fundamentally *wrong* with a tax on capital—a large number of countries levy an annual wealth tax which is a superior way of putting an extra charge on those whose income is derived from capital as against those who have to work for their incomes. The question to be asked is whether, when looked at in this way, the tax is a heavy one—i.e. whether it is a greater burden than an annual wealth tax would be; and whether its incidence compares well or badly with that of a straightforward tax on capital levied at progressive rates. On the first question the amount collected at present in Capital Gains Tax is of the order of £300–£400m. per annum which amounts to, say, $1–1\frac{1}{4}$ per cent. of the total value of assets which would be liable to a wealth tax and is, in fact, not very different from what the yield of the proposed wealth tax of the previous Government was estimated to be.[1]

On the second question, it is a positive advantage, from the equity point of view, that the tax charge is concentrated on those wealth-holders who succeed in appreciating the value of their capital and thereby preserve its real value in the face of inflation; while those who fail to do so (e.g. the holders of Government bonds) and thus become exposed to the full ravages of inflation, are not called upon to pay any tax.

Three other papers reproduced in this volume were prepared as evidence for official Committees. The first of these, written jointly with Robert Neild, was submitted to the (second) Royal Commission on the Press which was appointed in 1961 to consider whether economic and financial factors "tend to diminish diversity of ownership and control" in the newspaper industry "having

---

[1] Green Paper, *Wealth Tax*, Cmnd. 5704, London 1974, para 4.

regard to the importance in the public interest of the accurate presentation of news and the free expression of opinions". Its predecessor, the 1949 Royal Commission, which was appointed with similar terms of reference, found that "the decrease in the number of newspapers, which is an aspect of the concentration of ownership, has not been so great as to prejudice the public interest; but any further decrease in the number of national newspapers would be a matter for anxiety".[1] Between the time the first Commission reported and the second was appointed "seventeen daily and Sunday newspapers have ceased publication in London and the provinces and the ownership of those which remain has become concentrated in fewer hands".[2] In our evidence we aimed at giving an exposition of how the existence of economies of scale leads typically to oligopoly—a situation where the market is divided between a small number of producers who compete with one another by means of advertising and sales promotion or by product variation (which may come to much the same thing), both of which have the effect of raising the "break-even-point", i.e. the smallest volume of sales at which both prime and overhead costs are covered—and thereby make it progressively more difficult for newcomers to break into an industry. We assumed that this result has particularly pernicious effects in the newspaper industry which justify the introduction of special measures in that industry that would not be justified if applied generally. The remedy which we recommended consisted of a tax on advertising which was "weighted" by the size of circulation, so that beyond a point it would not pay a newspaper to enlarge its circulation. The proceeds of the tax would have been retained by the industry in the form of a subsidy of so much a copy sold up to a maximum circulation of 2 million copies a day. The Commission examined the proposal[3] and rejected it, whilst admitting that it could be effective in providing "more opportunity for the survival of a number of independent newspapers and also give some encouragement for the establishment of new ones",[4] on the ground that it would be intolerable "to force the proprietors of the two news-

---

[1] Cmd. 7700, para 674.
[2] Cmd. 1811 (1962 Royal Commission Report), para 2.
[3] Cf. *op. cit.*, paras 293–300.
[4] *Ibid.*, para 298.

papers primarily affected[1] to have for decades a major objective of progressively reducing their circulation". Clearly the sight of the omelette was not attractive enough to justify breaking the eggs.[2] The second Royal Commission, like the first, thus failed to come up with any answer to the question for which it was called into existence.[3]

The two papers written for Parliamentary Select Committees are of more recent origin. The first was submitted to the Select Committee on the Corporation Tax which Mr. (now Lord) Barber, Chancellor of the Exchequer in Mr. Heath's Government, appointed in order to decide which of the two alternative systems of giving "distribution relief" from corporation tax was to be preferred. The Conservative Government was determined to abolish the apparent "double taxation" of dividends inherent in the "classical" system of the Corporation Tax, since, in their view, this introduced a "discrimination in favour of retained as against distributed profits" which, in turn, distorted the allocation of "scarce investment resources".

All this was based on highly specious reasoning and the main purpose of my memorandum was to set out the case in favour of the "classical system" which is far more likely to benefit the dynamic and fast-expanding companies than either of the alternatives proposed by the Government. The arguments do not seem to have had much effect on the Committee whose main concern seems to have been to select the particular system likely to reduce the total tax burden on companies and shareholders most. Though in theory it would be possible to collect the same total revenue under any alternative system, in practice the system which gave distribution relief in some form or another had the

---

[1] The reference was to the *Daily Express* and the *Daily Mirror* which at that time dominated other papers in terms of circulation.

[2] The Commission, I gather, was much influenced in these views by its Chairman, Lord Shawcross.

[3] Since that time the problem of how to secure the survival of a competitive newspaper industry has been examined by Professor Fred Hirsch and D. Gordon, *Newspaper Money*, London, Hutchinson, 1975. A third Royal Commission on the Press (under the Chairmanship of Professor McGregor) was appointed in July 1974 and it issued its final report in July 1977. This had wider terms of reference than the earlier Royal Commissions in that it examined the quality of news coverage, newspaper ethics etc. On the matter of competition and new entry it noted the problems arising out of the tendency to concentration described by earlier Royal Commissions, but did not really have anything new to offer by way of solution.

advantage of making the corporation tax appear heavier than it was in fact. Hence under that system it became politically easier to reduce the burden of taxation on companies and politically more difficult to raise it.

In the event, whilst the Committee opted for the softest solution (the pre-1965 system) the Revenue managed to safeguard their interests by ensuring that, under the new dispensation, taxes would have to be paid by companies on the dividends distributed, under the system of the so-called "advanced corporation tax" already referred to, irrespective of the overall tax liability on their profits. And so it has remained to this day—despite the pledge of the Labour front bench, when in Opposition, to restore the Corporation Tax to its original form—a pledge which was never carried into practice.[1]

The next paper is the submission to another Select Committee of the House of Commons—on the proposed system of tax credit. This related to an ingenious scheme put forward by the Conservative Government in 1972 in the form of a Green Paper,[2] which was largely the work of Mr. (now Lord) Cockfield, the tax adviser to the then Chancellor, Mr. Barber. The scheme sought to put into effect a type of "negative income tax" which at that time was much canvassed in academic circles (on both sides of the Atlantic) as a simple and relatively effective method of securing for everybody a minimum standard without a means test—by the simple device of transforming income tax personal allowances into tax credits which would be paid to all wage and salary earners (in or out of employment) as a straight deduction from tax liability, with a net payment by the revenue whenever the credits exceeded the tax.

The advocacy of a scheme of this kind has a long history. Lady Rhys-Williams advocated it in numerous pamphlets toward the end of the War[3] and later it was made part of the official pro-

---

[1] The introduction of the concession for "stock relief" (made necessary by the exceptional financial strains on companies caused by the rapid rise of wages and commodity prices in the summer and autumn of 1974) made the issue rather an academic one. As a result of this relief the companies' liability to tax was greatly curtailed so that the effective liability would not have been very different under the one system than under the other. In addition, the introduction of dividend restraint in the summer of 1975 made it (temporarily) unnecessary to provide the same kind of discouragement to dividend distributions through tax provisions.

[2] *Proposals for a Tax-Credit System*, Cmnd. 5116, London 1972.

[3] For example, *Proposals for Financing Family and other Social Allowances and Simplifying Income Tax*, London 1944.

gramme of the Liberal Party. However the idea was rejected on numerous occasions (not least by the Royal Commission on Taxation in 1954[1]) partly on the ground that it was little different from a "cash supplement" to wages, the cost of which is clawed back through higher rates of taxation, which has undesirable effects for the same kind of reasons as the Speenhamland system had in the eighteenth century; partly because it would not be possible to pay credits on a scale that would make supplementation through means-tested benefits unnecessary—any more than was the case with the existing social security system. However, the obnoxious feature of the concrete scheme put forward in the Green Paper in 1972 was that it amounted to a thinly disguised shift in the burden of taxation in a regressive direction—the low income earners would have paid more, while taxpayers higher up the scale would have been considerably relieved, on account of the higher personal allowances (the benefits of which, in the case of the *lower* income groups, would have been more than offset by the saving in supplementary benefits and other social insurance payments consequent on the new scheme.[2]

However, the one great merit of the scheme was that it involved, as part of the scheme, the introduction of a unified system of family endowment (in replacement of the income tax child allowances and the inadequate and complicated schemes for family allowances) and this, after various delays, was finally put into effect in 1978 by the Labour Government; it is a reform which, once on the Statute Book, is not easily removed.

The paper on "The Income Burden of Capital Taxes" was written during the war as part of the study on *The Burden of Taxation* sponsored by the National Institute of Economic Research.[3] Its ostensible purpose was to work out the appropriate method for expressing the burden of Death Duties in terms of an equivalent income tax; the method previously employed (the so-called "insurance method" advocated by the Colwyn Committee) was based on arbitrary assumptions concerning saving behaviour and

---

[1] Cf. references on p. 151 of this volume.
[2] Cf. pp. 155 ff. below, particularly Tables 5 and 6.
[3] It also appeared as an article in the *Review of Economic Studies*, 1942.

had in any case become inapplicable since it would have involved, in case of large estates, tax rates in excess of 100 per cent. But the paper covered a wider ground in that it set out to clarify the relationship between taxes on capital and taxes on income, and it showed that the important distinction is between recurrent and non-recurrent taxes (like the Capital Levy advocated after the First World War); and on this basis an *annual* tax on capital should be regarded as a tax on income: a species of tax, which, though its incidence is different from a tax which is directly levied on income, is in many respects—both from the point of view of equity and economic effects—a superior way of levying an annual tax on the benefits derived from property. This theme has since been taken up by a large number of writers,[1] and the last Labour Government intended to introduce an annual wealth tax in Britain (this was announced in Mr. Healey's first Budget in November 1974) but did not get around to doing so before the necessary Parliamentary majority for passing such a measure had evaporated.[2] The paper is reproduced here as a contribution to the discussion on whether the existing capital taxation in Britain is "oppressive, harmful to business and a real deterrent to initiative and enterprise"[3] or whether it is in fact at a moderate level in comparison with the capital taxation of numerous other countries. The paper suggests a method of estimating the burden of capital taxes in terms of income foregone—which is a necessary step for any dispassionate examination of such questions.

The paper on "The Economics of the Selective Employment Tax" was prepared for this volume in the spring and summer of 1979 and is published here for the first time. It is intended to set out the assumptions concerning the mode of operation of competition in particular sectors of a capitalist economy such as Britain, and the considerations which led up to this tax, not just as a convenient

[1] Peacock, Alan. "Economics of a National Wealth Tax for Britain", *British Tax Review*, 1963; C. T. Sandford and Associates, *An Annual Wealth Tax*, London 1975; A. B. Atkinson, *Unequal Shares*, London 1972.

[2] A Green Paper on the Wealth Tax was published in 1974 (Cmnd. 5704); this was followed by the appointment of a Select Committee of the House of Commons which, however, failed to issue an agreed report (A Select Committee on a Wealth Tax), *Report and Proceedings, House of Commons Sessional Paper 696-1*, November 1975).

[3] A statement by the Chancellor of the Exchequer, Sir Geoffrey Howe, *Hansard*, 12th June, 1979, col. 255.

way of raising revenue but as an instrument for the more efficient allocation of resources.

When the tax was first introduced in the Budget of May 1966 it came as a complete surprise; and though the initial reception on the morrow of the Budget was not unfavourable, there was little understanding (and a great deal of confused thinking) concerning its purposes or likely effects even among trained economists. Gradually a strong and vocal opposition to the tax was built up by the traders affected by it, who declared almost in unison that the tax will "fail in its object since it will be passed on in higher prices in full"—not realising that this in itself is not valid argument against the tax—any more than it would be against indirect taxes of the ordinary kind, such as Excise Duties or V.A.T., all of which are "passed on" in prices. It became pretty evident that the real source of opposition by wholesalers, retailers, the hotel and restaurant trade, etc. was that they were *not* able to pass on the tax, or not fully; though no economist was able to explain satisfactorily why this should be so, as compared with other indirect taxes. As I was, if not the inventor, at least the driving force behind its introduction (the tax like almost everything coming out of Whitehall is more properly regarded as the joint product of inter-departmental committees or working parties), I was naturally concerned that the widespread misapprehensions concerning its effects should be investigated by a competent body, and I recommended that the Government should appoint an independent enquiry for the purpose. W. B. Reddaway was chosen to conduct this enquiry—which in due course came up with some striking conclusions (described on pp. 223 below) even though Reddaway resolutely refused to go into the question of explanation—i.e. the kind of assumptions concerning competition, prices formation, etc., that would be necessary in order to explain his results. For this reason I felt that despite the work of the Reddaway enquiry there was need to set out the underlying hypotheses, or the "theoretical model" that prompted its advocacy—even though this is now a matter of historical interest only since the tax was abolished by the Conservative Government in 1972 and the circumstances which made its introduction advisable in 1966 are not likely to recur in the foreseeable future.

The main idea behind the scheme was that a combination of taxes and subsidies on employment (or payrolls) applied in different sectors and regions of the economy would make it possible to effect a considerable improvement in the performance of the economy, and to raise its overall rate of productivity growth. The tax on employment in the service trades was to be combined with a general subsidy on employment in manufacturing (with a differentially high rate in the high-unemployment "development" areas) which would have the effect of improving the rate of growth of the manufacturing sector, its competitiveness in foreign trade and thereby make it possible to sustain a higher rate of economic growth. The Regional Employment Premium introduced a year later (in the Budget of 1967) was intended as a companion-piece to S.E.T.—it proved more difficult to secure support for this latter measure (simply because it appeared to increase *expenditure* rather than add to *revenue*); if it nevertheless reached the Statute Book this was mainly due, I think, to the support it received from the then Permanent Secretary to the Treasury, Sir William (now Lord) Armstrong.

R.E.P. was sacrificed when the first wave of "expenditure cuts" came "on stream" in 1976, under the influence of the new monetarism which swept the City, the media and important parts of the Establishment, and which dominated the philosophy of the I.M.F. The fact that it was an item on the expenditure side of the Budget and not on the revenue side (it appeared as an addition to expenditure rather than as a reduction in taxation) made it appear as a "burden" on the private sector of the economy, even though it was a subsidy to business, the effects of which were no different from that of a devaluation confined to particular regions of the country.

The experiment of using taxes and subsidies on employment as a means of improving the performance of the economy was thus brought to a premature end before the potentialities of this instrument could be properly explored. Such studies as appeared on the effects of R.E.P.[1] (as distinct from S.E.T.) suggest that it

---

[1] For example, John Rhodes and Barry Moore, "The Effects of the Regional Employment Premium and Other Regional Policy Instruments" in *The Economics of Industrial Subsidies*, Department of Industry, ed. A. Whiting, HMSO, 1976.

had a positive effect in stimulating production and employment in the development areas—though in terms of magnitude the results were uncertain and could not be satisfactorily isolated from those of other regional incentives such as investment allowances. It was fairly clear, however, that to achieve dramatic results on regional unemployment the magnitude of the subsidy would need to have been much greater.[1] On the whole we could say, here as elsewhere, that the response of the economy to price and cost incentives proved to be less than economists were apt to assume on the basis of econometric studies.

The last paper included in the present volume reproduces the substance of a talk I gave at a Brookings Institution Conference on Income versus Expenditure Taxes in the autumn of 1978. My book on the subject published in 1955 (referred to above) attracted quite a lot of attention at the time—more perhaps for its general analysis of the issues of taxation than for its particular proposals for reform—though some countries (such as India and Ceylon) which suffered from the combination of a dearth of savings, a highly concentrated distribution of wealth and a great deal of luxury consumption, were anxious to explore the possibilities of a tax which could be highly progressive in its incidence and yet leave the incentive and ability to save unimpaired.[2]

In the developed industrial countries, however (where tax administrations are far more competent to cope with a tax of this kind), there was not much interest in the Expenditure Tax until its merits in comparison with income taxes were discovered (or rediscovered) in the last five to ten years, simultaneously—though independently—in a number of countries. In the United States, Treasury circles began to take a practical interest, following the publication of a book by a U.S. Treasury official, Mr. Griffin, in 1974; the interest rapidly spread to the well-known group of tax-experts of the Harvard Law School and to specialists on

---

[1] At its highest, the incidence was less than that of a 10 per cent. subsidy on payrolls, which in turn (owing to the relatively small share regional value added in the final price) was less than that of a 5 per cent. devaluation.

[2] The Government of both India and Ceylon adopted an expenditure tax along the lines I recommended, but in both countries the tax was largely evaded or "avoided" and was withdrawn after a comparatively short time. (In Ceylon it was reintroduced only to be withdrawn again.) Cf. also the Introductions to Vols. 3 and 8 of these Essays,

taxation and public finance at various universities. In Britain, quite independently of this, James Meade formed a working group under the aegis of the Institute of Fiscal Studies which examined the whole idea afresh and came up with much the same recommendations as I did in my book. The Meade Report—which contained a thorough evaluation of the defects of the existing British tax system, similar in character to the minority report of the Royal Commission reprinted at the beginning of this volume (though possibly broader in scope and far more detailed), did not receive the attention it deserved. It appeared at a time when public mood in Britain—which is really the mood of its ruling classes as expressed through the regular "opinion-formers" of the media—was against distributive justice and turned a deaf ear to proposals which, by getting rid of numerous anomalies, were bound to make the tax system more "oppressive" and not less so.

To anyone who reads both my original book and the recent essay, it will be evident that, while I have not changed my views on the analytical plane, I have become far more sceptical of the possibilities of improving the distribution of income and wealth through taxation or of introducing effective reforms when these are perceived, in anticipation, as affecting adversely the interests of the property-owning classes. In Britain the tax reforming ardour of Liberal and Labour Governments—beginning with Harcourt's Death Duties in 1892 and Lloyd-George's surtax in 1909—brought about very little effective change in the distribution of wealth and income. Society has clearly become far more equal— or far less unequal—than it was in the nineteenth century: but this was more the result of the sustained rise in real wages (accompanied by the rise in the collective provision of welfare services) than of any restriction of the spending power of the rich brought about by taxation.

As far as taxation is concerned, the practical application of a new principle—such as the taxation of individuals according to their total personal expenditure rather than their income—even if it were to reach the Statute Book, would be hedged around with so many specific concessions or exceptions—introduced for reasons of political expediency, more or less thinly disguised by specious appeals to particular cases of hardship, the "efficient" allocation of resources, or of difficulties of administration—that it is doubtful whether the upheaval caused by the change would be worthwhile in terms of making the system significantly more equitable. The intellectual work of tax reformers, as Myrdal once pointed out,[1] can rarely take into account the precise form in which the basic ideas will be carried into practice; and this may well mean that the results diverge greatly from the original intentions, so that the objectives of the tax have not really been met and yet the illusion may have been created that they have—"one has paid the price, but one is cheated of the goods".

A further problem—which seems to plague Britain more than other countries—resides in the discontinuities and sharp changes of direction—U turns—caused by the operation of a two-party system of Government, in circumstances in which the two parties are increasingly closely associated with, and dependent upon, the opposing economic interests of Capital and Labour. This problem has intensified since 1970 when the Conservative Party first became dominated by doctrinaire reformers (in the style of the old nineteenth-century Liberals) as against the traditionalists and pragmatists, so that from now on successive Governments are bound to spend a great deal of their energies in undoing the work of their predecessors.

March 1980                                    Nicholas Kaldor

[1] *The Political Element in the Development of Economic Theory*, English ed., London 1953, p. 188.

# 1

## MEMORANDUM OF DISSENT
## TO THE FINAL REPORT OF THE
## ROYAL COMMISSION ON THE TAXATION OF
## PROFITS AND INCOME[1]

1. Though we participated fully in the discussions with our colleagues, and endorse a number of their recommendations (which will be listed below), we find ourselves unable to sign the final Report of the Commission, because of a fundamental difference of view between ourselves and the Majority as to the basic requirements of an equitable system of income taxation.

### I. INTRODUCTION

2. The purpose of progressive income taxation is to allocate the burden of tax fairly between different members of the community. As the Majority point out in the Report[2] a graduated tax differentiated according to personal circumstances is necessarily a tax on persons according to their respective total incomes, and not a tax on a "body of income . . . as such", considered impersonally under some system of classification. It follows that equity between persons cannot be secured—however nicely the effective rate of tax is graduated according to an individual's total taxable

---

[1] Published with the *Final Report of the Royal Commission on the Taxation of Profits and Income*, London H.M.S.O., Cmd. 9474, June 1955, pp. 354–424. This memorandum was drafted by me in the months February–April 1955 and signed by three members of the Commission, G. Woodcock, H. L. Bullock and myself, on 20th May, 1955.

[2] Para. 33.

income and however meticulously it is differentiated to allow for personal circumstances—unless the tax base itself (that is to say, the definition of income for tax purposes) provides a measure which is uniform, comprehensive and capable of consistent application to all individuals. Impartial assessment of the relative taxable capacity of individuals is impossible if the definition of taxable income is unduly restricted, ambiguous or biased in favour of particular groups of taxpayers.

3. A system of personal income taxation which operates without any clear definition of what constitutes "income" is exposed to a double danger. On the one hand the simple view that income is an unambiguous word, not subject to various interpretations, may ensure general complacency, and the particular notion of "taxable income" hallowed by legal tradition tends to become identified with taxable capacity as such. On the other hand, in the absence of any clear underlying principle, revisions and interpretations of the law proceed, in the light of particular considerations, to introduce successive concessions which have the effect of constantly shifting the tax burden in a manner which is no less far-reaching for being unobtrusive. Lacking a firm basic conception, neither the public nor the legislature nor the Courts are conscious of the extent to which the tax system, behind a façade of formal equality, metes out unequal treatment to the different classes of the taxpaying community.

4. It has therefore seemed to us most important to state at the outset what, in our view, is the "true conception of income"[1] required to secure an allocation of taxation that is in accordance with taxable capacity, or "ability to pay".

*The Definition of Income*

5. In our view the taxable capacity of an individual consists in his power to satisfy his own material needs, i.e., to attain a particular living standard. We know of no alternative definition that is capable of satisfying society's prevailing sense of fairness and equity. Thus the ruling test to be applied in deciding whether any particular receipt should or should not be reckoned as taxable income is whether it contributes or not, or how far it

[1] Cf. para. 28 of the Report.

contributes, to an individual's "spending power" during a period. When set beside this standard, most of the principles that have been applied, at one time or another, to determine whether particular types of receipt constitute income (whether the receipts are regularly recurrent or casual, or whether they proceed from a separate and identifiable source, or whether they are payments for services rendered, or whether they constitute profit "on sound accountancy principles" (or whether, in the words of the Majority,[1] they fall "within the limited class of receipts that are identified as income by their own nature"), appear to us to be irrelevant. In fact no concept of income can be really equitable that stops short of the comprehensive definition which embraces all receipts which increase an individual's command over the use of society's scarce resources—in other words, his "net accretion of economic power between two points of time".

6. Definitions of income giving expression to this basic principle have been offered by various writers on public finance, all of which, subject to minor differences, agree in regarding "income" as the sum of two separate elements, namely personal consumption and net capital accumulation. In the words of one writer income can be looked upon either as "(a) the amount by which the value of a person's store of property rights would have increased, as between the beginning and the end of the period, if he had consumed (destroyed) nothing; or (b) the value of rights which he might have exercised in consumption without altering the value of his store of rights". Hence income is the "algebraic sum of (1) the market value of rights exercised in consumption, and (2) the change in the value of the store of property rights between the beginning and the end of the period in question".[2]

7. The above definition focuses attention on two fundamental aspects of the concept of income which reflects the increment of "spending power" or "economic power" in a period. One is that income is a measure of the increase in the individual's command over resources in a period, irrespective of how much or how little of that command he actually exercises in consumption. The private choice of an individual as to how much he spends and

[1] Para. 31.
[2] Simons, *Personal Income Taxation*, (Chicago, 1938), pp. 49–50.

how much he saves is irrelevant to this notion: income is the sum of consumption and net saving. The second is that "net saving" (and hence income) includes the whole of the change in the value of a man's store of property rights between two points of time, irrespective of whether the change has been brought about by the current addition to property which is saving in the narrower sense, or whether it has been caused by accretions to the value of property. From the point of view of an individual's command over resources, it is the change in the real value of his property which alone matters, and not the process by which that change was brought about.

8. In applying the basic conception of income as the power to satisfy material needs to any workable tax system, a number of guiding principles need to be introduced.

(1) The first of these is, in the words of the Majority,[1] that "no income [should be] recognised as arising unless an actual receipt has taken place, although a receipt may take the form of a benefit having money's worth received in kind as well as of money or of a payment made to a third party in discharge of another's legal debt". The obvious corollary to this principle is that no deduction should be recognised from any gross receipt in arriving at the net receipt unless an actual outlay has taken place, whether in money or money's worth.[2] Hence improvement or deterioration in the market value of a man's property should not be recognised until it is reflected (as in the long run it must be) in his actual receipts, or in the outlays that he can properly charge against those receipts. (We shall refer to this point more fully in our treatment of the problem of capital gains.)

(2) The second guiding principle is that receipts which cannot reasonably be brought within the scope of taxation because

---

[1] Para. 29.

[2] Our tax system generally obeys this principle subject to two important exceptions. The first consists (as is stated by the Majority) in the taxation of the owner-occupier of a house or land in respect of the annual value represented by his occupation. The second consists in the concession which allows a reduction in the market value of unsold stock-in-trade below its actual cost of acquisition to qualify as a deduction against the year's receipts from trading activities.

their control and enforcement is beyond the power of any efficient tax administration are better ignored altogether (even though they are beneficial receipts) since their inclusion creates unfairness to the disadvantage of the honest taxpayer. (Gambling winnings may be regarded as an example of this.) The obvious corollary to this principle is that outlays or expenses chargeable against gross receipts which cannot be efficiently and uniformly administered (because it is beyond the powers of an efficient tax administration to control or check whether (a) they have actually been incurred or not; or (b) whether they have actually been laid out for the purposes stated; or (c) whether they are properly deductible as necessary expenses incurred in connection with, and for the purpose of obtaining, the receipts) should similarly be ignored, since their inclusion may create more unfairness between taxpayers than it remedies. (We shall refer to this point more fully in connection with the difference in the definition of income charged under Schedules D and E.)

(3) Thirdly, under a progressive system of taxation, recognition needs to be given to the fact that unique or non-recurrent receipts obtained in any particular period do not confer the same spending power on the recipient within that period as recurrent receipts of like amount.

*The Present Legal Definition of Taxable Income*

9. Our tax system has not been developed in obedience to such general principles; and to the extent that they do receive recognition in the tax code, it is more the result of ad hoc considerations or of administrative necessities than of any systematic application of a basic conception. The current legal definition of what constitutes taxable income has been arrived at by a process of piecemeal statutory revision and judicial interpretation of the provisions of Five Schedules, introduced by the Income Tax Act of 1803, under which the various kinds of taxable receipts and benefits are enumerated and which collectively define the limits of taxable income. As the Majority state, "While the fundamental structure remains signally unaltered, additions and alterations

have, of course, been made from time to time either by changing or enlarging the list of sources or by ad hoc provisions to the effect that a particular kind of receipt is to rank as taxable income".[1] But the original Act of 1803 already included a "sweeping up clause", in Case VI of Schedule D, under which "any annual profit or gain" is taxable which is not enumerated under any of the other Cases or Schedules. Since the law employs the terms "income", "profit" or "gain" interchangeably, the very insertion of such a clause is incongruous within a system which identifies income only by a process of categorisation and which in consequence nowhere defines what it is that is to be swept up.

10. The circularity inherent in this legal conception is well illustrated by the juxtaposition of two well-known judicial interpretations of the statute. "Income tax", according to Lord Macnaghten's famous dictum,[2] "is a tax on income". But "as regards the word income" said Lord Wrenbury,[3] "it means such income as is within the Act taxable under the Act". The law faces the same dilemma as the medieval Schoolmen who were forced to deny to exotic birds and beasts, captured by travellers in strange lands, the status of birds and beasts, since they relied for their definition on an exhaustive list of birds and beasts reported by tradition to have entered the Ark with Noah.

11. The inclusion or exclusion of particular types of receipts assumed an entirely different significance as income tax was gradually transformed from a small flat-rate impost to a steeply graduated tax calculated with reference to an individual's total income from all sources. Yet the trend towards the comprehensive tax base implied in the very notion of progressive taxation has been checked at various points, mainly on the basis of two distinct considerations. First, as the Majority point out[4] there has been a tendency to avoid the special problem of the heavy incidence of a steeply graduated tax on receipts which by their very nature are realised irregularly, instead of being spread evenly over the years in which they may be regarded as accruing, by the simple expedient of excluding such receipts altogether from the tax

[1] Para. 31.
[2] Attorney-General v. London County Council, (1900), 4 T.C. at p. 293.
[3] Whitney v. C.I.R., (1925), 10 T.C. at p. 113.
[4] Para. 32.

charge. Secondly, the ancient constricted conception of income as something which recurrently emerges and is separated off from its perpetual source, like the harvest from the soil, has lingered in the tax code from times when, by and large, income was the harvest from the soil. It has only been abandoned gradually, through the piecemeal adoption of basically inconsistent provisions, and without the consequences of its abandonment ever having been systematically taken into account. Thus the old view of the rigid separation between the income flow and its permanent source has been blurred by the allowances introduced for capital wastage and even losses, as permissible deductions in the calculation of income. The old boundary-line afforded by the regularity or recurrence criterion has been discarded in judicial decision which have established that casual or isolated gains are taxable provided that they are not of the character of "capital profits".

*Casual and Capital Profits*

12. Indeed this question of the status of "casual" and of "capital" profits has been a matter of uneasiness in this country for at least forty years; and the accession of case law, far from gradually evolving any clear principle, has left matters in greater uncertainty than they were before.[1] The exploitation of exceptional opportunities to make and enjoy profits which emerged from no regular profession or trade, during and after the First World War, brought into public question the justice of exempting from taxation fruits of luck and speculation which, in the economic benefits their possession conferred, seemed indistinguishable from taxed earnings more hardly won. The 1920 Royal Commission on the Income Tax recommended[2] that "a transaction in which the subject matter was acquired with a view to profitseeking, should be brought within the scope of the Income Tax, and should not be treated as an accretion of capital simply because the transaction lies outside the range of the taxpayer's ordinary business, or because the opportunities of making such profits are not likely, in the nature of things, to occur regularly or at

[1] Cf. also Appendix I of the Board's Memorandum on Capital Gains [not reprinted here].
[2] Cmd. 615, para. 91.

short intervals". On the other hand they stated[1] "profits that arise from ordinary changes of investments should normally remain outside the scope of the tax, but they should nevertheless be charged if and when they constitute a regular source of profit". In the view of the 1920 Commission therefore (1) the basic test of whether a particular gain is taxable should lie not in the regularity or recurrence of its character, but in the question whether the subject matter of the transaction was acquired with a view to profit-seeking or not; (2) when the subject matter of the transaction is an "investment", the motive of profit-seeking should not be presumed, unless such transactions occur with sufficient frequency to constitute a regular source of profits. (The second of these propositions is not stated in this form in the Report of the 1920 Royal Commission. But in our view it is the only interpretation of their position which makes the two recommendations, quoted above, consistent with one another.)

13. No subsequent action was taken by Parliament on these recommendations; and we agree with the Majority[2] that the line of approach adopted by the 1920 Commission is unsatisfactory. We consider a test based on motive to be not merely defective in its vagueness and the uncertainty of proof, but irrelevant. The sole relevant test, in our view, as to whether a gain is to be taxable or not is whether it secures a net material benefit to the recipient. From the point of view of taxable capacity it is irrelevant whether an increase in spending power occurs as a result of an unexpected windfall, or whether it was expected, planned or achieved in the course of a business organised for the purpose.

14. As the Majority explain[3] a series of Court decisions since 1920 have radically changed the state of the law. We believe however that these developments have only served to increase the ambiguity and uncertainty in the status of non-taxable "capital profits" without effecting any notable advance towards equity. The position now appears to be that a purely isolated profit is taxable, if the underlying transaction carries with it "the badges of trade". But the question whether it carries such a badge or not, appears to be decided not on motive, nor on whether a business had to be organised for the purpose, but simply on

---

[1] *Ibid.*, para. 90.     [2] Para. 113.     [3] Para. 86.

whether the transaction involved speculation of a rare kind (such as the purchase and sale of toilet paper by a money lender;[1] of whisky in bond by a woodcutter;[2] or of farms by a motor engineer[3]) rather than speculation of the more usual kind involving operations on the Stock Exchange or the produce exchanges. In the case of the purchase and sale of investments, "an accretion to capital" as Lord Buckmaster put it, "does not become income merely because the original capital was invested in the hope and expectation that it would rise in value".[4]

15. The Majority defend what appears to be the present position of the law by a more subtle piece of reasoning. According to this view[5] "referability to a defined source is essential to permit of a receipt being categorised as income". Though "all profits that arise from the utilisation of property are made in a sense out of capital"[6] only those profits are income "which arise out of something more substantial than the mere occasion of the profit itself. Income, it has been said, is the fruit that ripens on and can be plucked off the tree. If there is to be income therefore there must not only be fruit but also a tree. This substance is to be found where the person concerned has been conducting a venture or concern in the nature of trade out of which the profit arises. That is equivalent to saying that he was a dealer, even if he made only one deal. But the profit that is taxed in such a case is the income arising from the venture: it is meaningless to say that what is taxed is the profit from the sale itself".[7]

16. We are unable to follow these arguments. It seems to us that the motor engineer who buys and sells a farm or the woodcutter who buys and sells bonded whisky is in no different position from the Stock Exchange operator who buys and sells particular shares. If the one is deemed to have committed his capital to a venture, so has the other; if the one is to be decorated for the occasion with the "badges of trade", so should the other. The ordinary man (whether he accepts it as adequate or not) might be able to follow a line of reasoning according to which the profits of a

[1] Rutledge v. C.I.R., (1929), 14 T.C. 490.
[2] C.I.R. v. Fraser, (1942), 24 T.C. 498.
[3] Reynolds's Executors v. Bennett, (1943), 25 T.C. 401.
[4] Leeming v. Jones, (1930), 15 T.C. 333, at p. 357.
[5] Para. 31.    [6] Para. 109.    [7] Para. 84.

B

regular business are to be distinguished from isolated or casual
profits which a man might obtain outside his regular activities
once or twice in a lifetime. But we submit that he would be quite
unable to appreciate the equity of regarding certain profits as
taxable even though they be isolated or casual, and other profits
as exempt, even though they may be recurrent or regular—
simply because in the one case the transaction is deemed to have
an atmosphere of a "venture in the nature of trade" about it,
and in the other case this atmosphere (owing to the very ease
with which the transactions can be conducted) is absent.

17. Nor are we satisfied that even if this distinction were a
tenable one, the question of the taxability of the so-called capital
profits could be dismissed on the ground that they are a fruit
without a tree. "Referability to a defined source", even under
present law, is not invariably required to "permit of a receipt being
categorised as income"; there is also that "limited class of receipts
that are identified as income by their own nature".[1] In our view
it would still be necessary to show cause why these profits should
not be admitted to the membership of that limited class.

18. Though the Majority do not propose to widen in any way
the present legal conception of taxable income, they are conscious
of the ambiguity created by the vagueness of the present boundary-
line that separates taxable from non-taxable profits. They
therefore put forward, without wishing to lay down any fixed rule,
a set of guiding considerations for determining whether any
particular profit is to be regarded as taxable or not.[2] We do not
share the expectation that these "relevant considerations" would
serve to reduce the present legal uncertainty surrounding the
notion of income, nor do we find that they clarify the meaning of
the "true conception of income" for tax purposes. If the six
considerations were to be regarded as six necessary constituents
of the definition of taxable profits, they would serve to make the
concept of taxable profits considerably narrower than it is under
present law. This clearly was not the Majority's intention. Nor did
they look upon them as six independent conditions, any one of
which should be sufficient in itself to establish taxability—
especially since some of the criteria are matters of degree rather

[1] Para. 31.        [2] Para. 116.

than of a kind (as, e.g., length of the period of ownership or the frequency of transactions). In fact, in all doubtful cases some of the tests suggested are bound to give results contradictory to the others; and there is no indication how such contradictions are to be resolved. Thus the profits of a man who speculated in a commodity on a produce exchange—by buying and selling tea, for example—would pass the first test (since the subject matter of the realisation is normally the subject of trading rather than investment) but completely fail in the fourth (since "nothing at all is done" to bring the commodity into a more marketable condition). In our view the enumeration of these "relevant considerations" serves not only to emphasise the uncertainty of the present legal border-line that separates taxable from tax-exempt profits, but to reveal how wide that border-line or border-area is, relatively to the area which it encloses.

*Treatment of Expenses*

19. Enough has been said to show that the present legal distinction between taxable and non-taxable receipts cannot be justified on any reasonable criterion of equity. The other main respect in which the present legal definition of taxable income causes inequality of treatment between classes of taxpayers concerns not receipts, but outlays. As the Majority point out[1] one particular source of these differences consists in the allowances given for the wastage of capital. The original theory which ignored the wastage of capital altogether "has been profoundly modified in the course of time, but not to the same extent or in the same way in respect of all the different sources of income".[2] While incomes derived from trades, vocations or professions "now receive a full allowance out of taxable income to make good money expended in acquiring assets that are used up in the production of the income",[3] no allowances are given with respect to the capital expenditure incurred in vocational and educational training or for the expenditure which a man incurs "in developing and improving his expert knowledge".[4]

20. We cannot follow the Majority in the argument which they put forward in justification of this difference in treatment[5]

[1] Para. 38.  [2] Para. 38.  [3] Para. 39.  [4] Para. 41.  [5] In para. 42.

according to which the wastage involved in the case of an individual's capital equipment "is the obsolescence of the human machine itself, not the obsolescence of its skill or experience". We agree however with their view[1] that it would be impracticable to extend the scheme of capital allowances to expenditure incurred on investment in the human person; and we believe therefore that short of withdrawing capital allowances altogether—a course that, on grounds of expediency, we should not favour—the difference in treatment cannot in this respect be avoided and ought therefore to be recognised and compensated for.

21. Another and, in our view, even more important cause of such inequality arises out of the difference in the legal definition of deductible expenses in respect of income from a trade, profession or vocation assessed under Schedule D, and in respect of income from an office, employment or pension, assessed under Schedule E. In the latter case only such expenses are deductible as are "wholly, exclusively and necessarily" incurred "in the performance of" the duties of the office or employment. In the former case all expenses are deductible which are "wholly and exclusively laid out or expended for the purposes of the trade". As we shall argue in more detail in Section IV below this difference in wording implies that in the case of incomes assessed under Schedule D the calculation of the individual's actual liability proceeds on the basis of provisions for deductions which are without parallel in the case of incomes assessed under Schedule E; and which bring it about that the true taxable capacity represented by a unit of taxable income is normally considerably greater in incomes assessed under Schedule D than in incomes assessed under Schedule E. Here again we are of the opinion that the difference in treatment ought to be openly recognised and compensated for in so far as, for administrative reasons or on grounds of expediencey, it cannot be eliminated.

*Tax Avoidance and Escape*

22. The full tally of inequities arising from the defects in the calculation of the tax base—whether on the side of receipts or on the side of the allowances for expenses—can be reckoned only

[1] In para. 43.

after those taxpayers who are in a position to do so have adjusted their activities and transactions so as to benefit from gaps and ambiguities in the definition of taxable income.[1] The incentive to make such adjustments (which may not be a matter of tax evasion, and frequently may not even be classed as tax avoidance within the accepted meaning of that term) is in direct proportion to the effective marginal rate of tax and is inevitably powerful at the present level of taxation. Thus the exclusion of capital profits from the tax base leads to the conversion of taxable income into tax-free capital gains. Since this manoeuvre can in fact be accomplished within wide limits and through various channels the taxpayer finds that his taxable income, and therefore the size of his tax bill, is left in large measure to his own discretion, provided he is a man of property.[2] Generous provision for business expenses invites the dressing up of personal expenses as business expenses and the dressing up of income payments as expense allowances.

23. Moreover, the social cost of defects in the tax base is to be reckoned not only in terms of inequity between different taxpayers, but in distortions of normal economic behaviour. Such distortions take two main forms. Firstly, the desire and pursuit of short-term speculative gains, artificially stimulated by the tax-free character of such gains, tends to distort the allocation of the community's

---

[1] The ambiguity of the law in this context is just as important as the gaps in the law. So long as the taxability of certain classes of profits is subject to so much uncertainty, it is hardly to be expected that the taxpayer will regard such profits as part of his income for tax purposes when he comes to make out his tax return. The question of the assessment of such profits is therefore largely dependent on information reaching the Revenue authorities independently of the taxpayer—which must necessarily be a rather chancy affair. We feel that quite apart from any change in the present legal conception of taxable income, the hands of the Revenue would be greatly strengthened if there were a statutory obligation on taxpayers to return all profits made in the year; non-taxable or capital profits being shown separately.

[2] Several pieces of legislation on the Statute Book have been devised to stop particular methods of converting taxable income into tax-free capital gains, but alternative facilities remain readily available, and as we shall argue (paragraph 47) the problem cannot be effectively dealt with by means of special anti-avoidance provisions. Thus the Finance Act of 1937, Part II, Section 12, is designed to prevent tax escape through the sale of securities "cum dividend" and their repurchase "ex-dividend" in so far as sale and repurchase is accomplished in the same agreement or any collateral agreement. The Finance Acts of 1922 (Section 21) and 1937 (Section 14 (2) (b)) attempted to check avoidance of surtax, by shareholders in closely held corporations, through failure to distribute profits and subsequent realisation of accumulated earnings through the sale of shares. The Finance Acts of 1936 (Section 18) and 1938 (Section 28) prevent tax avoidance through transfer of securities to controlled foreign holding companies for the purpose of converting earnings into capital gains under the guise of repayments of capital, etc.

savings between different forms of investment. Secondly, the liberal provision for expenses of kinds that are not directly and inevitably associated with the making of the profits against which they may be offset, involves encouraging, by means of a considerable subsidy from the Exchequer, expenditure (e.g., on advertising and entertaining) of doubtful value which might not have been incurred at all in the absence of taxation.

*The Erosion of the Tax Base*

24. When the base on which a tax is levied lacks precise definition the system is particularly exposed to the danger that successive concessions, designed to take care of special situations, will cause a progressive erosion of the tax base until its efficacy as an instrument of taxation is seriously weakened. For once a new principle is admitted into a tax system on the basis of which additional concessions are given, the pressure for further concessions based on arguments of close analogy becomes well-nigh irresistible. Every time some particular interest can make out a case of inequitable treatment under the existing provisions of the law and a fresh concession is granted, it invariably follows that some other interest finds itself disadvantageously treated as a result and can make out an even stronger case for a further concession that can be shown to follow logically from the original concession made.

25. It could not be maintained that as a result of this whittling down process the allocation of the tax burden became any more equitable than it was before unless it could be shown that each new principle introduced was consistent with, and logically followed from, a comprehensive basic conception of taxable income. In the absence of any such conception the allocation of the tax burden is likely to become less rather than more equitable. In some cases a new "principle" may be officially recognised, and a range of concessions deduced from it, without it being realised that the principle conceded is but one aspect of a larger principle: with the result that it narrows the concept of taxable income for certain groups of taxpayers while leaving a wider concept applicable to others. In other cases a new "principle" may be induced from a particular concession granted in special circumstances for a

specific purpose, and originally conceived as of strictly limited application: with the result that in time the grounds for an exceptional concession are elevated into a general principle. The net result of the whole process is that the Government has to impose higher rates of taxation to obtain a given amount of revenue without any compensating gain in the general equity of the tax system.

26. There is less danger of this happening when a new tax instrument of wide application is introduced for an avowedly economic purpose, as for example in the case of initial or investment allowances or of non-distribution relief in connection with profits tax. Such concessions can be withdrawn at any time (as indeed the initial allowances were withdrawn in 1951 for a period). Their presence in the tax code is apparent and unlikely to escape notice and their retention needs continued justification on grounds of public expediency. But with concessions granted in response to pressure from particular interests, and whose justification is regarded, or comes to be regarded, as lying in equity rather than economic expediency, the situation is different. Once they are introduced it is difficult to withdraw them and they become the focal point of agitation for further concessions.

27. The last twenty years have witnessed the introduction of a whole crop of new concessions of this kind. One of these was the introduction of relief from foreign taxation which grew out of a concession originally granted (mainly for economic reasons) to Dominion taxation; that led to an extension covering other countries on the basis of reciprocity, and then to a full extension to all countries, and this in turn to demands for an extension of the range of foreign taxes that qualify for the relief; and finally, when the anomalous consequences of these concessions had been demonstrated, to arguments for the complete exemption of overseas profits from home taxation. Another example is provided by the great extension of the scope of capital allowances in the 1944, 1945 and 1949 Acts and the consequent demand for still further concessions, described in paragraph 193 of the first Tucker Report.[1] Indeed the Tucker Report acknowledges the validity of the general principle that the "Income Tax system should give

[1] Cmd. 8189.

relief in respect of the wastage of all assets that are used up or consumed in the course of carrying on a business". The incorporation of such a general principle in the tax code would logically carry with it (in our view) the tax recognition of the assets built up (and not only of the assets consumed) in the course of carrying on a business—in the form of goodwill for example. Another example is the extended recognition of losses for tax purposes, and the offsetting of losses against income from other sources (described by the Majority in paragraph 483 of the Report), the consequences of which we shall consider in Section v (A) below.

28. The present Royal Commission has been faced with a series of demands for further concessions and exemptions of this character. We shall confine our treatment of these issues to the cases in which we dissent from the conclusions of the Majority, though we are not always in agreement with the reasoning of the Majority in the other cases.

*Income or Expenditure as the Basis of Taxation*

29. As was explained in paragraphs 6 and 7 above, income taxation sets out to tax each individual according to the increase, in a period, in his command over society's scarce resources—irrespective of how much of that command he actually exercises in consumption and how much he leaves unspent, in the form of saving or capital appreciation. To the extent that this spending power is actually exercised in consumption its measurement raises no difficulty in principle, since it can be assumed that equal expenditures in terms of money in a given period represent claims of equal real value on the resources of society. But with regard to that part of a man's spending power which is not currently spent but saved up for the future (irrespective of whether this is the result of a deliberate act of saving or of capital appreciation or capital gains) there is an additional problem that equal amounts of such unspent income in terms of money value need not represent equal additions to the command over real resources in the hands of different individuals. In times of rising prices, the real increase in "spending power" represented by a given addition to the value of a man's store of rights will vary, not only with the size of that addition, but with the ratio of that addition to the

value of his store of rights at the beginning of the period. Analogous problems arise from the fact that the real value of a man's store of rights at any particular point of time may be looked upon either as the amount of goods and services it represents in terms of purchasing power at that moment or as the flow of such goods and services (i.e., the flow of real income) it commands over time. When interest rates are changing, measurement of the "command over resources" in the one sense will not yield consistent results with measurement in the other sense; and it depends on a man's future disposition of his resources (and not on his resources as such) whether the proper measure of his spending power is in terms of the stock of goods his resources command at any one time or the flow of goods they command over time.

30. In the light of these considerations it is a matter for examination whether any definition of the term "income" capable of translation into a measurable tax base could approximate an individual's spending power as closely as his actual spending does; and whether a tax assessed on personal expenditure might not secure a more equitable distribution of the burden of taxation than a tax assessed on income, whatever the definition of income chosen as the basis of taxation. Such an examination could take into account the spending power realised through dis-saving (living on capital) which must be ignored under a system which sets out to tax Income rather than Consumption—even though dis-saving may in fact be an important source of spending power, and despite the fact that large property owners are likely to dis-save extensively when marginal rates of taxation have reached a level which makes it rational for them to do so.

31. Since, however, the consideration of a personal expenditure tax (which would bring spending out of capital within the tax net) has been explicitly ruled out from the Commission's terms of reference we shall not consider this aspect of the problem but shall limit ourselves to the question of how the present system of charging a tax on income could be reformed so as to mitigate the existing inequities.

*Scope of the Present Memorandum*

32. The major inequities, in our view, arise from the present tax immunity of capital gains, and from the differences in the treatment of the trader assessed under Schedule D, and the treatment of the wage and salary earner assessed under Schedule E. Accordingly our main recommendations are concerned with these matters. The taxation of capital gains raises related issues concerning the reform of company taxation and we shall discuss these two problems in direct sequence. The differences in tax treatment between profits and other kinds of income arise partly out of general differences in the definition of taxable income which call for general remedies; partly out of specific provisions such as those concerning losses, capital allowances, stock valuation or double taxation relief which need to be considered in detail. Finally there are a number of particular issues concerning the taxation of individual income—expense allowances and benefits in kind, superannuation, covenants, etc.—on which we wish to comment as we are not in entire agreement with the Majority's views.

33. Before turning to particular issues we feel impelled, in the light of the discussion of Tax Avoidance in the Report,[1] to record unequivocally our view that the existence of widespread tax avoidance is evidence that the system, not the taxpayer, stands in need of radical reform. We agree with the basic view expressed in that Chapter that it would be wrong to assert that a man owes a duty to the community not to alter the disposition of his affairs so as to reduce his liability to taxation. It is up to the community, acting through Parliament, so to frame the tax laws that they do not leave wide loopholes or open broad avenues for tax avoidance.

## II. THE TAXATION OF CAPITAL GAINS

### THE GENERAL CASE FOR THE TAXATION OF CAPITAL GAINS

34. The tax exemption of the so-called capital profits of various kinds represents the most serious omission in our present system of income taxation.

[1] Chapter 32.

35. The basic reason for the inclusion of capital gains in taxation is that capital gains increase a person's taxable capacity by increasing his power to spend or save; and since capital gains are not distributed among the different members of the taxpaying community in fair proportion to their taxable incomes but are concentrated in the hands of property owners (and particularly the owners of equity shares) their exclusion from the scope of taxation constitutes a serious discrimination in tax treatment in favour of a particular class of taxpayer. The manner in which capital gains (of certain kinds at any rate) augment the taxable capacity of the recipient, has been convincingly shown, in our view, in the memorandum by the Board that is reproduced as an Annexe to the present Memorandum[1] and we do not therefore consider it necessary to argue this at length.

*Arguments against Taxing Capital Gains*

36. The main arguments habitually used to justify the exclusion of capital gains from taxation are:

(a) that the rise in capital values in the course of, or in consequence of, inflation represents illusory, and not real gains;

(b) equally the capital gains arising as a result of a fall in interest rates may be illusory, since they do not increase the investor's future income;

(c) capital gains are not only irregular, but may also be unsought or unexpected, and do not therefore represent the same kind of taxable capacity as regular and expected income;

(d) only a tax on realised capital gains is administratively feasible, and this is inequitable because (i) it imputes the gains on any realised asset to the particular year in which the realisation takes place, whereas the appreciation may have accrued over a series of years; (ii) the realised capital gains of any particular year may be offset by the depreciation in the value of unrealised assets in that year; (iii) if in a particular year the realised losses exceed realised gains, it would not be practicable to allow such losses to be set off

---

[1] Printed on pp. 425–70 of the *Final Report*; not reproduced here.

against other income, and yet it would be unjust merely to allow such losses to be carried forward as an offset against future gains.

The Majority base their recommendations mainly on arguments connected with (*b*), (*c*) and (*d*) above. We shall deal with all four types of argument in turn.

### (*a*) Capital Gains in an Inflation

37. We do not deny that the rise in capital values that occurs in the course of an inflation does not increase the taxable capacity of the recipients in the same way as a rise in capital values during a period of steady prices. But we cannot regard this as a justification for excluding capital gains from taxation within the general framework of a tax system which sets out to tax income and not consumption, and which therefore taxes that part of income which is saved as well as that part which is spent—although, as we shall argue below, it does constitute a case for certain well-defined exceptions. If the proceeds of the gain are spent the recipient derives the same benefit as he does in spending taxed income. If the gains are saved, the argument about their illusory character applies equally to all saving, and not merely to capital appreciation. If a man regularly saves up a part of his earnings by adding to his savings deposits or paying premiums on a life assurance, it may equally happen that as a result of inflation the real value of his accumulated savings is constantly shrinking. He is in no different position from another man who attains the same increase in the money value of his capital as a result of capital appreciation. The fact that in times of inflation money appreciation will not mean a corresponding real appreciation may be regarded as an argument against the taxation of savings as such. It is not an argument for the differential treatment of capital appreciation as against other forms of saving.

38. It must also be remembered that taxable capacity is essentially a relative concept, and those property owners who make capital gains during an inflation are undoubtedly in a better position than those who own fixed interest securities, and who therefore lose part of their real capital as a result of the rise in

prices. Equity cannot be secured by ignoring relative changes in the taxable capacities of different property owners; and, if it were held to be desirable (and possible) to exempt that part of capital appreciation which was commensurate with the general price rise, it would follow that any lesser degree of capital appreciation should be regarded as a loss. It is not our view that the tax code should be so devised as to insure tax-payers against the risk of inflation. Indeed we should consider any such intention singularly inappropriate, for taxation must be regarded as one of the principal weapons in the armoury of the central government for combatting inflation. In the event of a drastic depreciation it might become necessary to revise the basis of all monetary obligations and commitments, including tax payments—as was done in Belgium after the First World War, and in Belgium and France after the Second World War. But we do not regard such a situation as within the foreseeable circumstances which tax regulations, or tax reforms, should take into account.

## (b) Capital Gains and Interest Rates

39. An appreciation of capital values which results from a fall in the "pure" rate of interest is not in the same category as a rise in values which merely reflects higher prices, since in this case the capital gain is real enough in the sense that it increases the gainer's command over goods and services. As the Majority emphasise, however, if the proceeds of the gain are reinvested "a reinvestment of sale proceeds has to be made upon the terms that the investor must accept a lower yield upon his money and he needs therefore all or most of his gain to maintain the same nominal income".[1] This is true, but ignores the fact that the holders of long-term bonds still gain on such occasions relatively to other savers who save out of current incomes, or whose past savings were not invested in long-term bonds. When rates of interest fall, some savers (e.g., those whose savings are invested in savings deposits) must accept a reduction of income, whilst other savers manage to offset the effect of the fall in interest by the capital gains on their existing holdings. We do not see that equity is better served by ignoring the relative improvement in the

[1] Para. 93.

position of the second group of taxpayers altogether rather than by recognising it; even though we would agree that a capital gain resulting from a reduction in the yield of long-term bonds does not add to taxable capacity as much as an equivalent gain on equity shares resulting from higher dividend payments.

40. Further, it should be noted that whereas general movements in the price-level tend to be irreversible, there is no reason to suppose that the long-term trend of interest rates is either falling or rising. Past experience suggests on the contrary that periods of falling interest rates alternate with periods of rising interest rates, with little net change on balance. The man or the beneficiary of a settled estate who is unduly heavily taxed as a result of a fall in interest rates is correspondingly lightly taxed as a result of a rise in interest rates.

### (c) Capital Gains and Taxable Capacity

41. We wish to emphasise, however, that—ignoring the exceptional periods following in the wake of great wars or great economic depressions—capital gains are not, to any important extent, the consequence of either rising prices or falling interest rates. The great bulk of capital gains in normal periods is the result of rising real incomes (higher profits and larger dividend payments) to which therefore none of the above considerations apply. In a modern industrial community such as ours a high proportion (four-fifths or more if American experience can be taken as a guide) of all capital gains are derived from transactions in securities, and mainly in ordinary shares of business corporations. There is a steady long-run trend of rising share values which simply reflects the growth of the real earning power and the growing dividend payments of companies.

42. We take the view therefore that the great bulk of capital gains is of a kind to which the description "neither anticipated at the time of acquisition nor sought for by the recipient"[1] does not apply. It may be true that at any one time the majority of ordinary shares are held by their owners in the hope of long-term appreciation rather than of any definite expectation of an early sale at a quick profit, but this does not mean that the expectation

[1] Report, para. 94.

of such long-run appreciation is not an important part of the
benefit which the owners expect to derive from the acquisition
or the holding of ordinary shares. The value which successful
businesses acquire in the form of "goodwill"—the excess of their
market capitalisation over their share capital and reserves—is not
an isolated windfall like a lucky draw in a sweepstake. It is part
of the normal reward of successful enterprise: indeed, under
present day conditions it is by far the most important part of that
reward, the expectation of which is a crucial factor in the supply of
risk capital and business ability to new ventures. We do not wish
to deny that the prospect of high rewards to successful enterprise
plays an important role in the economic progress of society. But
this does not alter the fact that it is grossly unfair to allow the
rewards to the successful property owner or business man to
remain so largely exempt from taxation when successful authors,
actors, inventors, lawyers, surgeons or civil servants are all fully
taxed on their earnings.

43. Our first concern has been to show that, in the circumstances of present day Britain, it is not a sensible view to look upon
capital profits generally as isolated and non-recurrent windfalls;
but we also unreservedly reject the view that by virtue of being a
windfall, incidental and unforeseen, a gain ought to be exempt
from tax. Windfall gains confer material benefit just as expected
gains do. The Majority argue that to tax a pure windfall "would
inflict very small proportionate sacrifice on the taxpayer" but it
would still leave open the question whether "a gain in respect of a
single piece of property, isolated and non-recurrent, bore any
recognisable sign of being income".[1] If this is taken to mean that
the recipient will not adjust his scale of living, as a result of the
receipt of such a non-recurrent gain in the same way as in the
case of an increase in his regular receipts, the point is obvious;
but it is hardly relevant to a tax system which sets out to tax
savings as well as spendings.[2]

44. In paragraph 98 on the other hand the Majority argue that

[1] Para. 94.
[2] As we shall argue below, there is a case (under a progressive tax) for taxing non-
recurrent receipts in a different way from recurrent receipts, since, as was stated in
paragraph 8 (3), they do not confer the same taxable capacity in a particular period.
This, however, is a problem common to all forms of non-recurrent or irregular receipts
and not just to gains of a windfall character.

even if a man does spend his capital gains it would be unfair to
tax him on that account so long as spending out of capital in
general is left untaxed. "Two persons, one with a capital of
£100,000 on which no gains are being made, the other with a
capital of £30,000 on which he is making gains, may each of them
be selling assets in order to finance their expenditure; but why
should the second be taxed on his excess expenditure while the
first is untaxed?" Here the Majority seem to be disputing the
justice of electing Income as the base for personal taxation. The
objective of income taxation is to tax a man, not in accordance
with his spendings as such, nor in accordance with his disposable
wealth as such, but in accordance with his "increment in economic power" over a given period. Under an income tax capital
gains represent taxable capacity precisely because they provide a
distinct addition to the amount of goods and services which an
individual is in a position to command, quite irrespective of
whether he chooses to spend them or save them.

*Capital Gains and Tax Avoidance*

45. The full significance of the omission of capital profits from
taxation only becomes clear, however, when it is appreciated that
the extent to which rewards take the form of tax-free capital
gains rather than taxed dividend income is not something that is
fixed by Nature, but is very much subject to manipulation
by the taxpayer. A community with a highly developed capital
market like Britain offers wide opportunities for an individual so
to arrange his affairs that the accrual of benefits from his ownership of capital takes the form of capital appreciation instead of
taxable income. It is well known (indeed it is constantly broadcast
by the financial press) that it "pays" a surtax-payer to select
securities which have a low dividend yield but a high degree of
expected capital appreciation, owing to rising dividend payments
over time; to purchase bonds that stand at a discount, or bonds
that can be bought in an "unassented" form (like German and
Japanese issues at the present time) so that the value of the interest
that is periodically paid on them appears as an appreciation of
capital, and not as taxable income; or to convert income into
capital appreciation in innumerable other ways.

46. The sale of securities "cum dividend" and their repurchase "ex dividend" can normally be accomplished through the Stock Exchange on terms that relieve the holder of surtax if not the whole of income tax. Indeed through transactions between parties one of whom is taxed on capital gains (as is the case with stock-jobbers or finance houses) whereas the other is not, or one of whom is exempted from tax altogether (as with pension funds) while the other is not, it is always possible for taxable income to be converted into capital gains at the cost of the revenue. For the stock-jobber can offset his dividend or interest income by a capital loss; the pension fund can reclaim tax on interest and dividends received. It pays therefore both stock-jobbers and pension funds to buy securities cum dividend and to sell them ex dividend so long as the capital loss on the whole transaction is less than the gross dividend or interest payment; it pays the ordinary investor to sell cum dividend and to buy ex dividend so long as his net capital gain is greater than the net dividend or interest (after deduction of income tax and surtax) which he sacrificed. The existing legal provisions against "bond-washing" prohibit this practice when the sale and repurchase is accomplished "by the same or any collateral agreement". But there is nothing illegal in buying and selling securities through two separate and unrelated transactions, and it would indeed be impossible to frame anti-avoidance provisions which prevented a man from selling one day and buying the next day, especially since he need not even buy back the identical security to accomplish his object.

47. An extreme example of the conversion of taxable income into tax-free capital gains which has come into vogue in recent years consists of the device known as "dividend stripping". This concerns companies (mainly private companies) which have accumulated large balances of profits; such profits having been subjected to income tax are available for distribution as a taxed dividend. If such companies are bought by a finance house at the time when the companies' assets have been converted into cash or financial investments it is possible to extract the accumulated reserve by means of a special dividend and to sell the residual assets immediately afterwards at a corresponding loss. Since the finance house's receipt of the (net) dividend income will be offset

(and may be more than offset) by its loss on the capital transaction the result is that an amount corresponding to the current income tax on the capital loss will be reclaimable from the Exchequer. Depending on the terms on which the original owner sold the company to the finance house, the gain from the repayment of income tax is shared between the finance house and the original owner, and amounts to a greater or less proportion of the income tax deemed to have been deducted at source from the special dividend. An analogous result is attained (with even greater effectiveness) if the company is sold to a charity or a pension fund which can reclaim the whole of the tax on the dividend by virtue of its tax exemption; and which makes it profitable to pay a price well in excess of the realisable assets of the company. No doubt extreme practices of this kind could be stopped by special anti-avoidance provisions. But in our view so long as capital gains remain exempt from taxation it is impossible to deal with the problem of the conversion of income into capital gains in all its possible forms by specific pieces of legislation.

48. All these opportunities, moreover, are far more readily available to the large property owner than to the small saver; and it is well known from American experience that capital gains are a major source of large incomes but unimportant as a source of smaller incomes. The Report, while it pays a great deal of attention to the alleged inequities that the taxation of capital gains would involve as between one property owner and another (discussed in paragraph 61 below), makes no mention of the far more serious inequities that arise as a result of the exclusion of capital gains from taxation as between those who can (and do) manipulate their affairs so as to augment their tax-free gains at the cost of their taxable income and those who are not in a position to minimise their tax liability in this manner. In fact the Majority find no occasion to refer to problems of tax avoidance in connection with capital gains at all.

*Capital Gains and Undistributed Profits*

49. With regard to the capital profits associated with ordinary shares, the Majority admit that as companies are growing through the steady retention of part of their current profits and the con-

sequent growth of their earnings and dividends, "a process is detected which has the effect of adding to the capital of the shareholder through savings made out of the company's income without his share of the savings ever having been subjected to surtax as income in his hands".[1] They argue, however, that since undistributed profits bear the whole of the profits tax as well as income tax at the standard rate, even though this charge "has no ascertainable relation to the benefit that some shareholders may obtain from the fact that their share of retained profits is, in effect, saved for them in the corporate pool", "it is impossible to ignore the countervailing circumstance that profits made in corporate form do in fact bear a supplementary charge which is not imposed on other forms of profit or income".[2]

50. This argument implies that undistributed profits are the source and the measure of the appreciation of ordinary shares so that the case for taxing the appreciation of these shares arises from the difference between the tax actually paid by the companies on undistributed profits and the tax that would have been payable if the aliquot share of undistributed profits had been imputed to the individual shareholders. This approach completely overlooks the fact that in the case of successful companies the growth in market capitalisation resulting from the growth in earnings and dividends may greatly exceed the growth in the companies' reserves through the continued ploughing back of profits. To show how important that fact can be it is sufficient to refer to a few leading equities. In the case of Woolworth for example the market capitalisation of the ordinary capital amounted (in February, 1955) to some £m280 whereas the share capital and accumulated reserves together amounted to £m39. In the case of Marks and Spencer the market capitalisation amounted to £m128 whereas capital and reserves amounted to £m20. In both these cases therefore 83 to 86 per cent. of the accrued appreciation in the value of the shareholders' capital has never borne any form of tax, however indirect; nor can that appreciation be described as bearing the character of isolated, unexpected or non-recurrent gains, considering that it has accrued over a long series of years—in fits and starts no doubt,

[1] Para. 96    [2] Para. 97.

with fluctuations in the sentiment of the capital market, but unmistakably as a by-product of the growth in the companies' profits and dividends.

51. The cases where the market capitalisation of companies' "goodwill" exceeds by as much as 7 to 1 its share capital and the accumulated reserves are no doubt exceptional. Indeed, under present circumstances and for reasons not unconnected with the present tax régime, which will be discussed more fully below in the Section on Corporate Taxation (paragraphs 98–100), the disparity is frequently the other way round. What is important in the present context is that such disparity is common and may be very marked; and that it is the growth of the companies' reserves only which is taxed under the present system.

52. We agree with the Majority that the tax which the companies pay on their undistributed profits bears no ascertainable relation to the benefits which the shareholders obtain in the form of capital appreciation. This is so not only because the growth in market valuation is likely to differ from, and may exceed greatly, the increase in taxed reserves. It is also because a shareholder is not indissolubly wedded to any particular holding of shares but can buy and sell shares at more or less frequent intervals so that the capital gains or losses that he may realise on any particular holding or shares need bear no relation whatever to his aliquot share of the undistributed profits during his period of ownership. It is true, however, that the taxation of undistributed profits, to the extent that it reduces the amounts which companies put to reserve, may reduce the rate of growth of businesses and in this manner exert an adverse effect on the long-run appreciation of share values. We believe therefore that if capital appreciation were brought into charge in the form of a capital gains tax there would be a case for reducing the present burden of taxation on undistributed profits and our recommendations in Section III below are directed to this purpose.

### (d) Realised and Accrued Gains

53. We should now like to turn to the objections against the taxation of capital profits that are particularly directed against a scheme of taxation of realised capital gains. As is explained in the

Report,[1] it is a basic principle both of the tax system and of business accounting not to take account of profits until they are realised. This means that ordinary trading profits are reckoned as the year's receipts (whether in actual money or in money's worth), less the expenses that are attributable to those receipts, the latter being evaluated by reckoning the difference between the opening and the closing stock at actual cost. Unrealised gains which take the form of an appreciation in the market value of unsold goods relatively to their costs of acquisition are not taken into account; though accountancy principles approve, and the tax system by special concession allows the anticipation of unrealised losses in permitting stocks to be valued at market prices, when market prices are below cost.

54. We agree with the view expressed in paragraph 12 of the Board's memorandum that both administrative and other considerations make it inevitable that a tax on capital profits should follow analogous principles. From an administrative point of view it would be extremely difficult, if not impossible, to make a periodic valuation of all capital assets with sufficient accuracy to permit a tax to be levied on the change in the market value of all assets between two points of time. A tax on realised capital gains does, however, come to the same as a tax on the profit accruing through capital appreciation: the difference being only that for the purpose of measuring this profit the various assets that compose capital at any one time are valued at cost (and not at current market price) until they are sold or otherwise disposed of by their owners. Hence but for the special concession of valuing stocks at market prices when these are below costs, the tax on realised capital gains follows the same principles as are followed in the determination of trading profits.

55. We do not share the view that a tax on realised capital gains when considered over a sequence of years is either a less comprehensive or less equitable measure of the benefit derived from capital appreciation, than a tax on accrued gains. As the memorandum of the Board shows (in paragraph 12), if the tax on realised capital gains is so framed that all forms of property transfer are reckoned as "realisation" for tax purposes (the transfer

[1] Para. 29.

of assets by way of gift or inheritance just as much as by way of sale) the difference between realised capital gains and accrued capital gains can only be one of timing. Over a taxpayer's whole life the accumulated total of realised capital gains must necessarily come to the same as the accumulated total of accrued capital gains; and in consequence, the cumulative tax liability on account of capital gains should also come to the same (provided the tax rates are stable) except in so far as the one measure shows a greater or lesser irregularity in time than the other.

56. In general, taxation based on realised gains means a postponement of liability as compared with taxation based on accrued gains since property owners may not realise some of their assets during their lifetime at all, or not for some years after the appreciation of value has occurred. Moreover, the very existence of a capital gains tax might tempt taxpayers to postpone the realisation of the gains (or encourage the early realisation of losses) since they thereby gain the interest on the taxes payable during the period of postponement. Net realised gains would therefore normally lag behind net accrued gains, though under a progressive system the taxpayer would have an incentive to even out in time the rate of realisation of gains, and this consideration would tend to moderate the extent of the postponement. It may be thought that the fact that an investor normally prefers to realise an individual holding when the market is favourable—selling those assets which have risen in value and holding on to those which have fallen, in the hope of subsequent appreciation—might cause his net realised gains at times to exceed his net capital appreciation on all holdings and thus expose him to a higher liability than that warranted by the net change in his capital assets. However, it is open to an investor to effect a purely formal realisation of losses—by selling depreciated assets and buying them back immediately afterwards—so that he is not likely to incur liability on a higher total of realised gains than his net accrued gains. Hence whilst the rate at which gains are realised may lag behind the rate at which they accrue, they are not likely to run ahead of it.

57. There is no presumption therefore that the man whose capital is invested in diversified holdings and in easily marketable

securities would be more harshly treated under a system of progressive taxation when capital gains and losses are imputed to the year of realisation than under a system which taxes gains as they accrue. Indeed the contrary is likely to be the case. It is true that a tax on realised gains imputes the gain on any particular asset to the particular year in which realisation occurs, whereas the appreciation in its value may have accrued over a series of years. However, what matters from the taxpayer's point of view is not the gain associated with the realisation of particular asset but the fluctuation in the annual net total of his taxable gains, since it is only to the extent that his net annual gains fluctuate that he is obliged to incur heavier charges (under a progressive system of taxation) owing to the timing of the gains.

58. These fluctuations would tend to be much greater, however, under a system which taxes all capital appreciation as it accrues than under a system which taxes gains only as they are realised. Under the former system the taxpayer would be exposed to the full incidence of short-period fluctuations in the market prices of securities. In boom years he would be charged on the net appreciation of all his assets (and would presumably have to realise some of his assets in order to meet his tax bill). If the appreciation were subsequently wiped out in a depression year, he would have established a corresponding loss, but—on the hypothesis of a progressive scale of charges—this would not entitle him to a corresponding rebate of tax. He would thus lose on balance as a result of a fluctuation in the market value of unrealised securities over which he had no control and which brought him in the end no net gain.

59. Under a system of taxation which taxes only realised capital gains the very fact that the timing of the realisation of gains is under the taxpayer's own control would serve to even out the fluctuations in his annual liability. If the gains on realised assets are reckoned as the gains of a single year, so are the losses; if losses can be offset against the gains, and unabsorbed losses carried forward against future gains, the taxpayer is given, in fact, full facilities for moderating the effects of fluctuations in his taxable gains over time.

60. On the other hand there are circumstances in which a tax

on realised gains inevitably involves a bunching of gains in time, and hence, under a progressive tax, would involve the taxpayer in heavier liability owing to the incidence of timing. This would obviously occur where the capital profits are derived from a single indivisible asset—as for example when a man who has gradually built up a business sells it as a going concern or it changes hands at his decease. But it may occur more generally in cases where the capital assets are not easily marketable and can only be realised infrequently or when a wholesale realisation of accrued but unrealised gains is deemed to have occurred through death. This familiar problem in equity under progressive taxation[1] arises in connection with capital gains whenever a property owner is not in a position to spread out or regulate the realisation of his net capital profits. It should be emphasised that the problem disappears under a flat-rate tax, and that it constitutes the main argument, in equity, for a flat rate rather than a progressive rate of tax on capital gains.

61. Independently of the above considerations we recognise the force of the argument which leads to the conclusion that it would be inexpedient to tax capital gains at the full progressive rate of income tax and surtax combined. The arguments in favour of confining the charge to income tax—which would mean in effect a flat rate of tax once total income (including capital gains) is above the point at which the taxpayer becomes liable to the standard rate—are more powerful in our view when considered from the point of view of expediency than when considered from the strict point of view of equity. The great bulk of capital gains accrue to the higher income groups; the fundamental reason for this is that the accrual of capital gains is closely linked with the investment of capital in risky ventures, and it is the large property owner, and not the small saver, who is able to commit his resources to ventures involving risk. If capital gains were subjected to both income tax and surtax the effect would be that a great part of these gains would be taxed at an extremely high rate (mounting at present to 19s. od. in the £) which would be bound

[1] Theoretically the problem could be met by an arrangement permitting the averaging of income over a series of years (in a manner similar in principle to the cumulative averaging of weekly income under the present P.A.Y.E. system); but we understand that for administrative reasons this solution is regarded as impracticable.

to have a destructive effect on the willingness to assume risks. Added to this is the consideration that since a great deal of capital investment is made in the expectation of distant and not immediate appreciation even those investors not currently liable to the higher surtax rates would be in considerable uncertainty as to the rate at which their ultimate gains would be taxed when realised. Finally the full charging of capital gains to both income tax and surtax would have a negative effect on the incentive to save and encourage capitalists to dissipate their capital. Though we do not share the view of the Majority[1] that capital gains are generally saved and do not contribute to the spending of the property-owning classes,[2] it is true of course that the present opportunity to save tax free in the form of capital appreciation must provide an incentive to the large property owner not to dissipate his capital, despite the strong temptations which the high taxation of income combined with the tax exemption on spendings out of capital provides in this direction. We think therefore that the taxation of capital gains beyond a certain rate would have highly undesirable effects on risk-bearing, saving and capital formation.

Para. 106.

[2] The Majority are much concerned to show (para. 106) that "on the whole, capital gains will be saved" so that a tax on capital gains would not in itself "contribute to the control of inflation". We do not know on what evidence this particular conclusion is based. It is certainly not in accord with the official view—as is shown for example by the Economic Survey for 1953 where the Government explicitly refer to the effect of the fall in Stock Exchange prices in the previous year in reducing consumers' expenditure (Cmd. 8800, para. 38). The view is plainly contrary also to the undoubted effect of the rise in Stock Exchange values on the level of consumption of luxury goods in the course of 1954. Nor is it correct to suppose (as the Majority suggest in para. 105) that any restraining effect of a capital gains tax would depend on the actual realisation of the gains on which the taxes are paid. If a property owner knew that half his gains would be payable in tax on realisation he would behave in much the same way as if he were making only half the gains; and as the Majority observe, the characteristic form of such spending follows upon the rise in capital values as such and is not dependent on the actual realisation of the gains. A capital gains tax will reduce "boom spending" precisely because it reduces the extent to which an "[individual's] position on capital account is strengthened" by the boom. Quite apart from this the Majority's view that people will live on capital whether they make capital gains or not and *therefore* the mere fact of capital gains does not add to the volume of spending (para. 104) is self-contradictory. If people live on capital, but do not make capital gains, their spending must come to an end when their capital is exhausted. But if their spending is offset by capital gains, it can continue indefinitely.

It is true on the other hand that a capital gains tax so severe in its incidence as to cause the property owner to wish to dissipate his capital would, for a short period, increase spending. But while such a tendency might become serious in case of a capital gains tax which taxed away nine-tenths or more of the gains, we do not believe that there is any such danger if the tax is limited to one-half or less of the gains earned.

62. We cannot agree on the other hand that these considerations of economic expediency justify the continued tax exemption
of an important source of income and the consequent grave
injustice in the distribution of the tax burden between different
groups and different social classes. We certainly do not share the
view of the Majority[1] that the gains should either be taxed at the
full progressive rate or else not at all. There is no principle of
equity which leads us to suppose that if something cannot or
should not be taxed at 95 per cent. it should be taxed at zero per
cent. We therefore recommend that subject to the qualifications
and on the definitions suggested below capital gains should be
subjected to income taxation but not to surtax.

### Short-term and Long-term Gains

63. Subject to the above recommendation that capital gains
should not be liable to surtax we recommend that no distinction
should be made between short- and long-term gains. Any such
distinction is bound to be arbitrary and an invitation to tax
avoidance. The distinction in the U.S. tax system makes it worth
while for the taxpayer to realise short-term losses in less than six
months and short-term gains in more than six months and has in
many cases the effect that the taxpayer's liability is less than it
would have been if short-term gains had been taxed at the long-
term rate. We do not share the view that long-term gains have
any inherent claim to more favourable treatment than short-term
gains. We agree with the view expressed in the memorandum of
the Board (paragraph 17) that "looking at the matter purely as one
of taxable capacity there may seem little justification for distinguishing between two gains of equal amount simply because in
one case the asset was held for a longer period than in the other".

64. As already indicated we strongly support the suggestion
that contrary to the existing American practice change of ownership of property by gift or bequest should count as realisation
in the same way as the transfer of ownership by way of sale (the
property being valued for the purpose by the same rules as apply
to stamp duties). Without this provision, not only would a large
part of capital gains escape the tax net altogether, but the tax-

[1] Expressed in para. 99.

payer would have every incentive so to manipulate the realisation of his losses and his gains as to make his net unrealised gains as large as possible.[1]

## Treatment of Losses

65. We agree with the suggestions made by the Board as to the treatment of losses. Realised losses ought to reckon as an offset to realised gains; net unabsorbed losses ought to be permitted to be carried forward indefinitely as an offset against the taxpayer's future gains. As the Board's memorandum explains (paragraph 13) it is always open to a taxpayer to turn a paper loss—at least in easily marketable securities—into a realised loss, and to cover himself (if he has no real desire to liquidate his investment) by repurchasing the security afterwards. So long as losses only count as an offset against current or future realised gains, the taxpayer's incentive to do so will be confined by the extent of the realisation of his gains, and will tend to have the effect of confining the concept of net taxable gains in any particular year to the excess of net realised gains over net accrued losses. If, however, losses could be offset against past gains, the taxpayer would find it worth while to "realise" paper losses as they accrued, so that the tax would become one where the recognition of accrued losses was not limited to the amount of currently realised gains. In those circumstances the taxpayer could so manipulate his realisations (by formally selling securities whenever their price happened to be low enough to show a loss) that in an extreme case he would avoid paying tax altogether during his lifetime even though he might enjoy a steady appreciation on the total of his assets and/or a growing total of net gains on "genuine" realisations. It is true

[1] According to the provisions of the American law a change in the ownership of property by way of gift or bequest does not count as realisation. In the case of gifts *inter vivos* there is a partial remedy in that the property so transferred is valued for the purpose of any future realisation at the donor's cost and not at its value at the time of its transfer to the recipient. In the case of transfer by inheritance, however, not only is no gain recognised in the hands of the deceased but the property is valued at probate value in the hands of the beneficiary. Hence all accrued capital gains are automatically wiped out for tax purposes whenever property passes by death.

We have little doubt that these provisions (together with the distinction between short- and long-term gains) have been responsible for the fact that net reported capital losses have continued to be so large in relation to net reported capital gains and largely explain why the yield of the American tax continues to be so small in relation to the probable rate of accrual of capital gains.

that all such manipulations will involve a correspondingly higher liability on his estate at death but under a flat-rate tax (unless he has a definite expectation of a rise in the rates of taxation) he can only gain by them, since he saves the interest on the tax during the period of postponement. Analogous considerations apply to the question of allowing capital losses as an offset against other income. In that case the taxpayer would not only be able to avoid paying tax during his lifetime on his capital gains but to "borrow" money from the Revenue during his lifetime to be repaid only when his accounts are closed on his death. These particular considerations might not be so important if capital gains were taxed at a full progressive rate since in that case the taxpayer would have a clear incentive to even out in time the rate of realisation of his gains. But under a flat-rate tax the need to regard the taxpayer's account with the Revenue in respect of liability for net realised capital gains as a separate running account is the more obvious.

66. The need for such restrictions on the manner and extent to which capital losses are taken into account seems to have weighed heavily with the Majority of the Commission in their rejection of the taxation of capital gains. In paragraph 99, which sums up their general view of the problem, the Majority state that "indeed no form of the tax that was based on realised gains and realised losses—and there is no alternative—would escape the serious objection to its foundation in equity that it would tax to the same extent a man who had realised a gain on one of his assets, though showing a net loss on others that he retained, as the man who had realised a similar gain without any current depreciation of his other assets to set against it". Here their concern seems to be misplaced, and the reasoning behind it somewhat circular, since the main reason, or one of the main reasons, for restricting the way in which losses are taken into account (which in paragraph 91 the Majority appear to recognise) is precisely the ease with which a man can realise a paper loss, and the likelihood that he will do so whenever by so doing he effects a reduction in his tax bill. The situation described would therefore only be likely to occur, in any particular year, in the relatively rare circumstance of the depreciated asset being of a

kind that is not readily saleable. Even so this "serious objection to its foundation in equity" is only an objection if equity is so narrowly conceived as to require full equality of treatment between different taxpayers for each particular year. Under a flat-rate tax a taxpayer's cumulative liability would be unaffected by any delay he experienced in realising his loss.

67. There may be cases, however, in which a taxpayer realises a true loss but has no opportunity during his lifetime to offset that loss against gains, since he makes no subsequent gain. This case may be what the Majority have in mind when they state that the result of the proposed treatment "would not be to hold the balance evenly as between capital gains and capital losses, for, whereas a [realised] gain would be chargeable even if there were no realised loss, a loss would not be allowable except so far as there was a realised gain".[1] We do not believe that such cases are likely to be numerous. But they undoubtedly could occur; and whenever they do, the taxpayer's estate will show net unabsorbed losses at his death. Any possible inequity resulting from this would be mitigated if the tax claim arising out of net unabsorbed capital losses shown by an estate at probate valuation were allowed to be credited against estate duty liabilities. Provided the tax on capital gains is a flat-rate tax (so that the Exchequer is not committed to bearing the major share of unabsorbed losses, in a manner which might indeed tempt the aged into a last speculative fling) we are prepared to recommend that this should be allowed.

*Other Considerations*

68. We agree with the Majority that in times of inflation a tax on capital gains would inflict hardship on the owner-occupier who for personal or business reasons has to sell his house and find a new home somewhere else, and who may need all the money received from the sale of his old house for the purchase of another house of the same quality and condition. If the scope of the capital gains tax were extended to the case of the owner-occupier this might have the further undesirable effect of hindering mobility since people might be deterred from accepting new jobs if it meant that they had to sell their existing home. We therefore

[1] Para. 91.

recommend that the gains arising out of the sale of owner-occupied houses, to the extent of one residence for each taxpayer, should be exempted from the capital gains tax.

69. We believe, on the basis of the consideration of the various alternatives suggested in the Board's memorandum (paragraph 20) that for the purpose of the capital gains tax assets purchased prior to the appointed day should, in the case of securities quoted on the Stock Exchange, be deemed to have been purchased at the middle price ruling at the appointed day. In the case of other assets, the actual cost of acquisition should reckon as the purchase price, but the taxable gain should be reduced to that fraction of the total gain which the period between the appointed day and the date of realisation beats to the total period of ownership.

70. We do not wish to enter into a detailed consideration of the administrative problems created by a capital gains tax except to record our view that we do not believe that these problems would prove so formidable as is sometimes suggested. The experience of several European countries—such as the Scandinavian countries—as well as of the United States show that a tax on capital gains is by no means beyond the powers of an efficient tax administration. We believe that the institution of an automatic reporting system in connection with property transfers (such as is already in force in some countries, e.g., in Sweden) would greatly ease the administrative task of checking the transactions recorded on the taxpayer's return. We are in accord with the view that for an initial period the tax should be limited to gains arising from the sale of businesses, securities of all kinds and real property and that there should be an exemption limit (of say, £50 or less on any particular sale, when the annual gain is £400 or less) to reduce the administrative task involved.

*Other Forms of Capital Receipts*

71. The argument for the taxation of capital gains on the above lines applies equally to various other forms of receipts which are now exempt from taxation as being receipts of a capital nature. Such receipts are premiums on leases, moneys received for the surrender of leases, receipts on account of the sale of terminable rights of enjoyment or possession such as the sale of mineral

rights, etc. We agree with the Majority that such receipts represent "a commutation of the future income which the vendor would have received had he retained it" and are "capable of being described as anticipations of future income in the hand of the recipient and, as such, as partaking of the nature of income".[1] We do not agree with the Majority, however, that "common fairness argues against [their] inclusion in the range of taxable income" merely on account of the fact that the receipt "is in substance the equivalent of the discounted income of several years". This argument could equally be applied to the sale of patent rights, for example, which under present law are fully subject to tax. But, whether or not it would be fair to tax them at the full progressive rate of income tax and surtax combined, we certainly cannot admit the validity of the reasoning which argues that if they would be too severely hit under the full progressive rate they should for that reason be exempted from tax altogether. We therefore recommend that the net receipts (i.e., after deduction of any sum that may have been paid for the acquisition of these rights) on account of the sale of terminable rights which are now exempted from taxation should be subjected to income tax in an analogous manner to capital gains.

72. This concludes our recommendations concerning capital gains. There are a number of smaller issues which we have not touched upon but on which we are generally in agreement with the suggestions made in paragraph 19 of the Board's memorandum. There is, however, one important matter on which we find ourselves unable to accept the conclusions of the Board and this relates to the prospective net yield of a capital gains tax. The Board's estimate of the yield of the tax is based on a calculation of the prospective rate of appreciation of the value of capital assets made by the then Director of Statistics and Intelligence and given in Appendix VI of the Board's memorandum on Capital Gains. Since our disagreement is with the assumptions and methods on which the Board's estimate rests, it will be necessary to present our views on this estimate in some detail before putting forward a different estimate for the prospective yield of the tax based on alternative assumptions.

[1] Para. 32.

## THE LONG-TERM YIELD OF A CAPITAL GAINS TAX

73. The Board estimated (paragraph 29) the average annual yield of a capital gains tax—on the assumption that capital gains were charged to both income tax and surtax—in this country at £m50 a year. It was assumed by the Board that in the long run net realised gains correspond to net appreciation. On a calculation that annual average capital appreciation would amount to £m150 the yield of a capital gains tax was put at £m80 a year, and the net yield to the Revenue, after a reduction of £m30 to take account of consequential loss of revenue from estate duties and stamp duties, at £m50 a year.[1]

74. The estimate of the appreciation of privately owned capital of £m150 a year was arrived at on the following basis:

(i) Estimates made by Mr. H. Campion[2] of the value of privately owned capital in 1926–28 and in 1936 showing a total appreciation of £m1,893 between those two dates, or £m210 a year. It was estimated that about £m100, or 0·6 per cent. a year reflected capital appreciation. The same percentage increase applied to the 1950–51 estimate of privately owned capital of £m36,000 yielded an estimate of £m216 a year. This estimate was then reduced to allow for the loss of development rights, rent control and the effects of stamp duties, to £m150.

[1] This estimate was made in 1951. The Commission has recently been informed by the Board that if the same estimate was made now, in the light of changes both in policy and the economic situation, and "assuming continuance of present policies at home and stable conditions abroad, some increase in the earlier estimate might be justified". Since the original estimate was made "the burden of taxation on industry has been reduced, development charges have gone, moderate increases in rents have become possible and the general economic strength of the country has increased". However, in the Board's view it would be "quite unrealistic to put the figure for assumed average capital gains, in present circumstances, at more than, say £m200 to £m250. On the basis adopted in 1951 such a figure would give a net yield of £m75–£m100. But changes in policy and external circumstances might conceivably be such as to destroy the basis for any revision of the earlier estimate. It should again be emphasised that the estimates are average figures and that the actual yield corresponding to an average of £m75–£m100 might fluctuate between −£m200 and +£m300". (The minus figure in the estimate is due to the assumption that losses could be carried backwards and offset against past gains—a provision which both the Board and the Minority of the Commission have expressed themselves against. Assuming that losses could be carried forward but not backwards the minimum yield of the tax could not fall below zero.)

[2] *Public and Private Property in Great Britain* (1939).

(ii) Statistics based on tax returns in the United States showing that the ratio of net capital gains reported to total income reported was 1·9 per cent. in the period 1917–37, and 1·7 per cent. in the period 1938–46. On the assumption that a similar ratio would apply (in the long term) to post-war Britain, annual capital appreciation would be at a rate of about £m200.

75. We are unable to accept either of the above methods of estimation as indicating the long-term rate of capital appreciation in this country. Precisely because the movement of capital values fluctuates so greatly with the trade cycle and with political uncertainties, any assumption that is based on the projection of past experience should in our view be based on the long-term trends and not on changes between arbitrarily selected dates. In Britain the slump following 1931 considerably reduced profits, with the result that in 1936 (as shown by assessments in 1937–38) gross trading profits were still below the level of the years 1926–28. Stock Exchange values of ordinary shares barely recovered in 1936 to their 1926–28 level—according to the Banker's Magazine Index they were, in fact, 10 per cent. below that level. Whilst gilt-edged prices had risen considerably with the fall in long-term interest rates this had only a limited effect on private fortunes owing to the large conversion operation of the 5 per cent. War Loan carried out in 1932. The period in question therefore can by no means be taken as representative of the rate of capital appreciation over longer periods.[1]

76. The same kind of objection applies to the American figures. The first of the two periods, 1917–37, includes the biggest and most prolonged slump in American history, whilst the war period 1938–46 is hardly relevant as an indication of the rate of appre-

---

[1] We are not discussing the question of how far the estimate of the actual capital appreciation in those years is in itself reliable enough for any firm conclusions to be based on it. While the methods employed by Mr. Campion and others to estimate the value of private capital from estate duty statistics and mortality rates may give a sound indication of the broad order of magnitude of the value of private capital at any one time, they are hardly accurate enough for measuring differences in values between two dates. The estimate of £m100 for net annual personal savings in 1926–28 to 1936—a step in arriving at the estimate of capital appreciation—was derived from a single figure of £m139 for 1938 which was itself a residual between the estimates of personal income and expenditure.

C

ciation of capital values in normal times. Moreover, American data on net realised gains reported to the Revenue authority are hardly relevant from the point of view of estimating the rate of capital appreciation, since, as was indicated above (paragraph 64) a large proportion of gains in the United States escape the capital gains tax altogether because all accrued capital gains are wiped out when property passes on death.

77. In our view any reasonable estimate of the long-term rate of capital appreciation in this country should chiefly be based on estimates concerning the long-term trend in trading profits, dividends and the value of ordinary shares. At the present time the total value of privately owned capital may be put at some £m40,000 of which some £m12,000 are in the form of ordinary shares whilst another £m8,000 are in the form of real property. Capital appreciation, in the long run, mainly reflects the appreciation on these two kinds of assets. The price level of gilt-edged and other fixed interest securities—if past experience is any guide —is not likely to give rise to any long-term appreciation or depreciation, since periods of rising and falling interest rates are likely to alternate with each other without any significant trend in either direction. Whilst the long-term rate of appreciation in real property is less predictable, the long-term rise in ordinary shares will be closely related to the rate of increase in dividends which in turn can be assumed to increase at much the same rate as company profits.[1]

78. In the 44 years 1870–1914 gross profits assessed to Schedule D increased at an average compound rate of over 3 per cent. a year. In the 33 years 1914–47 the rate of growth was 4½ per cent. a year. In the six years 1947–53 company profits grew at a compound rate of 8 per cent. a year. The first of these periods included a long period of falling prices between 1870 and 1900, and a subsequent period of rising prices up to 1914; but this only

[1] As we explain in paragraphs 98 et seq. below this has not been the case since 1938 owing to dividend limitation and related factors. There is no reason to suppose, however, that, unless it be the result of deliberate Government policy, there will be any further decrease in the proportion of profits distributed as dividends. The experience of the last four years has shown, on the contrary, that despite the discriminatory tax on dividend distributions, dividends have increased at a faster rate than profits, and this is likely to continue for some years. According to figures recently published by the Stock Exchange ordinary dividends, since 1950, increased at a rate of 12 per cent. a year. The rise in company profits in 1950–53 was only 6 per cent. a year.

brought the wholesale price level to around 80 per cent. of its 1870 value. The second period included the two inflationary periods following the first and second World Wars as well as the prolonged slump of the 1930s. The third period was one of full employment and rising prices. It appears to us that any estimate of the long-term growth of profits in this country would have to take into account the fact that Governments since the war have assumed responsibility for maintaining high and stable levels of employment. To the extent that future Governments will succeed in carrying out this policy the rate of growth in industrial production will be higher than in the past and the long-term trend of prices is more likely to be rising than falling.

79. We believe that the rate of growth of industrial production in this country cannot be put at less than 3 per cent. a year. On this basis the long-term rate of growth of profits is unlikely to be below 3–5 per cent. a year. The lower of these estimates assumes that the inflationary trend in prices experienced since the war will be completely eliminated in the future. The upper estimate also assumes that Governments will succeed in controlling inflationary trends more successfully in the future than in the past; but it takes into account the possibility of the continuance of a moderate degree of price inflation. Assuming that dividends keep pace with the rise in earnings, this implies an annual increase in dividend payments of the order of £m25–£m40, and an average increase in the value of ordinary shares of £m500–£m800 a year.[1]

80. The percentage rise in the value of real property cannot be estimated with any such confidence but is not likely to be as great. Assuming an increase of the value of real property of the order of 1–2 per cent. a year and taking into account capital gains on the sale of unincorporated businesses, capital appreciation in forms

[1] We have chosen the figure £m25–£m40—in preference to the figure of £m20–£m30 which represents 3–5 per cent. of *current* dividend payments—simply because we do not believe that the relationship of dividends to earnings will remain at its present ratio. Since the ending of dividend limitation in 1950 ordinary dividend payments have increased by some £m210, £m100 of which occurred in 1954. In the four years ending 31st March, 1954 the increase in the value of securities quoted on the Stock Exchange was £m5,000 of which about £m3,000 represented the rise in the value of ordinary shares. The rise in the market value of *all* ordinary shares in personal ownership over the period may be put at £m4,000 or £m1,000 a year. (According to figures recently published by the Stock Exchange the ordinary shares of United Kingdom registered and managed companies, quoted on the London Stock Exchange, excluding investment trusts, rose by £m1,500 in the second half of 1954.)

other than ordinary shares cannot be put at less than £m100–£m200. Hence the long-term rate of capital appreciation in this country in all forms should be put at a minimum of £m600–£m1,000 a year.

81. An alternative approach which yields much the same results takes the rate of accumulation of company reserves as its starting point. While the market values of shares at any particular time can move independently of the underlying assets of companies, past experience suggests that over longer periods the rise in share values keeps pace with the growth of assets: indeed to the extent that the market puts a value on companies' "goodwill" the rise in market values should outstrip the rate of increase in reserves.[1] The current rate of increase of undistributed profits of companies (after deduction of depreciation measured in terms of current replacement cost) is of the order of £m800 a year. Hence additional dividend payments of £m40 a year represent no more than a return of 5 per cent. on the additional capital annually reinvested by shareholders through the ploughing back of profits; and that in turn involves the appreciation in the value of shares by £m800 a year.[2]

82. Assuming that the rate of capital appreciation will be of the order indicated, there will be a long gestation period before the appreciation is fully reflected in realised capital gains. But, for reasons explained in paragraphs 55–56 above, the ultimate rate of realised capital gains should correspond with a time lag of a number of years, with the rate of accrual of gains.

83. We understand from the Board that after making allowance for the effect of stamp duties in reducing the extent of the gains, and allowing for gains accruing to exempt bodies and to non-resident holders, and assuming an average marginal rate of 7s. 6d. to 8s. 0d. in the £, the ultimate annual yield of the tax on our calculation of the rate of appreciation of capital would be between

---

[1] If this has not been the case since the war, the reason is again to be found in the great reduction in the proportion of earnings distributed as dividends. Earnings of companies have risen fully as much as reserves.

[2] The Board's estimate implies in effect that the sums annually reinvested by companies on behalf of their shareholders is "money down the drain", from which the owners derive no appreciable benefit, present or future. Otherwise it would be impossible to regard as "quite unrealistic" an average appreciation of more than £m200 to £m250, when ploughed back company profits alone represent £m800.

£m200–£m350 (including £m20–£m30 payable by companies at the 33⅓ per cent. rate suggested in paragraph 109 below). This does not allow for the consequential loss in the yield of estate duties. The Board estimate this consequential loss at 35–40 per cent. of the yield of the capital gains tax, or £m65–£m130 a year. In our view the consequential loss from estate duties could not exceed 25–30 per cent. of the total revenue from estate duties after a lapse of 30 years from the initial introduction of the tax;[1] hence the Board's estimate would be consistent only if the annual yield of estate duties were also assumed to be twice as large as at present. This in turn implies that there would be no spending out of capital gains, that estate duties would be paid out of saved-up income rather than out of capital and that there would be no avoidance of duties through *inter vivos* settlements.

84. In putting forward this estimate we do not wish to deny that international political uncertainties, world economic crises or domestic elections may interrupt or reverse for prolonged periods the trend in the rate of accrual of the investors' capital appreciation. The capital gains tax is certainly not a tax that could be relied on as a steady source of revenue. Nevertheless we believe it right to estimate the yield of such a tax on the assumption that Governments, of whatever political party, will be bent on, and will succeed in maintaining the state of economic prosperity of the nation. It is precisely this newly-assumed responsibility for maintaining the economy on an even keel which makes the case for the imposition of such a tax so much stronger than it was in the past. The risks which were formerly associated with the holding of ordinary shares—the risks that profits are wiped out, or that companies go bankrupt, during the periodic economic crises of capitalism or during prolonged periods of economic

---

[1] Assuming that estates become liable for death duties on the average once every 30 years, the average capital appreciation on all estates, on the above assumptions as to the annual rate of capital appreciation, will be 60–100 per cent. in 30 years' time. Assuming further that the gains will be concentrated on the top 50 per cent. of estates, the average appreciation on those estates will be 120–200 per cent. The reduction in the dutiable value of those estates due to the capital gains tax assuming a marginal tax of 9s. od. in the £, will therefore be between $\frac{220-100}{220} \times 0.45$ and $\frac{300-100}{300} \times 0.45$, or between 25 and 30 per cent. Assuming the present yield of £m140 from estate duties on the top 50 per cent. of estates, the loss of estate duty will be £m35–£m42.

stagnation—have been largely removed as a result of the new methods of economic control, and the new responsibilities assumed by the State. If the owners of risk capital profit from these policies, as in the long run they are bound to do, fairness demands that part of the benefit of these gains should be shared by the taxpaying community in general.

### III. CORPORATE TAXATION

85. We agree with the Majority that the present situation under which companies are subjected to two different taxes, the standard rate of income tax and the profits tax, is unsatisfactory.

### The Case for Separating Personal and Company Taxation

86. The charging of companies to income tax on the whole of their profits at the standard rate is a survival from the days when income tax was a proportional tax and the tax was levied on the benefits accruing from certain sources without regard to their destination. In present circumstances it cannot be asserted that the companies' payment of income tax at the standard rate equalises the tax burden as between corporate profits and other incomes. Whilst the actual tax liability on the profits distributed is adjusted in accordance with the total income of the individual shareholder, the rate at which the shareholders' dividend is deemed to have been taxed in the hands of the corporation, and the rate at which it has actually been taxed are not necessarily the same, the identity between the two existing only in legal fiction. That legal fiction has been subjected to increasing strain in recent years when, as a result of double taxation agreements, the effective rate of income tax payable by companies has come to differ in varying degrees from the standard rate to which they are formally liable. While shareholders continue to be credited with payment at the standard rate whenever their tax liability is equal to, or exceeds the amount deducted at source, in cases where their liability is less than the amount deducted or when they are exempt altogether (a charity for example) the amount of tax credited is limited to the effective rate paid. This in itself is

inequitable. With regard to undistributed profits, as we have argued earlier (paragraph 52) there is no reason to suppose that the taxation at some particular rate such as the standard rate, provides an equitable measure of the benefits which shareholders individually derive from retained profits in the form of capital appreciation.

87. We feel therefore that there is a strong case for abolishing the existing system under which companies are formally liable to income tax at the ruling standard rate on the whole of their profits whilst any dividends subsequently paid by the companies are deemed to have paid income tax at the rate current at the time of distribution for purposes of surtax, and at some other rate for the purposes of tax repayment. Since the graduated income tax levied on individuals is in fact an entirely different tax from the proportional or flat-rate tax imposed on companies, there is everything to be said for a formal separation of the two kinds of taxes which would at once simplifiy considerably the whole tax structure and, by abolishing the artificial link between personal and company tax rates, make it possible to vary the rates of company taxation in either direction without varying personal taxation and vice versa.

## Double Taxation of Dividends

88. The Majority record in the Report[1] the attempts made by the Commission to work out a scheme for a uniform corporation profits tax in replacement of the existing income and profits taxes paid by companies. Such a scheme would have brought the United Kingdom system of company taxation into line with those in force in a large number of other countries. This scheme was finally rejected by the Majority of the Commission because it was not possible to overcome a number of technical difficulties[2] which the particular scheme favoured by the Majority had encountered.

89. All these technical difficulties emerged, not from the conception of a separate corporation profits tax as such, but solely on account of the desire of the Majority to incorporate into the scheme a special feature whereby an appropriate share of the

[1] Paras. 542 et seq.
[2] Explained in some detail in para. 546 of the Report.

corporate tax was to be credited to the individual shareholder as
an offset against his income tax liability. As the Majority explain
no such plan of crediting the one tax against the other proved
administratively feasible.

90. In the view of the Majority it would constitute "double
taxation" if the shareholder were subjected to income tax on his
dividends without allowance for the fact that "the profits from
which the dividend is drawn have paid corporation tax in the
company's hands".[1] It seems to us that this view rests on a mis-
conception. Once we recognise that the profits tax paid by
companies is a different tax from the income tax paid by individuals, and therefore the one can be levied at rates which are
quite independent of the other, the principles of equity no more
require us to offset the payment of the profits tax against the
individual's liability to income tax than to call for such a tax
credit in connection with the many other taxes (such as local
rates, the petrol duty or the stamp duty) the incidence of which
directly or indirectly falls on the individual income tax payer.

91. Nor does it follow that the individual shareholder would be
in a better position if such offsetting arrangements were made
than if they were not made. The Majority argument assumes in
effect that the Government would levy the corporation profits
tax at the same rate (whatever that rate is) irrespective of whether
the tax is credited against the shareholder's income tax or not.
But since the net revenue from the tax would be very different in
the two cases, no such supposition would be justified. From the
shareholder's point of view, on the other hand, what matters is
the amount by which his profits are reduced through corporate
taxation, not the precise form in which they are reduced. Since
not only the rates of profits taxation but the nominal dividends
declared by the companies can be expected to be adjusted to the
difference in the mode of charging, it is not clear why the shareholder is put under any disadvantage under the one system as
against the other. We greatly regret therefore that the Majority
felt themselves unable to recommend a scheme which would
have brought about a considerable improvement in both the
equity and the administrative simplicity of the tax system.

[1] Para. 544.

*A Corporation Profits Tax*

92. We therefore recommend that company profits should be made subject only to one tax, the Corporation Profits Tax, which should be drawn up on principles appropriate to company taxation and levied at rates that are independent of personal income tax. No income tax should be levied on companies as such, but companies should be asked to act as agents to the Revenue and deduct income tax at the ruling standard rate on all interest and dividends paid out.

93. Assuming that companies are only charged with a Corporation Profits Tax the primary questions to be considered are (i) the manner in which the tax should be levied—i.e., whether it is to be levied at a proportional rate or a progressive rate, and whether there should be a differentiation according as the profits are distributed or retained; (ii) what should be the total amount of taxation levied on companies having regard to the amount of taxation borne by individuals, the needs of revenue and the ultimate incidence of the taxes charged on companies.

94. With regard to the first question we do not believe that either considerations of equity or of economic expediency would justify taxation at a progressive rate. The considerations which require a rich individual to be taxed at a higher rate than an individual of more moderate means do not apply to comparisons between large and small corporations. Considerations of economic efficiency on the other hand undoubtedly favour the levying of tax at a rate or schedule of rates which is independent of the total profits earned by the corporation. This still leaves the question open, however, whether the tax should be at the uniform rate on the whole of profits, or whether the part of the profits that is distributed should pay tax at a higher rate or at a lower rate than the part which is undistributed. The existing profits tax (charged in addition to income tax) levies a tax of $22\frac{1}{2}$ per cent. on distributed profits and $2\frac{1}{2}$ per cent. on undistributed profits. The Majority of the Commission felt that if this matter were considered on equity considerations alone the differentiation ought to be the other way round, the tax being confined to that part of the profits which is retained.

95. It seems to us that whilst equity considerations are un-

doubtedly relevant to the issue, it is impossible to arrive at an ideal method of taxation of companies by applying the same principles to the consideration of this problem as are appropriate in the case of personal taxation. Whilst it is true that the ultimate burden of the taxes levied on a corporation falls on individuals (in much the same way as in the case of any other tax) it cannot be assumed without qualification that a tax levied on a corporation is merely an indirect way of levying a tax on a definite body of individuals, who are the owners of the corporation at any one time. No conclusive evidence was before us that would enable us to say whether or not the incidence of taxes on company profits is shifted in the form of higher prices. To the extent that it is, the burden of the tax does not fall on the shareholders but on the ultimate consumers of the products of industry. But even if one assumes that the taxes are not shifted but effectively reduce the net profits of corporations, it does not always follow that the incidence of these taxes falls on any particular group of shareholders. This is the case when the tax is directly passed on in the from of lower dividends. To the extent, however, that the effect of the tax is to reduce not the dividends but the net amount retained by corporations, the incidence is borne by future, rather than by present shareholders; and it takes the form of a lower rate of long-run appreciation in share values (resulting from a lower rate of growth of assets and earning power) than would have occurred otherwise.

96. In the case of any particular company, however, the connection between accumulated reserves and share values can vary within very wide limits, so that it is uncertain how quickly or slowly the growth in reserves is transmitted into market valuations. Since shareholders may switch their holdings from one company to another at any time, the "future" shareholders of a company need not be the same persons as the present shareholders, so that it is not possible to assert that any definite group of shareholders suffers discriminatory treatment when the *retained* profits of one company are subjected to a different rate of effective taxation than the retained profits of another. For this reason one cannot apply the same notion of "fairness" when it comes to the allocation of the tax burden between corporations as one can and should

apply to the allocation of taxation between different individuals. For, as the Majority emphasise[1] the benefit that individuals derive from retained profits is in the form of capital gains; the amount of capital gains which particular individuals make on particular shares depends on their timing of purchases and sales, and not on the amount of undistributed profits during any particular period. Hence fairness in company taxation does not ensure fairness in the taxation of individuals; nor does "unfairness" in the form of unequal incidence of tax on the undistributed profits of different companies cause "unfairness" in the taxation of individuals. All that can be asserted is that a given total amount raised in taxation from corporations taken as a whole imposes a corresponding burden on the body of shareholders of companies as a whole.

97. For these reasons, as the Majority state, it is not possible "to find a satisfactory basis of taxation for corporate profits by any line of reasoning that would treat companies as if they were the same sort of taxpayers as individuals".[2] Nevertheless they criticise the existing discriminatory tax on distributed profits on the ground that it is "not calculated to produce an equitable distribution of the tax between different companies",[3] since the burden falling on undistributed profits will be all the heavier the greater the ratio of preference dividends to ordinary dividends. From the point of view of the burden of the tax falling on companies, however, it is not the relation of preference dividends to ordinary dividends that matters, but the ratio of dividends of both kinds to total profits; a company paying a high ratio of preference dividends is not placed at any special disadvantage if the ratio of its ordinary dividends to its profits is correspondingly low. A system which differentiates against distributions is only "unfair" therefore in the sense that it discriminates against companies which distribute a high proportion of their earnings, and in favour of companies which retain a high proportion. To regard this as "unfair" presumes, however, that there is a particular allocation of the tax burden between companies which has a claim to be regarded as a standard of fairness; and this, as we have seen, is not the case.

[1] Para. 51.    [2] Para. 56.    [3] Para. 523.

*Effects of the Discriminatory Tax on Distributions*

98. The appropriateness of any particular form of company taxation (as distinct from the weight of taxation) cannot therefore be judged from the point of view of its fairness or unfairness to different individual taxpayers but only from the point of view of its general economic effects. The purpose of a differential profits tax on distributions is to keep down dividend distributions in relation to earnings, and it can be a most efficacious instrument for the purpose. This is because with any increase in distributions the amount of tax falling on the companies is automatically increased, and the amount retained is reduced out of proportion to the additional amount distributed. Thus while (at present rates) a company that distributes one-third of its gross earnings pays 14 per cent. of its gross retained profits in profits tax, for a company that distributes one-half of its earnings the corresponding charge is 25 per cent., whilst for a company distributing two-thirds of its earnings, it is no less than 48 per cent. This means that, allowing for income tax, while a company distributing one-third of its gross earnings pays 59 per cent. of its retained profits in taxation, a company distributing two-thirds pays 93 per cent., so that in the latter case its net retentions amount to only 2½ per cent. of its pre-tax earnings.

99. The existence of the differential profits tax has undoubtedly been a major cause of the relative modesty of dividend distributions as compared with the rise in earnings. Thus if we compare 1953 with 1938, the growth in gross trading profits of companies (excluding companies in the nationalised industries for both years) from £m669 to £m2,688, was just over fourfold. The growth in dividend distributions (before deduction of income tax) over the same period (including both preference and ordinary dividends) from £m430 to £m609, was under one and a half times. Though the over-all tax charge had increased from about 30 per cent. to 53 per cent. of taxable profits, undistributed profits after taxation grew from £m215 to £m1,221, or nearly sixfold, whilst net savings of companies (after depreciation and initial allowances) rose from £m95 to £m811, or almost 8½ times. Moreover, whilst in 1938 company savings and depreciation roughly balanced the domestic investment of companies in fixed capital and in stocks,

in 1953 their gross savings after taxation exceeded their gross domestic capital expenditure (including stock appreciation) by £m540.

100. There can be little doubt therefore that but for the discouragement provided by the differential tax system the rise in dividends would have been more in line with the increase in earnings. Such an increase in dividends would have had the most undesirable effects, not so much on account of the increased spending out of dividends in itself—for distributed dividends may be subject to a surtax charge, as well as income tax, in the hands of the shareholder—but because of the far greater untaxed benefit which shareholders would have obtained in the form of capital gains. As the Majority state, Stock Exchange values of securities depend on dividend payments far more than on earnings: "the market makes little difference in valuation for differences in the earnings cover of dividends if plainly adequate".[1] This is confirmed by the movement of Stock Exchange values since the war. Despite the fact that total net earnings after all taxation have risen more than three times, this has not been reflected in the Stock Exchange prices of ordinary shares which only approached double the pre-war level in the course of 1954 when the payment of ordinary dividends also approached double the pre-war amount.

101. The Majority admit that the differential profits tax restrains dividend distributions and encourages retentions but they dispute the fact that a policy of dividend restraint checks inflationary tendencies, since "it does not follow that smaller distributions will reduce consumption demand".[2] They also argue that "the mere retention of profits cannot be rated as an economic advantage: on the contrary it would better serve the public interest that a company should be encouraged to distribute those profits which it cannot put to fruitful use, in order that there may be a chance that they may be invested effectively elsewhere. Nor is it advantageous for the economy that the level of dividends should be kept down. Whatever other considerations bear upon the problem, the market value of shares in industrial and commercial enterprises is artificially depressed and an obstacle placed in the way of raising new capital".[3]

[1] Para. 55.    [2] Para. 535.    [3] Para. 536.

102. We believe that these arguments would carry more weight if the Majority had not been so emphatic in their rejection of the taxation of capital gains. It is true that the purchasing power placed in the hands of the public through larger dividend payments is not likely to be large enough, taken by itself, to represent any considerable addition to consumption demand. The doubling of all dividend payments—which would do no more than restore the pre-war relationship between dividends and earnings—would mean a gross addition of some £m600, and a net addition (after income tax and surtax) of not much more than £m200 to the total of incomes. Even if all of this were spent, it would only add something of the order of 2 per cent. to total consumers' expenditure. If one ignored (as the Majority ignore) the undoubted psychological link between dividend payments and wage claims, it would be correct to say that spending the proceeds of higher dividends is not likely to make a great difference to inflationary pressure. But the doubling of dividend payments would also involve a doubling in Stock Exchange values; and this would mean an addition, not of £m200, but something of the order of £m12,000 to the disposable wealth of shareholders, none of which would bear any tax. If only 10 per cent. of that were spent, the consequences on inflationary pressure would by no means be negligible. The rise in Stock Exchange values in the course of 1954 was undoubtedly responsible (in part at any rate) for the inflationary symptoms which developed towards the end of that year and which endangered our balance of payments position.

103. We do not disagree with the Majority's view that the artificial encouragement of the retention of profits by companies is not necessarily an economic advantage. Beyond a certain point it does not in itself stimulate the rate of capital formation—as is shown by the fact that in the last few years the net amounts retained by companies have greatly exceeded their financial requirements, both on account of capital expenditure and of investment in working capital. It can be argued also that the system of financing capital expenditure so largely out of the undistributed profits of companies, does not ensure the best use of the community's savings. It makes it more difficult for fast-expanding firms to raise funds in the capital market; it strengthens

the monopolistic tendencies in the economy, and it encourages wasteful expenditure on behalf of those firms who have more money than they can use and who are yet prevented (by custom and tradition as well as by the instruments of public control) from channelling these funds to their most profitable potential use.

104. At the same time we consider that, in the special circumstances of the post-war years, the measures taken since the war by successive Governments for the prevention or discouragement of dividend increases were an ineluctable necessity in order to maintain full employment without serious inflation—the measure of wage restraint in the years 1948–50 would not have been attained without dividend restraint; and to prevent an enormous untaxed increment to the wealth of a particular group in the community. The social and economic inequalities which such a shift in the distribution of wealth would have created would not have been compatible with the sense of fairness and equity of a modern democratic community. In the absence of the taxation of capital gains there is no alternative but to discourage the making of capital gains through appeals to dividend restraint and through institutional measures of various kinds. Once capital gains are brought within the scope of taxation, however, the problem takes on an entirely different aspect. For in the long run a private-enterprise economy is likely to function more efficiently if neither higher dividend distributions nor the emergence of capital gains is prevented by discriminatory measures.[1]

105. We are strongly opposed therefore to the recommendation

[1] One consequence of the policy of dividend restraint followed since the war has been that the special provisions concerning the undue withholding of distributions by closed corporations (originally introduced in the 1922 Finance Act and amended in numerous further Acts) have been left more or less in abeyance as far as trading companies are concerned though they have continued to be enforced as regards investment companies. In our view this has led to the exploitation by taxpayers of the policy of dividend restraint for the purpose of surtax avoidance since it has enabled successful men in the professions, etc., to form themselves into one-man trading companies and thereby avoid paying surtax on an arbitrarily chosen proportion of their income. (By liquidating such companies on later occasions it is possible moreover to claim the unhindered enjoyment of that income without any surtax charge.) We are in agreement with the recommendation of the Majority [para. 1038] that in future the Special Commissioners should have power to charge surtax on that proportion of the income of such companies which in their view could reasonably be distributed (without being required to direct that the whole of the income should be deemed to have been distributed in such cases). We feel strongly however that subject to this recommendation the official policy of dividend restraint should not be regarded as being in conflict with the full application of the provisions of the Income Tax Acts concerning closed corporations.

of the Majority that the differential profits tax should be abolished forthwith, quite independently of whether capital gains are taxed or not; though we would favour such a change as part of a wider reform which included the taxation of capital gains on the lines recommended in Section II above. We do not agree with the view expressed by the Majority that the tax is not necessarily effective in discouraging higher distributions.[1] The increase in dividend distributions since 1953, to which reference is made by the Majority, can, in our view, be adequately accounted for by the reduction in the standard rate of income tax, the reduction in the rates of profits tax and the subsequent repeal of the Excess Profits Levy. Besides, from the point of view of the effectiveness of the device, it is the principle that matters and not the particular schedule of rates that is chosen to give effect to the principle. When the Majority argue that the present difference between the distributed and undistributed rates "can have only a minor influence on distribution policy when other influences combine to pull in the opposite direction" they are saying, in effect, that a differential rate of 20 per cent. is not enough. Nobody would dispute that a differential rate of say, 50 per cent. would not only prevent increased distributions but force companies to reduce the existing level of dividends.

106. We recommend therefore that after the introduction of the capital gains tax, the corporation profits tax should be charged at a uniform rate on the whole income of companies. Income tax should be deducted at the standard rate on the payment of rent, royalties, interest and dividends, such payments received by companies should be "grossed up" for the purpose of calculating the taxable income, and the income tax credited against the corporation profits tax liability. We agree with the Majority's recommendation[2] that the existing provisions relating to the exemptions and abatement of profits tax should be abolished.

107. Simultaneously with the imposition of a capital gains tax on individuals the realised capital gains of corporations should be subjected to the corporation profits tax. Realised capital losses of companies should be offset against capital gains or carried forward against future gains in the same way as in the case of individuals.

[1] Para. 537.    [2] Para. 557.